Jewish Family Celebrations

Jewish Family Celebrations

The Sabbath, Festivals, and Ceremonies

Arlene Rossen Cardozo

St. Martin's Press | New York

PERMISSIONS

The definitions of words in the Glossary that are marked with an asterisk are reprinted with the permission of the *Encyclopedia Judaica,* Keter Publications, Jerusalem, 1971.

All Hebrew blessings are excerpted from:
Hertz, Dr. Joseph H. THE AUTHORIZED DAILY PRAYER BOOK. Copyright © 1948, renewed 1975, Ruth Hecht. Bloch Publishing Company Inc. New York. Reprinted by permission of the publisher.

Songs on pages 17–18, 18–19, 65, 66, 92, 94, 95, 101, 108–9, 119–20, 148–9, and 151 were published previously. Music, courtesy of Tara Publications–Board of Jewish Education, N.Y. cassette and holiday music series.

"Eliyahu Ha-navi" is reprinted with the permission of Behrman House Publishers, New York.

The words to the "Ballad of the Four Sons" by B. Aronin appear in *More Songs We Sing* by Harry Coopersmith and are reprinted with the permission of the United Synagogue Commission on Jewish Education, United Synagogue of America, New York.

Library of Congress Cataloging in Publication Data

Cardozo, Arlene.
Jewish family celebrations.

Bibliography: p.
Includes indexes.
1. Judaism—Customs and practices. 2. Fasts and feasts—Judaism. 3. Family—Religious life (Judaism) I. Title.
BM700.C37 296.4 82-5568
ISBN 0-312-44231-9 AACR2

First Edition
10 9 8 7 6 5 4 3 2 1

To Grandma and Grandpa—
Mary Witebsky Cohen and
Henry Benjamin Cohen—
in whose home I fondly recall
the Jewish celebrations of
my childhood

Contents

Acknowledgments

While the following persons bear no responsibility for the contents of this book, each has in some way been of help to me.

I am most indebted to Rabbi Bernard Raskas, Temple of Aaron Synagogue, St. Paul, Minnesota, for his continued moral support, for reading many portions of the manuscript in draft, making helpful suggestions, and for answering countless questions. I am also grateful to Rabbi Mordecai Miller, Shaary Torah Synagogue, Canton, Ohio, whose suggestion that I teach a course for Jewish families started me on the whole project, and whose continuing counsel was of great help.

I would also like to thank Professor Dov Noy, Hebrew University, Jerusalem, who extended wonderfully gracious hospitality to my husband and me in Israel while answering my questions on potential sources for the book; Professor Jonathan Woocher, Brandeis University, and media specialist Sheree Woocher, who were great sources of encouragement from the beginning; Professor Tzvee Zahavy, University of Minnesota, whose directed readings course on life cycle material was most helpful and whose statement, "Sending the kids to Jewish schools, courses, and camps isn't the answer; they need to learn within the family," stayed with me throughout the writing of the manuscript; Professor David Blumenthal, Emory University, who responded most helpfully to my requests for source information; Felicia Weingarten, oral historian and Holocaust survivor, in whose excellent lectures I came to feel in a new way the enormity of what happened to European Jewry; and University of Minnesota anthropologist Riv-Ellen Prell, for her advice on life cycle sources.

In addition, I am most grateful to Professor Geoffrey Wigoder, editor of the *Encyclopedia Judaica,* who made numerous files of pictures of Jewish families through the ages available to me, and to Mia Ben-Giora and Arlene Yaacov, who spent many hours helping me track down particular pictures in the Keter Publishing Company library; to Varda Mor, Bar-David Literary Agency, Tel Aviv, who conveyed enthusiasm for the manuscript since its inception, and to Daphna Avnon, Jerusalem, whose interest at a crucial time was most welcome.

I am most indebted to Cantor Morton Kula, Adath Jeshurun Synagogue, Minneapolis, Minnesota, for the time he spent providing me with information on Jewish music and for putting me in touch with Velvel Pasternak; and to Velvel Pasternak, of Tara Publications, for his great generosity in providing me with almost all of the songs that appear in this book.

My special thanks to Mary Lund-Anderson, who typed draft after draft of the manuscript and who became a "teammate" to me in this whole undertaking; to my good friend Marge Roden, who frequently commented on the manuscript during its various stages of development; and to my delightful Aunt Tissy, who critiqued the latkes and the manuscript with equal zeal, improving both.

My love and thanks to my live-in consultant/research staff—my husband, Dick, who spent hundreds of hours talking to me about the structure and contents of the manuscript and almost as many hours reading and rereading drafts; and our daughters: Miriam, who located appropriate transliterations and translations of blessings from Hebrew to English, and who compiled the Glossary; Rebecca, who searched for definitions, helped double-check recipe ingredients, and made lists of songs and blessings; and Rachel, who helped compile the bibliography, and, most important, cooked dinner while I wrote.

Once a manuscript is completed, the real work begins. My thanks to my agent, Peter Ginsberg, for his enthusiasm and selection of the right publisher; to my editor, Ashton Applewhite, for her excellent advice on additions, deletions, and countless details; and to Estelle Laurence, a terrific copyeditor.

Author's Note

My father raised me on a story about a young man who left home to search for diamonds. The man traveled the world over until he happened one day, decades later, to return worn and weary to his home town. His parents had passed on years before; his former fiancée had long ago given up waiting for him, married another, and was now a grandmother. But his abandoned home was still standing, so there he slept. When he got up the next morning he went outside and, as he had done in all of the countries of the world throughout his long and lonely lifetime, began digging. And there were the diamonds—in his own back yard.

Nearly fifteen years ago my husband, Dick, and I began to feel that our assimilated American life-style was not sufficient to give our children a feeling of purpose in today's world. What heritage did we have to transmit to them to give them feelings of rootedness? What experiences could we offer them to reinforce our values? What activities could we share with them so that we might grow together, rather than in separate directions?

The answers, we found, were in our own back yard. For, although neither Dick nor I came from traditionally observant families, we had each been raised with enough Jewish background (I through observant grandparents, Dick through his family's synagogue affiliation) to know that the heritage was ours if we were willing to unearth the information we needed to incorporate Jewish observances into our home.

As we did so, we found that celebrations of the Jewish calendar year provided us with a framework for solidifying our own family unit. Although this discovery was new to us, the basic structure has, in fact, nurtured Jewish families in nearly every country of the world and has been adapted over the years to meet the needs of various families, living in different cultures, throughout the ages.

When we first began incorporating Jewish observances into our home, I searched for a book that would explain the origins of the festivals and would include under one cover, recipes, blessings, and songs for each occasion. No one book was available. But, fortunately, from the moment we showed an interest in having our family become more actively involved in the observances of our ancient heritage, another family took us under their wings and introduced us, by example, to ways in which they celebrated Shabbat and festivals within their home. As we grew comfortable with their rituals, we gradually began incorporating first one, and then another, into our own family.

Because not everyone has friends nearby to provide this kind of support, I hope that this book will provide other families with the kind of family-celebrations-by-example that our friends provided for us. It is also meant to give families who already incorporate Jewish practices into their home information on the origin and development of these observances.

Throughout the book, I've used examples of the ways many different families interpret and participate in Jewish celebrations. In addition, I have, for two reasons, drawn heavily on our own family's experiences. First, because in our family we *all* do the work and *all* enjoy the preparation for Shabbat and festivals, whereas in previous times it was the wife and mother who did the preparation, while the rest of the family enjoyed the celebration.

The second and more powerful reason is that like many Jewish-Americans, we have arrived at our Jewish celebrations through a period of transition: from highly assimilated Jews with few Jewish observances as part of our lives fifteen years ago, we have developed a strong appreciation of the ways in which Judaism can provide our family with a means of unification, a deep sense of enrichment, and a feeling of rootedness in an age when all of these are essential.

Introduction

For centuries the family has been the means through which traditional Jewish celebrations have survived and flourished. Just as the family has preserved these celebrations through the ages, today these observances can greatly enhance and unify the family.

For example, when a family marks Shabbat, making Friday night a special kind of family evening, and Saturday a particular kind of day, then the family is participating together in something both historical and unique, over one hundred times a year.

When, in addition, a family prepares for and celebrates a full cycle of Jewish festivals—Rosh Hashanah, Yom Kippur, Sukkot, Simchat Torah, Hanukkah, Purim, Pesach, Shavuot, Yom Hasho'ah, and Yom Ha'atzma'ut—well over a third of the year is spent in some kind of shared Jewish activity; one that is rooted in the past, which enjoys the present and looks toward a future.

The shared participation in the weekly and annual cycle gives rise to an understanding of what it means to be not only a family at this moment in time but a Jewish family with a 3,500-year-old past. The same holds true for ceremonies of the life cycle. Participation in particularly Jewish ceremonies of birth, death, coming of age, and marriage enables each family member to realize his or her place within a many-thousand-year-old heritage.

Each celebration is composed of a variety of practices that developed through the centuries and continue into our own time. Trying to analyze which customs were superimposed upon which is like participating in an archaeological dig in which layer upon layer of civilization is unearthed.

At the root of each ancient custom is first a universal theme that gave rise to practices from our ancient past, predating the Israelites and relating to man's most basic dreams, fears, hopes, and superstitions. Some of these ancient practices are still present in our modern celebrations.

Layered upon those universal practices are particular customs that developed as the Israelites became a people, traceable to First and Second Temple times, from roughly 1000 Before the Common Era (B.C.E.) to the beginning of the Common Era (C.E.). Although the Israelites may have borrowed practices in part or in total from their neighbors, they endowed those practices, many of which are integral parts of today's festivals, with unique meanings.

Following the destruction of the Second Temple in 70 C.E., new interpretations were superimposed upon old celebrations. The Israelite/Hebrews, now known as Jews, were widely dispersed and continued to practice their beliefs in their new environments. After the dispersion, the customs of the Sephardic Jews, who settled in the Mediterranean countries, developed in part independently from those of the Ashkenazic (Eastern European) Jews, from whom most American Jews trace their ancestry. Consequently, many customs and ceremonies are attributable to one or another branch of Jewry but not necessarily to both.

Frequently, during the Middle Ages mystical beliefs became attached to old customs, resulting in new practices.

Now that many of us trace our American heritage back three, four, and more generations, the Jewish-American community has developed its own character and as a result some of its own distinct customs.

The beauty of our multi-layered history is that when we participate in a Passover Seder, build a sukkah, or have a family Rosh Hashanah dinner, in each celebration we can trace centuries of our family's far distant past straight into our own homes. Each present-day celebration is a culmination of many centuries' layering of custom onto a basic festival, so that while the basis is preserved, a variety of changes in circumstances has produced the different practices we observe today.

A Shared Shabbat

A Shared Shabbat

A Family Day

Shabbat, the weekly day of rest, which gives family members time together away from the ordinary activities of the week, has never been more valuable than today in this fast-paced age of individuality. For, while each doing one's own thing may be fine when practiced in moderation, each family member doing his or her own thing to the exclusion of all else leads to the inevitable theme songs of the twentieth century: "My parents don't take time to sit and talk to me." "My family never did anything as a group." "We each went our own way," and so on.

Through its various rituals, Shabbat provides a means for family members to spend leisurely time together—to talk, eat, sing, and relax—away from outside pressures of school and work.

For parents, one or both of whom may be heavily involved in careers, and/or personal and community concerns, Shabbat can provide an opportunity to sit back, breathe deeply, and appreciate being with the people who matter most in their lives. For older children and teens, it is similarly a time to relax with their families, away from engulfing school and peer group activities.

To young children, Shabbat means a happily anticipated routine, for they adore rituals and the knowledge that something meaningful that involves fun-filled preparation will occur and reoccur. They enjoy having family and friends for meals on Shabbat; it means more activity, more attention, good things to eat, and probably a later bedtime. Shabbat can be wonderful for little children for whom no day is a workday anyway, simply as a happy occasion on which to enjoy life more than ever, surrounded by loved ones.

Just how a family celebrates Shabbat is a matter of that particular family's interpretation of what a day of rest should be. What works for one family group may not work for another. What is important is that each family finds the way that works best for it; that provides the most opportunity for harmonious activities, and leaves members with the most complete feeling of relaxation and refreshment.

There is ample historical precedent for a variety of ways in which a family may choose to spend Shabbat, for there are many theories about the origin and purpose of the day of rest. As Shabbat evolved and was observed through the ages there was much debate about what constituted work and what didn't; what contributed to rest and what was considered counterproductive.

Origin and Evolution

The word Sabbath comes from the Hebrew word Shabbat. The Hebrew root of the word "Shabbat" (S-B-T) means "cease or desist," and may originally have been linked to the Babylonian Shabbatum, the day of the full moon, when the ancients believed that the moon stood still. This standing still is in part what Shabbat is all about: a time when work ceases, when the individual can remain "in place" for twenty-four hours, to rest and regenerate.

Information about the origins of the Hebrew/Jewish Sabbath is sketchy. Nobody knows when or how the observance of the seventh day of the week as a particularly different day to be marked in a specific way originated. It seems clear from the fourth biblical commandment, "Remember to keep the Sabbath Holy" that by the time the Bible was written the Sabbath was already an established institution, and that the seventh day of the week was to be "remembered" and "kept" as though it had always been there.

A particularly interesting theory holds that the Hebrew Sabbath was originally linked to the Babylonian superstitions regarding certain phases of the moon as "evil" or "unlucky" days. On these "unlucky" days, which fell on the seventh, fourteenth, twenty-first, and twenty-eighth of some months, the king, as representative of the gods, was prohibited from doing certain things lest he arouse the gods' anger and evil befall him and his subjects. The king's abstentions included eating any food touched by fire, riding in his chariot, changing his clothes, and discussing affairs of state.[1]

Similarly, the Hebrews were commanded, "Ye shall kindle no fire throughout your habitations on the Sabbath day" (Exod. 35:3), and to "abide every man in his place, let no man go out of his place on the seventh day" (Exod. 16:29). Nevertheless, scholars note major differences between Babylonian "unlucky" days and the Hebrew Sabbath in that the latter referred to the final day of each seven-day interval irrespective of the phase of the moon; in addition, the Hebrew Sabbath was viewed as a memorial of creation which ensured all men and their animals a day of rest from their labors.[2]

If Shabbat originally resembled some aspects of the Babylonian "unlucky" days, it seems our Hebrew ancestors regularized the occurrences of our special days and completely altered their meaning by imbuing the days with a positive spirit and humane considerations. Rather than being an "unlucky" day, the Hebrew Shabbat became the most happily anticipated day of the week; a day during which man and his animals rested completely from the toils and rigors of their customary routines.

As Shabbat evolved throughout the ages, the ways in which families implemented this special day also changed. In the days of the First Temple (tenth to sixth century B.C.E.) people stopped their labors in the fields as well as their commerce in the villages as the Sabbath approached. The Temple area was crowded, and families traveled about freely since Sabbath restrictions on distance and modes of travel hadn't yet been developed. The Sabbath was not as important to families of First Temple times as were the major pilgrimage festivals—Pesach, Shavuot, and Sukkot—the latter being occasions of joyous festivities combined with pilgrimages to the Temple in Jerusalem.

The Babylonian Exile in 586 B.C.E. strengthened the Sabbath.[3] Whereas in Israel the Sabbath couldn't compete with the major pilgrimage celebrations, in exile the other festivals, which had relied heavily on the Temple, obviously couldn't be celebrated in the same way. The Sabbath, however, was a celebration that took place within the home and didn't require the Temple. It provided families with feelings of hope and peace as well as with a sense of identity in a strange land. Thus, the Exile elevated to new and ever-lasting positions both the home, as the center of celebration, and the Sabbath, as central to the Jewish family.

In fact, families of the Exile found the day of rest so important that when their descendants returned to Israel a century later they were appalled at what they perceived as the desecration of Shabbat throughout their land. In some parts of the country laborers toiled in the fields. In Jerusalem most people didn't work, for the Sabbath had become a merchant's holiday. Except for those selling their wares, everyone else was free to buy.

Phoenician merchants, too, enjoyed the Hebrew Sabbath as a perfect day to visit Jerusalem to sell their goods.[4] The prophet Nehemiah preached vehemently against this abuse of the Sabbath day, and when his words went unheeded, he sent guards to the gates of the city to prevent the intrusion of visiting merchants. After that time, the Sabbath became much more heavily protected through the incorporation of strict Sabbath rest laws into the priestly code.[5]

Rabbinic Period: Liberalizations and Restrictions

After the destruction of the Second Temple in 70 C.E., the rabbis of the first three centuries of the common era clarified biblical statements regarding Sabbath rest laws in two equally important ways: first, they liberalized phrases regarding light and movement; second, they developed a thirty-nine-point policy on Sabbath restrictions.

The liberalizations included the rabbinic decree that the biblical injunction "Ye shall kindle no fire throughout your habitations on the Sabbath day" (Exod. 35:3 be interpreted to mean that such fires could be lit before sundown Friday and could remain lit throughout the Sabbath. The rabbis further decided that the word "place" in the biblical command, "abide every man in his place, let no man go out of his place on the seventh day" (Exod. 16:29), could be interpreted to mean "town." They also devised the *eruv tehumin*—blending of Shabbat limits—a legal fiction for extending the walking distance allowed on the Sabbath. (Eruv, which literally means "mixing, blending, or intermingling," is a term applied to rabbinic legislation that makes permissible otherwise prohibited acts on Shabbat and festivals.)

While the foregoing interpretations of the biblical statements concerning light and movement were obviously liberalizations, rabbinic institution of a thirty-nine-point policy defining what kinds of acts constituted work, and what, therefore, should be avoided to ensure a labor-free Sabbath, has been perceived by many people throughout the ages as stringent.

The rabbinic definition of work, based on interpretations of biblical phrases, meant anything that was necessary to build the desert sanctuary (the portable Ark of the Covenant, which the Israelites carried with them during their wanderings in the desert). Examples of those forbidden acts included plowing, sifting, tying a knot, and building and kindling a fire. Besides the thirty-nine acts, any other actions which derived from or could be confused with them were also rabbinically forbidden. A major theological premise underlying these prohibitions is that in order truly to appreciate his limitations in a divinely created universe, on one day each week man should relinquish control over all that he has mastered.

Rabbinic interpretations of biblical statements gave rise to the Halachah: the Talmudic code. (This is a generic term for the whole legal system of Judaism which encompasses the laws and observances.) After this development much of what families did or did not do on the Sabbath was a result of reinterpretations of that original code by future generations of rabbis.

The liberalizations of interpretations regarding light and movement on the one hand, the restrictions on a multiplicity of activities on the other, have given rise to vigorous debate throughout the centuries as to who is a "Sabbathmaker" and who is a "Sabbathbreaker." It depends upon whom you ask.

To this day some of the few remaining Karaites (a sect dating from the eighth century, who interpret the Bible literally and perceive rabbinic interpretations as a corruption of Mosaic teachings) permit no light on the Sabbath. They and the Samaritans (the oldest of the dissenting sects, who base their beliefs on the

Law of Moses and reject the authority of the Jewish sages) leave their homes on Shabbat only to attend religious services.[6] To them, because they believe the rabbinic law authorizes the violation of biblical statements, what we have come to call Orthodox Judaism (the most strictly adherent form of Judaism) is lax indeed. Yet to many traditional Jews who live in strict accordance with rabbinic law, those Jews who observe the spirit of the Sabbath, but not the letter of rabbinic ordinance, are in continual violation of Shabbat.

Rabbis have been kept busy throughout the centuries interpreting what activities are and are not compatible with the Sabbath. It's great fun to listen to two or more Jewish scholars discuss a question of permissible Shabbat activity. On one such occasion I queried two Jewish Studies professors (each held a doctorate and, in addition, each held a rabbinic degree, one from an Orthodox yeshiva, the other from a Reform seminary), on the question of whether or not cross-country skiing was an "approved" Sabbath activity.

"I can make a case for it because I love skiing," the Orthodox-trained scholar said, and proceeded to do so with Halachic examples ("Using a cane is okay, so why not a ski pole . . . you need not carry the ski if you put it on outside the door as you would a boot," etc.). The scholar trained in the more liberal Jewish tradition was not so sure: he hates winter, and for him being outside in cold weather infringes on his Shabbat enjoyment anyway; skiing would desecrate it! He thus proceeded with counter-arguments and examples to show that cross-country skiing could, in fact, be "wrong" on Shabbat. ("After all, creating is prohibited on Shabbat and you'd be creating a path moving the snow with the skis," etc.)

Shabbat through the Ages

Because Shabbat has been celebrated in nearly every country throughout the world, we see a great deal of variation in how it is observed, particularly with regard to Shabbat foods and the words and melodies of Shabbat songs. Yet, occasionally, constants develop when something becomes so meaningful to so many people that it passes from community to community, and country to country, becoming a permanent part of the Shabbat ritual in many lands.

An example of such an addition occurred during the Kabbalistic movement of the sixteenth century, when the table songs *(zemirot)* reached great popularity. These songs, which many families today love to sing on Friday night and at the noon and late afternoon meals on Saturday, contribute to the mood and the uniqueness of Shabbat and reinforce it as a day of joy.

Eighteenth- and nineteenth-century Eastern European Jewish families put their mark on the Sabbath as well, in a very real sense putting into practice the long-held idea that the whole week looks to Shabbat. While the sixteenth-century Kabbalists personified the Shabbat as a spiritually present Bride or Queen, many Eastern European Jews interpreted the day as a taste of the hereafter.

Thus, during the entire work week—from sundown Saturday until sundown Friday—family members anxiously awaited Friday night and Saturday; and the best of whatever the family could afford of food, wine, and clothing was put aside and readied for *Shabbos,* as it was then called.

The cohesiveness of the Jewish communities of eighteenth- and nineteenth-century Eastern European shtetls contributed to a homogeneous interpretation of Sabbath observance. Families saw Shabbat as a day to rest from the rigors of the week, a day to put aside money matters, a day that offered a haven of retreat from the often harsh routines of daily life. The community defined the manner in which Shabbat was observed, and things were done in very much the same way from family to family.

By late Friday afternoon shtetl fathers had come home from work, bathed and readied themselves for shul (synagogue). After services they returned home to bless their wives and children, and rejoiced in the finest meal of the week. The following morning groups of black-frock-coated fathers and sons walked to shul; many mothers, dressed in Sabbath best, went, too, although those with babies and small children remained at home (unless an older daughter stayed at home with the younger children).

After services, groups of families walked to their homes together; each family enjoyed a Shabbat lunch followed by a long nap. During the latter part of the afternoon families visited back and forth, sipping tea and eating fruit and cake, until the men departed for shul to bid the Sabbath farewell.[7]

Preparation

Challah-making and Baking

In our home, as in countless other Jewish homes, preparation for the day of rest begins with the ancient custom of the making of Sabbath bread loaves called *challah.* In biblical Hebrew, challah means a round loaf or cake, and pertains to the cake of new dough which the Israelites were required to give as Temple offering (Num. 15:17–21). In traditional Judaism, one pulls off a small piece of unbaked challah dough and blesses and burns it, in recollection of the ancient requirement. A folkloric interpretation is that the dough was thrown into the fire to appease evil spirits.[8]

In later times the word challah came to mean not only the Sabbath bread but also any white bread, as distinct from the rye breads usually made for weekdays.[9]

When our girls were preschoolers, challah dough-making was a laughter-filled time that began right after Friday breakfast as the kitchen table was transformed into a mess of yeast, flour, and broken eggs. Nowadays, I mix and kneed the challah dough either first thing Friday morning or sometime around noon, when I leave my typewriter until Sunday morning.

By the time Miriam and Rachel, now in their teens, and Rebecca, now ten, arrive home from school Friday afternoon, it's time to "punch down" and mold the challah dough—a project we all enjoy. Sometimes one of the girls takes over and does it all, but more often than not, we all sit around the kitchen table, everyone talking at once about her day. While we talk, and mold the bread dough, tensions seem to relax; conversation becomes quieter and sometimes ceases in the same way that playing with a ball of clay becomes an all-consuming, absorbing, thoroughly relaxing activity.

Sometimes we form the bread dough into twists, a shape that became popular in Germany during the early Middle Ages and which in some locales has come to be considered synonymous with challah. Other times the girls feel inspired to try new forms and mold the dough into such shapes as a Magen David (six-pointed Star of David) or Chai (symbol of life).

After we mold the bread dough, we brush the unbaked loaves with egg white, then sprinkle them with poppy seeds (said to symbolize the manna which fell as the Israelites wandered in the wilderness after the Exodus from Egypt) before baking.

Challah

There are hundreds, if not thousands, of available challah dough recipes. This is one we use because it is so low in eggs and shortening.

1½ cups warm water
1 package yeast
1 tablespoon sugar
1 teaspoon salt
1 egg
1 tablespoon corn oil
6 cups flour
Additional egg white and sesame or poppy seeds (optional)

Pour 1½ cups warm water into large mixing bowl. Add yeast and let stand for 10 minutes. Add sugar, salt, egg, and oil. Mix in flour 1 cup at a time. Knead for several minutes. Turn the oven on to 300°F. Transfer the dough to a greased bowl. Place the bowl on top of the stove, cover it with a towel, and let the dough rise for 2 or more hours. Punch down. Let the dough rise again, for at least an hour. Punch down again.

Place dough on greased cookie sheet. Divide dough into two equal parts. Braid or mold the dough into the desired shapes. Cover with a towel and let the dough rise again another hour. Brush with egg white and sprinkle with sesame or poppy seeds if desired. Place the pan in a 375°F. oven and bake for 50 to 60 minutes until the bread is golden brown. Makes two small loaves, each of which serves four to six persons.

Variation: Do not divide dough before molding into the desired shape. One loaf will serve ten to twelve. For two large loaves, double the recipe.

Table Setting

While our challah is in the oven, Rachel, our resident perfectionist, sets the dining-room table so that it will be "just right" for Shabbat. By the time we're ready to sit down she has everything done, complete with candles in the candlesticks, wineglasses at every place, and the challah plate ready so that two loaves of hot bread can be placed on it, then covered with a napkin or special challah cover until it's time to bless and eat them.

Our Friday night dinner menu varies, within the limits of trying to have something that *everybody* likes. In addition to whatever we're having as a main course, on either Thursday night or Friday afternoon Rebecca and I make a big pot of soup so that we have a soup course preceding the main part of our Friday night meal. (That in itself lends a festive touch since weekday meals are usually one course.)

The soup also forms the mainstay of our Saturday noon meal served along with either sandwiches or a salad—which we also make in advance, ensuring that everybody can enjoy his or her day of rest with minimum time spent in the kitchen.

Celebration

Shabbat Dinner

Candle-lighting

The Jewish day is reckoned from sundown to sundown; thus Shabbat begins when the sun sets on Friday and lasts until sunset Saturday. (Sunset is traditionally determined when three stars can be sighted in the sky. Our great-grandmothers used to say Shabbat was concluded when they "couldn't tell a black thread from a white one.") In ancient times, candles were lit at sundown for purely utilitarian reasons; when the wicks were lit on the sixth night of the week, the day of rest was officially ushered in.[10] Later the rabbis imbued this lighting of the candles with special significance. At least two candles were to be lit in honor of the Sabbath—one to "remember the Sabbath day," based on Exodus 20:8, the other to "observe" it as in Deuteronomy 5:12.

In our home we light Shabbat candles when everyone has gathered for dinner at the dining-room table. Candle-lighting time signals a separation from the week, a familiar feeling of peacefulness. It's usually the woman of the home who lights and sings a blessing over the candles, but in our family, although I light the candles, Rebecca says the blessing, which she's been doing since she was old enough to talk.

The Blessing over the Candles

בָּרוּךְ אַתָּה יְיָ אֱלֹהֵינוּ מֶלֶךְ הָעוֹלָם · אֲשֶׁר קִדְּשָׁנוּ
בְּמִצְוֹתָיו וְצִוָּנוּ לְהַדְלִיק נֵר שֶׁל-שַׁבָּת :

Baruch ata adonai eloheynu melech ha-olam, asher kidshanu b'mitzvotav vitzivanu l'hadlik ner shel Shabbat.

Praised are You, O Lord our God, King of the universe, Who has sanctified us by Your laws and commanded us to kindle the Shabbat light.

The custom of reciting or singing a blessing over the candles is not nearly so ancient as many of us suppose, but rather derives from the eighth or ninth century and was not universally accepted in Jewish communities until after the twelfth century.[11]

Some scholars believe the blessing came about as a reaction of the rabbis to the then-powerful sect of Karaites, who, in observing the literal biblical translation of Exodus 35:3, "Ye shall kindle no fire throughout your habitations on the Sabbath day," spent the entire Sabbath in the dark.[12] The rabbis mandated that not only could lights be lit before sunset to burn during the Sabbath, but that to kindle them was divinely decreed!

Our family began observing Shabbat in our home when Dick's Grandma Bess was eighty-eight years old. From then until almost the Sabbath before she died at ninety-six, we were frequently fortunate to have her at our Shabbat dinner table. Luckily for us, as Grandma Bess got older her memory of her long-distant past became clearer. So, while she sometimes couldn't readily remember details of recent events, she had vivid recall of times before she left Eastern Europe as a small child, and shared many stories of those long-gone years with us.

The story we all loved best, and beseeched her time and again to retell, explained how the brass candlesticks we use every Friday night happen to be on our table (and provided us with a kind of capsule history of how countless Jews and pairs of candlesticks came to the United States).

In the mid-1880s life was difficult for Grandma's family in Russia; economic problems were complicated by the fact that her teen-age brothers would soon be eligible for the Czar's army, in which Jews regularly suffered severe discrimination and mistreatment. Her parents, Moses and Molly Katchuk, finally planned to escape with their eight children.

They were able to take little with them but the clothes they wore, and knapsacks with a couple of changes for each person—only what was necessary and could easily be carried. As they prepared to leave their home forever, Grandma remembered her mother gathering her brood to her, holding the baby in one arm while clutching the Shabbat candlesticks with her free hand. Then they fled.

And so Molly Katchuk's great-great-granddaughters—our Miriam, Rachel, and Rebecca—feel a deep sense of their own roots as they place the Sabbath candles in her candlesticks on our dining-room table one hundred years later.

Blessing the Children

Following the candle-lighting and blessing, Dick chants the traditional Sabbath prayer over the children:

The Blessing of the Children

To Sons say:— : יְשִׂמְךָ אֱלֹהִים כְּאֶפְרַיִם וְכִמְנַשֶּׁה

To Daughters:— : יְשִׂמֵךְ אֱלֹהִים כְּשָׂרָה רִבְקָה רָחֵל וְלֵאָה

To Sons and Daughters:— יְבָרֶכְךָ יְיָ וְיִשְׁמְרֶךָ : יָאֵר יְיָ פָּנָיו

אֵלֶיךָ וִיחֻנֶּךָּ : יִשָּׂא יְיָ פָּנָיו אֵלֶיךָ וְיָשֵׂם לְךָ שָׁלוֹם :

To Sons: Y'simcha elohim k'Ephraim v'che-Menasheh.
To Daughters: Y'simeych elohim k'Sarah, Rivka, Rachel v'Leah.
To Sons and Daughters: Y'varech-cha adonai v'yish'mrecha. Ya'er adonai panav eylecha vichunecha. Yisa adonai panav eylecha, v'ya-seym l'cha shalom.

Fathers say to their sons: "May God make you like Ephraim and Menasheh" (Joseph's sons); and to their daughters: "May God make you like Sarah, Rebecca, Rachel, and Leah" (the virtuous matriarchs). The rest of the blessing for both sons and daughters is:

> The Lord bless you and keep you. The Lord make His face to shine upon you and be gracious to you. The Lord turn His face to you, and give you peace.

Kiddush

After the blessing of the children, Dick leads us in the singing of the Kiddush—the sanctification of the Sabbath—sung over a cup of wine, symbol of Sabbath joy.

Kiddush—The Blessing over the Wine

בָּרוּךְ אַתָּה יְיָ אֱלֹהֵינוּ מֶלֶךְ הָעוֹלָם · בּוֹרֵא פְּרִי הַגָּפֶן׃

בָּרוּךְ אַתָּה יְיָ אֱלֹהֵינוּ מֶלֶךְ הָעוֹלָם · אֲשֶׁר קִדְּשָׁנוּ
בְּמִצְוֹתָיו וְרָצָה בָנוּ · וְשַׁבַּת קָדְשׁוֹ בְּאַהֲבָה וּבְרָצוֹן
הִנְחִילָנוּ זִכָּרוֹן לְמַעֲשֵׂה בְרֵאשִׁית · כִּי הוּא יוֹם תְּחִלָּה
לְמִקְרָאֵי קֹדֶשׁ זֵכֶר לִיצִיאַת מִצְרָיִם · כִּי־בָנוּ בָחַרְתָּ
וְאוֹתָנוּ קִדַּשְׁתָּ מִכָּל־הָעַמִּים וְשַׁבַּת קָדְשְׁךָ בְּאַהֲבָה
וּבְרָצוֹן הִנְחַלְתָּנוּ · בָּרוּךְ אַתָּה יְיָ · מְקַדֵּשׁ הַשַּׁבָּת׃

Baruch ata adonai eloheynu melech ha-olam borey p'ri ha-gafen.

Baruch ata adonai eloheynu melech ha-olam, asher kidshanu b'mitzvotav v'ratza vanu, v'shabbat kodsho b'ahava uv'ratzon hinchilanu zikaron l'ma'asey v'reyshit. Ki hu yom t'chila l'mikra-ey kodesh zeycher litzi'at Mitzrayim. Ki vanu vacharta v'otanu kidashta mikol ha-amim, v'Shabbat kodsh'cha b'ahava uv-ratzon hinchaltanu. Baruch ata adonai m'kadeysh ha-Shabbat.

Praised are You, O Lord our God, King of the universe, Who creates the fruit of the vine.

Praised are You, O Lord our God, King of the universe, Who has sanctified us through Your commandments and has taken delight in us. In love and favor You have given us the holy Shabbat as a heritage, a reminder of Your work of creation, first of our sacred days recalling our liberation from Egypt. You chose us from among the people and in Your love and favor sanctified us in giving us Your holy Shabbat as a joyous heritage. Blessed are You, O Lord our God, Who hallows the Shabbat.

Just as it's been traditional for women to bless the candles, tradition has held that the man of the home raises his cup of wine and recites the Kiddush when the family has gathered around the Shabbat table. However, even among highly observant Jews variations are developed by individual families. We have frequently enjoyed Shabbat dinner with friends of ours who rotate the honor of reciting the Kiddush among their four children. The child who recites Kiddush also leads the singing at the conclusion of the meal.

Some scholars believe the practice of pronouncing the Kiddush over a cup of wine originated in the first centuries of the common era when a cup of wine began each meal. Then, when it was no longer a routine prelude to the meal, the practice of drinking a cup of wine before the Sabbath meal was kept on as a religious rite.[13] (As with so many customs, the practice is retained and imbued with new meaning long after the original reason is gone.)

Blessing over the Bread

We keep the challah covered with a napkin or special challah cloth until after the Kiddush when we bless the two loaves—a thanksgiving for the food about to be eaten.

Ha-Motzi—The Blessing over the Bread

בָּרוּךְ אַתָּה יְיָ אֱלֹהֵינוּ מֶלֶךְ הָעוֹלָם · הַמּוֹצִיא לֶחֶם מִן הָאָרֶץ׃

Baruch ata adonai eloheynu melech ha-olam ha-motzi lechem min ha-aretz.

Praised are You, O Lord our God, King of the universe, Who brings forth bread from the earth.

One rabbinic explanation for covering the challah is so that it won't be "insulted" that the wine is being blessed first. Actually, there is an excellent practical reason: when covered with a heavy napkin or cloth the challah retains its heat. A good thing, since those who baked it would suffer insult if they weren't praised for the wonderful still-warm-from-the-oven bread!

The practical reason for the use of two loaves of bread on Shabbat is that in ancient times there was always one loaf of bread to accompany each cooked dish (probably to absorb the liquid in the way we serve a hot dish over rice, potatoes, or noodles) and on Shabbat, the most festive day of the week, two cooked dishes were served.[14] A rabbinic explanation for the use of two loaves is that they symbolize the double portion of manna which the Israelites found in the wilderness on the sixth day of the week to eat on both the sixth and seventh days.

Songs

Although there are many songs which we sing between dinner courses and afterward, there is one stand-by that we sing every week before our meal officially begins. It is "L'Ha Dodi," composed by Sholomo Alkabetz, one of the Kabbalists of sixteenth-century Safed. These Kabbalists were religious mystics who took literally a passage in the Talmud which related that certain third-century sages would ready themselves for the Sabbath, then say: "Come, let's go and meet the Sabbath Queen" or the "Sabbath Bride." The Kabbalists, thirteen centuries later, put this passage into practice by walking in procession to the outskirts of town—as the sun went down late Friday afternoon—to greet the "Sabbath Bride." "L'Ha Dodi" is considered the best-known Hebrew poem and supposedly has been set to more tunes than any other poem the world over.[15]

Of the "L'Ha Dodi" melodies with which we're familiar our favorite is:

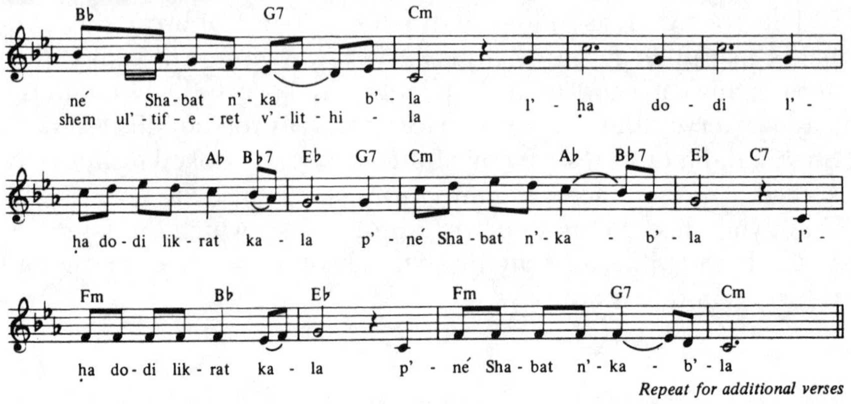

לְכָה דוֹדִי לִקְרַאת כַּלָּה פְּנֵי שַׁבָּת נְקַבְּלָה
שָׁמוֹר וְזָכוֹר בְּדִבּוּר אֶחָד הִשְׁמִיעָנוּ אֵל הַמְיוּחָד
יְיָ אֶחָד וּשְׁמוֹ אֶחָד לְשֵׁם וּלְתִפְאֶרֶת וְלִתְהִלָּה
לְכָה דוֹדִי לִקְרַאת כַּלָּה פְּנֵי שַׁבָּת נְקַבְּלָה

Come my friend to meet the bride; let us welcome the Sabbath. "Observe" and "Remember," in a single command, God announced to us. The Lord is One, and His name is One, for fame, for glory, and for praise.

It is the custom in many homes to sing "L'Ha Dodi" when everyone first gathers at the table, before any of the blessings are recited. In fact, we have friends who begin singing it as they get up from their living-room chairs and walk toward the dining room table to begin their Shabbat dinner; a symbolic re-creation of the processional of old.

One of our favorite table songs (zemirot) is "Tsur Mishelo," which we often sing at the table following our Shabbat dinner.

Tsur Mishelo

צוּר מִשֶּׁלּוֹ אָכַלְנוּ בָּרְכוּ אֱמוּנַי שָׂבַעְנוּ וְהוֹתַרְנוּ כִּדְבַר יְיָ.

Bless the Lord Whose food we ate. We ate and have some left, as God has said.

At the conclusion of our Shabbat meal we all enjoy participating in the Birkat Ha Mazon, which we also recite or sing after Shabbat lunch and at the conclusion of festival meals. There are many renditions of the Birkat Ha Mazon. The following version begins and ends with Hebrew verses, and includes four English paragraphs in the middle.

Birkat Ha Mazon—The Grace after Meals

בָּרוּךְ אַתָּה יְיָ אֱלֹהֵינוּ מֶלֶךְ הָעוֹלָם · הַזָּן אֶת־הָעוֹלָם כֻּלּוֹ · בְּטוּבוֹ בְּחֵן בְּחֶסֶד וּבְרַחֲמִים · הוּא נוֹתֵן לֶחֶם לְכָל־בָּשָׂר · כִּי לְעוֹלָם חַסְדּוֹ : וּבְטוּבוֹ הַגָּדוֹל תָּמִיד לֹא־חָסַר לָנוּ וְאַל יֶחְסַר־לָנוּ מָזוֹן לְעוֹלָם וָעֶד בַּעֲבוּר שְׁמוֹ הַגָּדוֹל · כִּי הוּא זָן וּמְפַרְנֵס לַכֹּל וּמֵטִיב לַכֹּל וּמֵכִין מָזוֹן לְכָל־בְּרִיּוֹתָיו אֲשֶׁר בָּרָא · בָּרוּךְ אַתָּה יְיָ · הַזָּן אֶת־הַכֹּל :

Baruch ata adonai, eloheynu melech ha-olam; hazan et ha-olam kulo b'tuvo, b'cheyn b'chesed uv-rachamim. Hu noteyn lechem l'chol basar, ki l'olam chasdo. Uv'tuvo ha-gadol, tamid lo chasar lanu v'al yechsar lanu mazon l'olam va-ed. Ba'avur sh'mo ha-gadol, ki hu zan umfarneys la-kol u'meytiv la-kol, u'meychin mazon, l'chol briyotav asher bara. Baruch ata adonai, hazan et ha-kol.

Praised are You, O Lord our God, King of the universe, Who feeds the whole world with Your goodness, with grace, with lovingkindness and tender mercy; You give food to all flesh, for Your lovingkindness endures forever. Through Your great goodness food has never failed us. O may it not fail us for ever and ever for Your great Name's sake, since You nourish and sustain all beings, and do good to all, and provide food for all Your creatures whom You have created. Praised are You, O Lord, Who gives food to all.

We thank You, O Lord our God, for the land, for the covenant and the Torah, and food in plenty. Praised are You, O Lord, for the land and for the food.
Have mercy, O Lord our God, on Israel Your people, and on the kingdom of the house of David. Grant us relief from all our troubles, and rebuild Jerusalem speedily in our days. Praised are You, O Lord, Who in Your mercy rebuilds Jerusalem. Amen.
Praised are You, O Lord our God, our Father, our King, Who deals kindly with all, and will deal kindly with us.
Let us inherit the day which will be entirely a Sabbath. Make us worthy of the days of the Messiah, and the life of the world to come.

עֹשֶׂה שָׁלוֹם בִּמְרוֹמָיו הוּא יַעֲשֶׂה שָׁלוֹם
עָלֵינוּ וְעַל כָּל־יִשְׂרָאֵל וְאִמְרוּ אָמֵן׃

Oseh shalom bimromav, hu ya'aseh shalom
aleynu, v'al kol Yisrael, v'imru ameyn.

May He who makes peace in high places make peace for us and for all Israel, and let us say Amen.

Shabbat Day

Our Sabbath eves are traditional and predictable—we always sit down to a better-than-usual meal in the dining room, with candles, wine, and challah, sing songs, relax and spend a leisurely evening, sometimes with friends joining us for Shabbat dinner, sometimes dropping by later in the evening, most of the time just at home with the family. How we spend the next day varies between what we call a "classical Shabbat" and what we have come to call a "contemporary Israeli Shabbat."

Classical Shabbat

Among our friends who observe a "classical Shabbat" are Myrna and Dan and their four children. On occasion we have enjoyed a most restful day with their family, going with them to services in the morning, then back to their home for a traditional noon meal, sitting around the table singing zemirot and participating in a study session with them.

Since their oldest child has been able to read, Myrna and Dan have had weekly Shabbat-study sessions with their children. When their younger children were babies and toddlers they napped during this part of the afternoon, but as they grew older and realized something meaningful was going on in the living room it became a kind of status symbol of advancing age to be able to skip or postpone napping and join in the studying. (Their oldest child is now in his late teens and, whereas in early years either Myrna or Dan led the afternoon study session, now the children take turns leading the study hour and selecting material, which ranges from Torah to current Jewish events.

While my father was alive and our children were young, we enjoyed a weekly "classical Shabbat" with him. We used to meet him at my parents' house and walk to the synagogue together, where we would participate in the services and the socializing afterward. We'd walk with him back to his house, then return home for a Shabbat lunch and nap, followed by an afternoon stroll.

We still often do spend Shabbat essentially in this way: going to services as a family, having lunch together, resting during the afternoon. But not always. Sometimes we enjoy a "contemporary Israeli Shabbat"—the kind of Shabbat we have spent frequently during the past few years, but for which we found a model only after our first visit to Israel.

Contemporary Israeli Shabbat

When in Israel, we are frequently invited to spend Shabbat with various friends. Each family celebrates Friday late afternoon and evening much as we do—with happy preparation and a leisurely, relaxing evening.

Shabbat morning does not begin at sunrise as does the Israeli workday, six days out of seven. Rather, our friends appreciate the chance to sleep later than usual, to ease into the day, have a relaxing midday meal, and spend the afternoon visiting on their only unstructured day of the week (Sunday in Israel is a full workday).

What's interesting is that on the face of it, this latter kind of Shabbat sounds as if it could be any day off. What makes it Shabbat? In Israel there is no question, for as in Eastern Europe in times past, the entire week looks to Shabbat. The Israeli work week is 5¾ days; the pace is hectic, the hours are long. When does an Israeli relax and wind down? When is there time to sit with family and see friends? On Shabbat, the most anticipated day of the week. Nobody works past early afternoon on Friday; everything closes early, not to reopen until Saturday night or Sunday morning. The entire environment is transformed from busyness to calm. There is no such day as Saturday: it is Shabbat.

This "contemporary Israeli Shabbat" is only part of the Shabbat picture in modern Israel. Throughout Jerusalem today one sees in microcosm the centuries of Shabbat philosophies, interpretations, and observances. Hassids (members of a particular group of highly observant Jews) wearing tall hats and long cloaks march ten abreast down main streets singing Shabbat melodies on their way to services; in the Orthodox sections such as Mea Shearim, women wear long-sleeved dresses and nylon stockings to the synagogue even in ninety-degree heat. In the Old City of Jerusalem, many men, women, and children congregate to pray at the remaining wall of the destroyed Temple. Within blocks of where the Temple once stood, families walk about visiting with one another, and children play. While the particulars of its observation vary from family to family, the spirit of Shabbat prevails in the land in which it was invented.

Shabbat in America

Observing Shabbat in America is very different. Externally, nothing changes. For our non-Jewish neighbors Saturday is just another day; albeit often a day away from offices, it is a time when another kind of work—getting the laundry and marketing done—takes place instead. So those of us who wish to make Saturday Shabbat must make our own internal changes. Once we do—and the concept that "this is Shabbat" is internalized—buses can run past the door, all the stores in town can be open, and it doesn't change Shabbat for us.

When the spirit of Shabbat becomes established, it is possible to enjoy the day by defining and doing the things that make it special and by omitting those activities that make it ordinary.

In addition to Friday night dinner, we practice three other Shabbat day traditions—Shabbat lunch, *se'udah sh'lishit* (the third meal), and the *Havdalah* (Separation) ceremony at the close of Shabbat.

SHABBAT LUNCH In our home we gather in the dining room for Shabbat lunch in the early afternoon; sometimes another family joins us, sometimes friends of the girls come, many times we're just our own family unit.

Blessings before the noon meal include the Kiddush (santification), said over the wine, and Ha-Motzi, the blessing said over the bread.

Kiddush—The Blessing over the Wine

בָּרוּךְ אַתָּה יְיָ אֱלֹהֵינוּ מֶלֶךְ הָעוֹלָם · בּוֹרֵא פְּרִי הַגָּפֶן׃

Baruch ata adonai eloheynu melech ha-olam
borey p'ri ha-gafen.

Praised are You, O Lord our God, King of the universe, Who creates the fruit of the vine.

Ha-Motzi—The Blessing over the Bread

בָּרוּךְ אַתָּה יְיָ אֱלֹהֵינוּ מֶלֶךְ הָעוֹלָם · הַמּוֹצִיא לֶחֶם
מִן הָאָרֶץ׃

Baruch ata adonai eloheynu melech ha-olam ha-motzi lechem min ha-aretz.

Praised are You, O Lord our God, King of the universe, Who brings forth bread from the earth.

Our menu is based on a variation of the Eastern European cholent. This long-simmering stew is similar to the Israelite *hamim* (Hebrew for hot), a kind of mixture which as far back as the second century was sealed and cooked in a slow oven, originally the still-hot embers of Friday afternoon's fire. The dish of stew was not opened until Saturday noon, when it was served hot. Jews took the slow-cooking concept with them into exile. They adapted the basic idea of a one-dish meal of meat, liquid, grain (barley, rice, etc.), legumes, and vegetables, all of which could be mixed, and baked overnight, according to the availability of the foods of the country in which they lived.[16] Families of Eastern Europe called their Shabbat meat and vegetable casserole "cholent," a word which comes from the Old French word *chald,* meaning warm.[17] In Germany it was known as *schalet.*

To keep the tradition of not lighting a flame on the Sabbath, families needed to have a specially built recess in the stove into which they could place a jar of hot water to hold the heat for food and drink. Not all stoves were large enough, nor were they all built with this feature, so often one neighbor heated the cholent for several families.

Since cooking is an everyday activity, we love the notion of preparing a double portion on Friday to keep Saturday free. Our cholent or hot food is a lighter version of the hearty Eastern European oven-casserole stew, which we find too filling for a midday meal. Instead, we have hot soup, which is, after all, simply stew made with more liquid. With it we usually serve a salad, and the second loaf of the challah. This menu easily expands for however many happen to be at our table.

Traditional Eastern European Cholent

2 pounds brisket or other cuts of beef
Salt and pepper to taste
3 medium onions, sliced
6 medium potatoes, peeled and sliced
1 cup dried Lima beans, soaked overnight in 6 cups of water

Place the meat in a 4-quart ovenproof casserole, season with salt and pepper, and cover with the sliced onions. Add the sliced potatoes and drained Lima beans. Cover with water. Then cover the casserole dish with a tight-fitting lid. Traditionally this is baked overnight in a 250°F. oven. For those who do not object to reheating food on Shabbat, it can also be prepared on top of the stove by cooking it over low heat for several hours. Makes 8 to 10 generous servings.

Our version of cholent, which I call a cholent soup, is far less heavy then the traditional Eastern European type. One can take a Shabbat walk after eating ours, whereas the traditional cholent is so filling it commands one to nap for the rest of the afternoon.

Cardozo "Cholent" Soup

Every Cardozo Shabbat soup is different from the one that preceded it, depending on what vegetables are readily available. A sample soup might be composed of:

2 beef bouillon cubes
1 pound beef, cubed
3 medium onions, peeled and sliced
3 potatoes, peeled and sliced
12 carrots, peeled and sliced
4 stalks celery with leaves, diced
½ pound fresh green beans, diced
2 sprigs fresh parsley
Salt and pepper to taste

Fill a 6-quart pot halfway with water and bring the water to the boil. Remove the pot from the stove. Add the bouillon cubes. Stir until they dissolve. Add the meat (browning is unnecessary as the meat is cooked for several hours on low heat so it remains moist), vegetables, parsley, and seasoning. Return the pot to the stove and bring the contents to a boil. Cover the pot and simmer the soup for about 4 hours on low heat. Makes 12–16 servings.

SE'UDAH SH'LISHIT In ancient times families ate two main meals per day; one at about ten in the morning, the other at the end of the afternoon. Because the Hebrew day begins and ends at sundown, every family counted on three Shabbat meals together —the Erev Shabbat Friday night dinner, the mid-morning meal, and the end-of-Shabbat evening meal. Later, this established routine gave rise to the rabbinic precept that one should eat three meals on Shabbat, and that no meal should precede morning prayers. The mid-morning meal was moved up a couple of hours and became our Shabbat lunch. The late afternoon meal became the se'udah sh'lishit—third meal of the day—and often concludes with Havdalah services.

The se'udah sh'lishit provides families with a perfect time to invite friends to share a leisurely visit. The menu for the third meal is usually very simple—an assortment of breads and cheeses, some relishes, tea, and sweets. Hard-boiled eggs seem to be universal for se'udah sh'lishit, perhaps because they are symbolic of the destruction of the Temple, something we remember even at the happiest, most relaxed times.

Se'udah sh'lishit is particularly popular in Israel with both religious (in Israel "religious" connotes those who are traditionally observant) and secular families. We experienced a most memorable se'udah sh'lishit with Orthodox Israeli friends in which our family and their family of six sat around their table eating eggs, challah, fresh fruit, and cakes, and singing for hours. We had an equally enjoyable time with another Israeli family in their apartment at "five o'clock Shabbat"—a secular term for se'udah sh'lishit. A number of families were invited; the younger children ate and played, the teen-agers and adults enjoyed tea, cakes, and conversation.

HAVDALAH This is the bittersweet time when, as the sun sets, just as on the evening before, we share a ceremony using candle-light and wine as our symbols to separate the Sabbath from the rest of the week. Whereas on Shabbat eve we light candles to begin the day of rest, at Shabbat's close we light a candle, pour wine, and sing songs to signify the Sabbath's end. On Shabbat eve we say a blessing over the challah, the bread which begins our meal; at Shabbat's end we say a blessing as we pass a spice box around one to another. Spices were used in ancient times at the end of meals.

Dick begins the Havdalah ceremony by raising a full cup of wine and leading us in the following blessing:

The Havdalah Blessing over the Wine

הִנֵּה אֵל יְשׁוּעָתִי אֶבְטַח וְלֹא אֶפְחָד כִּי עָזִּי וְזִמְרָת
יָהּ יְיָ וַיְהִי־לִי לִישׁוּעָה׃ וּשְׁאַבְתֶּם מַיִם בְּשָׂשׂוֹן מִמַּעַיְנֵי
הַיְשׁוּעָה׃ לַיְיָ הַיְשׁוּעָה עַל־עַמְּךָ בִרְכָתֶךָ סֶּלָה׃ יְיָ
צְבָאוֹת עִמָּנוּ מִשְׂגָּב־לָנוּ אֱלֹהֵי יַעֲקֹב סֶלָה׃ לַיְּהוּדִים
הָיְתָה אוֹרָה וְשִׂמְחָה וְשָׂשׂוֹן וִיקָר׃ כֵּן תִּהְיֶה לָּנוּ׃
כּוֹס יְשׁוּעוֹת אֶשָּׂא וּבְשֵׁם יְיָ אֶקְרָא׃

בָּרוּךְ אַתָּה יְיָ אֱלֹהֵינוּ מֶלֶךְ הָעוֹלָם · בּוֹרֵא פְּרִי הַגָּפֶן׃

Hiney eyl y'shu'ati evtach v'lo efchad ki azi v'zimrat
yah adonai va-y'hi-li lishu'a. Ushavtem mayim b'sason mima'ainey
ha-y'shu'a al-amcha birchatecha sela. Adonai
tz'va'ot imanu misgav-lanu elohai Ya'akov sela. La-y'hudim
haita ora v'simcha v'sason vikar. Keyn tih'yeh lanu.
Kos y'shu'ot eh-sa uvsheym adonai ekra.

Baruch ata adonai eloheynu melech ha-olam
borey p'ri ha-gafen.

Behold, God is my salvation; I will trust, and will not be afraid: for God the Lord is my strength and song, and He is become my salvation. Therefore with joy shall you draw water out of the wells of salvation. Salvation belongs to the Lord: Your blessing be upon your people. The Lord of hosts is with us. The God of Jacob is our refuge. The Jews had light and joy and gladness and honor. So be it with us. I will lift the cup of salvation, and call upon the Name of the Lord.

Praised are You, O Lord our God, King of the universe, Who creates the fruit of the vine.

The custom of pronouncing the Havdalah blessing over the wine apparently originated in much the same way as the Kiddush: just as a cup of wine began the meal, so a cup of wine ended it. Thus, the Havdalah blessing, which was recited at the conclusion of Shabbat anyway followed the third meal of the day. The meal concluded with a cup of wine, served at the time of the Havdalah prayer.[18]

Dick then lifts the spice box and passes it among us as we bless the spices:

The Blessing over the Havdalah Spices

בָּרוּךְ אַתָּה יְיָ אֱלֹהֵינוּ מֶלֶךְ הָעוֹלָם · בּוֹרֵא מִינֵי
בְשָׂמִים׃

Baruch ata adonai eloheynu melech ha-olam, borey miney b'samim.

Praised are You, O Lord our God, King of the universe, Who creates various kinds of spices.

There are various explanations as to the origin of the spices as part of the Havdalah ceremony. One view is that in ancient times the burning of incense always concluded the meal, and therefore the spices were literally always there. Another view is that before the advent of the fork, the fingers were cleansed with spices over a bed of hot coals; so the spices were brought in after the last Sabbath meal and hands were cleansed.[19]

Following the passing of the spice box, a blessing is recited over the light of a multi-wicked candle (many wicks signify the many manifestations of light), which was lit to provide light as darkness descended.

The Blessing over the Havdalah Candle

בָּרוּךְ אַתָּה יְיָ אֱלֹהֵינוּ מֶלֶךְ הָעוֹלָם · בּוֹרֵא מְאוֹרֵי הָאֵשׁ:

Baruch ata adonai eloheynu melech ha-olam borey m'orey ha-eysh.

Blessed are You, O Lord our God, King of the universe, Who creates the light of the fire.

One explanation for the custom of reciting a blessing over the Havdalah candle is that it demonstrates that Shabbat restrictions are no longer in force. (Lighting a fire is forbidden on Shabbat; we light the Havdalah flame hence terminating Shabbat.)

Havdalah concludes with a blessing that emphasizes the separation theme:

The Hamavdil Prayer

בָּרוּךְ אַתָּה יְיָ אֱלֹהֵינוּ מֶלֶךְ הָעוֹלָם · הַמַּבְדִּיל
בֵּין קֹדֶשׁ לְחוֹל בֵּין אוֹר לְחֹשֶׁךְ בֵּין יִשְׂרָאֵל לָעַמִּים ·
בֵּין יוֹם הַשְּׁבִיעִי לְשֵׁשֶׁת יְמֵי הַמַּעֲשֶׂה · בָּרוּךְ אַתָּה
יְיָ · הַמַּבְדִּיל בֵּין־קֹדֶשׁ לְחוֹל׃

Baruch ata adonai eloheynu melech ha-olam. Hamavdil beyn kodesh l'chol beyn or l'choshech beyn Yisrael la-amim beyn yom ha-sh'vi'i l'sheyshet y'mey ha-ma'aseh. Baruch ata adonai ha-mavdil beyn-kodesh l'chol.

Praised are You, O Lord our God, King of the universe, Who makes a distinction between holy and profane, between light and darkness, between Israel and the heathen nations, between the seventh day and the six working days. Blessed are You, O Lord, Who makes a distinction between holy and profane.

Dick then takes a drink of wine, extinguishes the candle in the wine, and we sing "Eliyahu Ha-navi." It's Eliyahu (Elijah) who, based on a verse at the end of the Book of Malachi, is expected to announce the coming of the Messiah. "Eliyahu Ha-navi" was originally sung at the conclusion of Shabbat because Jewish mystics believe the Messiah will not come on Friday while Jews are preparing for Shabbat nor on Saturday while they are resting, but rather begin to expect him immediately following the Sabbath. When we sing this Eastern European folk song at our table we think of Elijah not as did the mystics of old but rather as a symbol of peace.

Ëliyahu Ha-navi

May the prophet Elijah come soon, in our time, with the Messiah, son of David.

From "Eliyahu Ha-navi" we go right into "Shavua Tov" (Hebrew for "a good week"), and follow that by singing "A Gut Voch" (Yiddish for "a good week"). Although these words have been set to various tunes we simply sing them over and over to the same melody as for "Eliyahu Ha-navi."

There is never a time we sing this song that I don't recall the voice of my grandfather H. B., who died over twenty years ago, telephoning us as he did every week at the close of Shabbat to wish us *a gut voch.* Since Grandpa would have liked his grandchildren to have been raised with more Jewish practices than any of us were,

I know that he would chuckle with delight to see his *great-*grandchildren singing "A Gut Voch" to one another, and at the sight of all of us joining hands and breaking into Israeli dances at the conclusion of our Havdalah ceremony.

The Ancient Fall Festivals

Rosh Hashanah
Yom Kippur
Sukkot
Simchat Torah

The Ancient Fall Festivals

The four fall festivals comprise a twenty-three-day celebratory cycle beginning with Rosh Hashanah, which ushers in the High Holy Days, the ten days of the penitential New Year's season. The solemn fast day of Yom Kippur, the Day of Atonement, closes this ten-day period. Sukkot, celebration of the ingathering of the harvest, comes four days after Yom Kippur ends. This delightful festival lasts for eight days and is followed directly by Simchat Torah, the day of rejoicing in the Torah.

Celebrating the entire cycle rather than simply observing some individual holidays greatly enhances the impact of the total season. Our family once observed the quasi-festive days of Rosh Hashanah, and the solemn day of Yom Kippur, while knowing nothing about the joyous celebration of Sukkot and Simchat Torah. Now, however, we find Sukkot the most colorful, totally involving festival of the entire year. Moreover, if I attended a synagogue one day a year that day would most certainly be the joyous day of Simchat Torah, when young and old sing, dance, pray, eat, and drink around the Torah.

The origins of these four festivals are complex and intermingled. While in ancient times each festival day no doubt marked some kind of celebration, only later did historical, religious, and/or cosmic significance become attached to each of them. For instance, little evidence can be found for the day we know now as Rosh Hashanah as originally having been anything more than a special new moon festival. Each new moon was celebrated with a fast; thus Rosh Hashanah may have been a kind of minor version of Yom Kippur as we now know it.

Sukkot, for thousands of years the fall agricultural festival, may once have been the Jewish New Year festival. In fact, some scholars maintain that in ancient times there was a Sukkot New Year celebration which became almost Dionysian; spiritual leaders realized toning it down would be impossible but felt that at least people could be penitent before the revelry—so a fast day, now known as Yom Kippur, was instituted a few days before the beginning of the Sukkot festival.[1]

Regardless of how these various festivals evolved and why, what is important to Jewish families today is that so much developed and was passed down that we have a twenty-three-day fall celebratory period. That gift, given to us by our predecessors, is ours to preserve and enrich.

Rosh Hashanah

The Jewish New Year provides each family member with the opportunity to take stock of his or her relationships with others and, when necessary, to make amends. It is the time to begin the year among those for whom we care, coming together with family and close friends to greet one another, to share a walk, a visit, or a meal.

Rosh Hashanah, the New Year festival, and Yom Kippur, the Day of Atonement, which follows ten days later, comprise what we call the High Holy Days. Although many of us think of them as two distinct holidays, the New Year festival and the Day of Atonement form the beginning and the end of a ten-day period of penitence. The beginning is a subdued New Year's celebration (a Day of Remembrance where we look backward at the past year as well as forward to the new one), and the end is a Day of Penitence and of complete fasting.

Origin and Evolution

The Torah (Five Books of Moses), the source book from which interpretations of the major festivals of the Jewish year derive, does not prescribe a New Year celebration. It does stipulate, however, that the first day of the seventh Hebrew month is to be a special day.

> And the Lord spoke unto Moses saying: Speak unto the children of Israel, saying: "In the seventh month, in the first day of the month, shall be a solemn rest unto you, a memorial proclaimed with the blast of horns, a holy convocation. You shall do no manner of servile work: and ye shall bring an offering made by fire unto the Lord" (Lev. 23:23–25).

Many scholars interpret this passage to mean that at the time the Torah was written, Tishri 1, the first day of the seventh Hebrew month, was no more than a new moon festival, albeit a special one. (The shofar—ram's horn—blown to mark the New Year was always blown on the new moon.) Some biblical critics think Tishri 1 was chosen as Rosh Hashanah, "head of the year," because it began the seventh month, and in ancient times the number "seven" had special meanings.

The point in time when Tishri 1 was specified as the New Year festival is also unclear, and various scholars set forth fascinating and often divergent views on the subject. Many of them seem to agree that the New Year may originally have been celebrated at another time and then moved backward or forward to Tishri 1.

These are among some of the more intriguing views: Pesach, which falls in Nisan, the first month of the Jewish year, was probably the original Jewish New Year festival;[1] Pesach was one of two New Year festivals, it being the spring festival, and Sukkot, which comes exactly six months afterward, being the fall New Year; Tishri 10, now Yom Kippur, was originally the New Year;[2] Purim, with all its carnival-like festivities, may have been an introduction to, or spillover from, the Pesach spring New Year festival.[3] Still another hypothesis is that Shavuot, the late spring festival, which celebrates the receipt of the Torah, was originally the New Year festival.

The only thing which seems at all certain from these theories is that a good case can be made for almost every major festival originally to have been a New Year celebration. Perhaps Tishri 1 was ultimately chosen as New Year's Day precisely because it did not already commemorate a major historical moment, such as the

Exodus from Egypt or the encounter at Sinai, and thus it stands alone as a day from which new time is reckoned.

We do know that by Second Temple times the official Jewish New Year festival was celebrated on Tishri 1, and that most of the characteristics of the holiday as we now know it were established by that time. In the eleventh century C.E. Palestinian Jewry added Tishri 2 to the New Year festival, since Tishri 1 and 2 were considered "one long day."

Preparation

Preparation for the Jewish New Year takes place within the self. It is a time of introspection and self-appraisal, designed to lead to positive change. Some scholars hypothesize that like the New Year in most ancient agricultural societies, Rosh Hashanah originated as a time when a hoped-for renewal of the lease on land was synonymous with a new lease on life. However, from what may have begun in the primitive reliance on myth and magic, Judaism evolved a psychologically and sociologically sound system of personal evaluation.

From ancient shepherds in the Judean hills, trying through ritual and sacrifices to exert some influence on the rains upon which survival depended, we have come a long way. Our fate is no longer completely bound to crops we plant and harvest with our own hands. However, our destiny *is* intimately connected to those around us; our family and friends, our community. Thus, the entire Hebrew month of Elul, which precedes the New Year, is designated as one of repentance for wrongs committed against family, friends, and neighbors, either knowingly or unknowingly—and restitution is to be made.

Interestingly, many ancient societies specified a preparatory period for evacuating the evil before one welcomed the New Year and with it new chances. Many of these societies concentrated on the physical cleansing of the premises (witch hunting and burning), and a bit of this remains in the Rosh Hashanah customs of *tashlich* (pages 49–50) and the Yom Kippur *kapparot* (page 52).

Basically, however, the Hebrew-Jewish way of "banishing the evil" entails a "spiritual cleansing" through personal evaluation, recognizing one's errors, and developing the humility to rectify them through asking forgiveness from one's fellow man.

The month-long penitential period preparatory to Rosh Hashanah is not a day too long for us moderns. Restitution takes time, not only for trying to right obvious errors of commission but also for correcting errors of *omission* concerning people we care about but with whom there never seems time to keep in touch.

The Jewish New Year provides the opportunity to maintain communication. The New Year season, which usually falls about the time when the school year begins, is the perfect time to make a date to see friends even if it is for weeks or months hence. There is the relatively new Jewish custom of sending greeting cards to out-of-town friends, which can be an effective means of maintaining contact if the card contains a message—to tell our news, to ask about our friends, and to wish them the best of health and happiness and peace during the coming year.

Life gets busy, and structured, and complicated. Life with small children is often that way; life with older children is *always* that way. Maintaining contact with friends and relatives is a two-way street—if we don't reach out, they may not either. If we do, they may. And maintaining relationships with those we love and like is at the basis of what life is all about, though often we get so busy with what seems important that we forget what's *really* important. The fall festival season gives us a time to get in touch, to stay in touch—and thus to look forward to a richer year ahead.

Celebration

When one thinks of the secular New Year in American society as well as in many other cultures, the immediate connotations are of partying, singing, fun, and merrymaking. While many of the festivals of the Jewish year are characterized by these very features, the Jewish New Year is not.

Consistent with its theme of solemn evaluation and personal

scrutiny, in comparison both with other Jewish festivals and with secular New Year's celebrations, this holiday is one of subdued joyfulness. One wishes one's friends *"L'Shanah Tovah Tikatayvou"* (May you be inscribed for a good year); there may be wine toasts of *L'Chaim* (To life), but that's about the extent of the revelry.

Yet Rosh Hashanah is most definitely an occasion for enjoying the warm companionship of one's immediate family, often augmented by extended family and close friends. This coming together ties the family unit to something larger than itself and provides its members with a sense of linkage to others of similar heritage.

Extended Family Celebrations

My earliest recollections of the New Year are of coming in from Hastings, the small Minnesota town in which we lived and in which we were the only Jewish family, to my grandparents' home in north Minneapolis, an area which in some ways was a re-creation of an Old World Eastern European community. The homes in my grandparents' area were spacious, and northside Minneapolis Jews were involved in occupations in communities outside their living area. Nevertheless, in the early 1940s, within walking distance of my grandparents' home, were several synagogues, representing varying degrees of orthodoxy and conservatism, the Hebrew school, the Jewish Children's Home, and the Jewish Community Center; most of the neighborhood grocery stores, drugstores, butcher shops, and most other places of business were Jewish-owned and operated.

We arrived shortly before sundown Erev (the eve of) Rosh Hashanah. The businesses had already closed and the men were starting to walk to the synagogue. Grandpa was pacing impatiently outside the house talking with Uncle Mel and waiting for my father to join them to walk to services. As we entered my grandparents' home, filled with absolutely delicious aromas, Grandma seated me at the kitchen table and gave me tastes—a miniature meal, actually—of the feast soon to come.

Then Grandma's sister, Aunt Lu, who lived with my grandparents, occupied me with stories until Auntie Ethel emerged from her bubble bath and sang down the stairs, "Is Arlene here? Well, please have her come up and help me dress." And thus followed one of my favorite holiday routines of "helping" my beautiful lighthearted young auntie brush her brown curls and select what to wear from among her pretty dresses and high-heeled shoes.

When the men came home, Grandma called us to the white-clothed dining room table, where she lit *yom tov* (holiday) candles. Grandpa then recited the Kiddush over the wine. We began the meal with Grandma's chicken soup, followed by chopped liver and gefilte fish, beautiful vegetable and fruit platters, roast chicken, oven-browned potatoes, lots of baked carrots, fresh green peas, and then Grandma's beautiful orange fluff dessert.

At dawn the next morning, Grandpa left for "shul," going first to an Orthodox service he preferred, in a synagogue of which he was a founder; then later in the morning to meet Grandma and the rest of us at a Conservative synagogue, which he also helped found, when Grandma and her friends decided the *mechitza* (the division between men and women) had—once and for all—to be removed.

Shortly after we were seated in my grandparents' pews in the large sanctuary Daddy took us downstairs to "visit Grandpa," who did not sit upstairs in the pretty red upholstered second-row seats. Praying in English? Listening to the cantor and the choir? Not Grandpa. He and a group of his contemporaries had their own service downstairs in the stark chapel.

After services we'd return to Grandma's for a huge lunch, then friends and relatives would drop in during the afternoon prior to the feast Grandma would serve that evening. (This would all be repeated on the second day of Rosh Hashanah as well.)

While to me these exciting holiday times of being with my parents, grandparents, aunts, and uncle were all-consuming, my mother was always a little wistful—she remembered the holidays of her childhood when all of Grandma's seven sisters lived nearby (now only two did) and there was constant visiting back and forth in their homes with dozens of cousins. Although I loved the holidays the way they were, she always wished that it were possible to re-create her childhood holiday memories both for me and for herself. As a parent I grew to understand this. Dick and I with Miriam, age four, and Rachel, age one, had just moved back to Minneapolis from Boston; my grandparents had both died and my parents lived in my grandparents' house. The neighborhood had changed but the synagogues were still there. For the next five years, we still went to Grandma's house for the holidays, but it was my mother who came to the door and scooped up her granddaughters; it was now my father, their grandpa, who waited for Dick to walk to services with him just as he once had with his father-in-law, my grandpa H.B. I was now the mother, and the two little girls devouring their grandmother's chicken soup weren't my sister and me; they were my daughters.

Even then, when we were in an actual sense re-creating the past in the identical surroundings, I wondered—will this be as memorable for Miriam and Rachel as it was for me?

A few years later my parents sold the house and shortly thereafter my father died. I then found myself no longer going to Grandma's or Mother's for the holidays. And, no matter how we celebrated at home it seemed to me that the holidays weren't for our children what I remembered them being for me.

I now realize that while we can't re-create our own happy memories for our children, our families can establish new, equally joyful traditions. What my children, like many other children of the mobile society, have lost in not having a "grandma's house" to move into as regular holiday guests, they have gained by being integrally involved in the holiday hospitality process. Sometimes we invite another family, other times two or three families with children similar in ages to ours for the holidays. Over the years our children have come to feel that these friends are like cousins. They interact with them in much the same way that they would with relatives whom they might not see on a weekly basis; by picking up their relationship on one holiday where they left off on the last one.

In addition to spending holiday time with other families, we also have single friends who enjoy having a home to come to on the holidays, and who take an interest in our daughters much in the way that my single aunt and uncle used to make holidays special for me.

We always have friends for a mid-afternoon late-lunch/early-dinner meal after services on the first day of the holiday. The second day of the holiday is usually a "play-it-by-ear day" with our having a meal with friends in their homes, or going visiting during the afternoon, or having friends drop by, on a casual basis.

Rosh Hashanah Dinner

Although we have a big festival meal in the latter part of Rosh Hashanah afternoon, I'm not my grandma. Usually everyone brings a part of the meal and I make a main course or two. We have a short ceremony before we eat. While we light the festival candles the first night of Rosh Hashanah, the first and second days are considered "one long day" and we therefore don't light candles again on the second night.

The Blessing over the Candles

בָּרוּךְ אַתָּה יְיָ אֱלֹהֵינוּ מֶלֶךְ הָעוֹלָם · אֲשֶׁר קִדְּשָׁנוּ
בְּמִצְוֹתָיו וְצִוָּנוּ לְהַדְלִיק נֵר שֶׁל (***on Friday add***: שַׁבָּת וְ) יוֹם טוֹב :

Baruch ata adonai eloheynu melech ha-olam, asher kidshanu b'mitzvotav vitzivanu l'hadlik ner shel (on Friday add: Shabbat v') Yom Tov.

Praised are You, O Lord our God, King of the universe, Who has sanctified us by Your laws and commanded us to kindle the (on Friday add: Shabbat and) Festival light.

On the first night of the festival we recite the Kiddush immediately following candle-lighting. On the second night we say the Kiddush as soon as we gather at the table.

Kiddush—The New Year Blessing over the Wine

בָּרוּךְ אַתָּה יְיָ אֱלֹהֵינוּ מֶלֶךְ הָעוֹלָם · בּוֹרֵא פְּרִי הַגָּפֶן :

בָּרוּךְ אַתָּה יְיָ אֱלֹהֵינוּ מֶלֶךְ הָעוֹלָם · אֲשֶׁר בָּחַר־
בָּנוּ מִכָּל־עָם וְרוֹמְמָנוּ מִכָּל־לָשׁוֹן וְקִדְּשָׁנוּ בְּמִצְוֹתָיו ·

וַתִּתֶּן־לָנוּ יְיָ אֱלֹהֵינוּ בְּאַהֲבָה אֶת [יוֹם הַשַּׁבָּת הַזֶּה וְאֶת]
יוֹם הַזִּכָּרוֹן הַזֶּה יוֹם [זִכְרוֹן] תְּרוּעָה [בְּאַהֲבָה] מִקְרָא
קֹדֶשׁ זֵכֶר לִיצִיאַת מִצְרָיִם · כִּי בָנוּ בָחַרְתָּ וְאוֹתָנוּ
קִדַּשְׁתָּ מִכָּל־הָעַמִּים · וּדְבָרְךָ אֱמֶת וְקַיָּם לָעַד · בָּרוּךְ
אַתָּה יְיָ · מֶלֶךְ עַל כָּל־הָאָרֶץ מְקַדֵּשׁ [הַשַּׁבָּת וְ] יִשְׂרָאֵל
וְיוֹם הַזִּכָּרוֹן׃

Baruch ata adonai eloheynu melech ha-olam borey p'ri ha-gafen.
(On Shabbat add the words in brackets.)

Baruch ata adonai eloheynu melech ha-olam, asher bachar banu mikol-am v'romamanu mikol-lashon v'kidshanu b'mitzvotav vatiten-lanu adonai eloheynu b'ahava et [yom ha-Shabbat ha-zeh v'et] yom ha-zikoron ha-zeh yom [zikaron] Teruah [b'ahava] mikra kodesh zeycher litzi'at Mitzrayim. Ki vanu vacharta v'otanu kidashta mikol ha-amim, ud'varcha emet v'kayam la'ad. Baruch ata adonai, melech al col-ha-aretz m'kadesh [ha-Shabbat v'] Yisrael v'Yom ha-Zikaron.

Praised are You, O Lord our God, King of the universe, Who creates the fruit of the vine.

(On Shabbat add the words in brackets.)

Praised are You, O Lord our God, King of the universe, Who has chosen us from all peoples and exalted us above all tongues, and sanctified us by Your laws. And You have given us in love, O Lord our God [this Shabbat day and], this Day of Remembrance, a day of blowing the Shofar [on Shabbat substitute for the last phrase—a Day of Remembrance of blowing the Shofar, in love]; a holy convocation, as a memorial of the departure form Egypt. For You have chosen us and have sanctified us above all nations; and Your word is truth and endures forever. Praised are You, O Lord, King over all the earth, Who hallows [the Shabbat and] Israel and the Day of Remembrance.

Following the Kiddush, we recite the Shehecheyanu, a blessing of Thanksgiving for our having reached a new season, or for something new that is used or eaten for the first time.

Shehecheyanu—The Blessing for the New Season

בָּרוּךְ אַתָּה יְיָ אֱלֹהֵינוּ מֶלֶךְ הָעוֹלָם · שֶׁהֶחֱיָנוּ
וְקִיְּמָנוּ וְהִגִּיעָנוּ לַזְּמַן הַזֶּה׃

Baruch ata adonai eloheynu melech ha-olam shehecheyanu v'ki-y'manu v'higianu la-zman hazeh.

Praised are You, O Lord our God, King of the universe, Who has kept us in life, and has preserved us, and enabled us to reach this season.

Next we say the blessing over the bread, called the crown challah, that we bake for this festival. We use the same recipe as for our Shabbat challah on page 10 but add a cup of raisins to the dough to make it more festive. We mold the bread dough into a round shape thought to have been originated by Jewish mystics of the eighteenth-century Ukraine to symbolize "the kingship of the Creator of the Universe."[4] The rounded form of the bread also symbolizes the complete year for which we hope.[5]

Ha-Motzi—The Blessing over the Bread

בָּרוּךְ אַתָּה יְיָ אֱלֹהֵינוּ מֶלֶךְ הָעוֹלָם · הַמּוֹצִיא לֶחֶם
מִן הָאָרֶץ׃

Baruch ata adonai eloheynu melech ha-olam ha-motzi lechem min ha-aretz.

Praised are You, O Lord our God, King of the universe, Who brings forth bread from the earth.

We then pass a double dish, one side filled with sectioned apples, the other with honey; we recite the blessing over the apples as each person dips his apple in honey and eats it.

The Blessing over the Apples and Honey

בָּרוּךְ אַתָּה יְיָ אֱלֹהֵינוּ מֶלֶךְ הָעוֹלָם · בּוֹרֵא פְּרִי הָעֵץ:

Baruch ata adonai eloheynu melech ha-olam
borey p'ri ha-eytz.

Praised are You, O Lord our God, King of the universe, Who creates the fruit of the tree.

After eating the apple and honey we say:

יְהִי רָצוֹן מִלְּפָנֶיךָ יְיָ אֱלֹהֵינוּ וֵאלֹהֵי אֲבוֹתֵינוּ
שֶׁתְּחַדֵּשׁ עָלֵינוּ שָׁנָה טוֹבָה וּמְתוּקָה:

Y'hi ratzon milfanecha adonai eloheynu veylohey avoteynu
shet'chadeysh aleynu shana tova um'tuka.

May it be Your will, O Lord our God, and God of our fathers, to renew unto us a happy and pleasant year.

The custom of having something sweet, and avoiding anything sour, during Rosh Hashanah no doubt prevailed throughout the ancient world because of the belief system that what one ate determined what the year would hold. The specifics of the apples and honey seem to be that the apple is a symbol of fertility and abundance; the honey is used because since ancient times it has been said to have regenerative powers, and even thought to confer immunity from illness.[6] (Not to mention the allusion to the "land of milk and honey.")

In addition to the apples and honey we serve a first fruit of the season—something which those assembled would likely not have tasted as yet during the late summer or early fall. When we get dates from Israel we usually pass a dish of them around; otherwise we serve pomegranates or something equally unusual.

The custom of the eating of the first fruits of the season probably goes back to the time when the New Year was associated with the gathering of the fruits, first brought to the Temple for offering. The analogy is often made that since the destruction of the Second Temple the altar has been represented as the family dinner table, and thus the first fruits would be most appropriately served at this time.

Another explanation for the eating of the first fruits of the season on the *second* night of Rosh Hashanah is that since the two days of Rosh Hashanah are regarded as "one long day," there is doubt as to whether or not one should recite the Shehecheyanu on the second night. So as not to recite a blessing in vain, a new fruit is placed on the table, then the blessing is recited. The blessing is valid since the new fruit would require the blessing whether or not a new holiday occurred.

Following the challah, apples and honey, and first-fruits, we help ourselves at a buffet table on which the main courses are placed.

One of my favorite Rosh Hashanah dishes is a fish recipe that I learned from my good friend, Israeli author Bina Ofek. Although we can't get the same kind of fish as she did, and don't have those magnificent Israeli tomatoes for the sauce, we still enjoy our adaptation of her recipe.

Bina's Fish Patties

Patties: 2 pounds ground freshwater fish
Salt and pepper to taste
½ cup bread crumbs
2 eggs
1 cup water
1 teaspoon ground cumin
¼ cup chopped fresh parsley
6 teaspoons oil

Sauce: 3 (16-ounce) cans tomato sauce
2 medium onions, peeled and chopped
1 green pepper, seeded and chopped

In a bowl, mix together all of the ingredients for the patties. Refrigerate for several hours. Then form the cold mixture into about 16 patties. In a frying pan, saute the patties, a few at a time, in hot oil until brown on both sides. Place the patties in one layer on a greased baking dish (layering them will cause them to crumble). In a separate bowl, mix together the tomato sauce, onions, and green pepper. Pour the sauce over the patties. Cover tightly with foil. Bake at 350°F. for 1 hour. Serves 8.

Eating fish on Rosh Hashanah is customary in both the Sephardic and Ashkenazic traditions because of its ancient association with fertility and with immortality. In some families, on Rosh Hashanah the head of the household is served the head of a fish, over which he recites a blessing that "we will become like a head, not a tail." One explanation for this custom goes back to the ancient belief that what one eats determines what will happen during the year; thus, eating fish, because they are so prolific, will cause us "to multiply."

An unusual food prohibition connected with Rosh Hashanah is that placed on the eating of nuts. The theory behind this was that eating them might cause too much phlegm in the throat, thus making prayer difficult.

Rosh Hashanah Customs

Two of the most ancient Rosh Hashanah customs are the blowing of the shofar, which takes place in the synagogue, and the tashlich ceremony, which is performed near a body of water.

SHOFAR-BLOWING On the first and second days of Rosh Hashanah the younger children shiver with mixed awe and delight as the shofar is sounded in two series of blasts during the morning services. In Temple times the shofar—(made of a ram's horn, or the horn of any other ritually clean animal except the cow, a reminder of the golden calf) was blown as a means of making announcements; folklorists note that similar horns were blown by ancient Near Eastern tribes to declare war, and/or to frighten the evil spirits.

By the tenth century C.E. much rabbinic significance had been attached to Rosh Hashanah shofar-blowing. Among scholar and leader Saadya Gaon's much-quoted reasons for the blowing of the shofar are a reminder of our stand at the foot of Sinai; the Temple's destruction; the binding of Isaac; and the gathering of the Dispersal of Israel.[7]

TASHLICH Tashlich is an ancient custom wherein one goes with other members of the community to a body of water, turns one's pockets inside out, and recites certain prayers. Symbolically it is man's attempt collectively to cast away his sins in hopes of divine forgiveness for his repentance. Some synagogue congregations hold tashlich ceremonies immediately following services on the first day of the holiday, except when the first day falls on Shabbat; then tashlich is held the second day. In other congregations members gather later in the afternoon to perform tashlich, while still other congregations ignore the custom altogether.

According to rabbinic interpretation, tashlich is based on the verse in Micah (7:19) where the prophet speaks of God casting the sins of Israel into the sea "and Thou wilt cast *(ve-tashlich)* all their sins into the depths of the sea."[8]

Some scholars trace the tashlich ceremony back to primitive roots and give a variety of reasons for it, including the shaking off and washing away of sins. One theory holds that the ceremony derives from the ancient belief that every stream or body of water was inhabited by a spirit who claimed a life each year. Thus people emptied crumbs from their pockets into the stream to feed the spirit, thereby hoping to appease it—a literal casting of their bread upon the waters.[9]

The first time I ever witnessed a tashlich ceremony, though I didn't realize immediately what was going on, was on a visit to New York City during Rosh Hashanah. When I saw thousands of black-garbed figures moving slowly toward the water it seemed, initially, that the entire population of the city was making an exodus into the East River. As I drew closer, and the service began, I realized that I was watching the ancient tashlich ceremony, performed for thousands of years by Jews in towns, villages, and cities the world over. This time it was taking place during what, for the rest of the city, were regular business hours, in the world's busiest metropolis.

Although we usually don't participate in an official tashlich ceremony, a Rosh Hashanah afternoon walk has become a family custom. Since we live across the street from the Mississippi River, we do, in fact, walk along the riverbank every Rosh Hashanah, often with friends with whom this New Year's walk has become a tradition.

Yom Kippur

Yom Kippur, the most solemn day of the Jewish Year, culminates the ten-day penitential season and provides families with a final chance to reflect together on the year gone past before participating in a fresh future. Yom Kippur—Day of Cleansing, of Purgation, of Atonement—derives from the biblical passages (Lev. 16:29–31) that state: on the tenth day of the seventh month ". . . Ye shall afflict your souls and do no manner of work . . . for on that day shall atonement be made for you; to cleanse you . . ."

To many, Yom Kippur is considered the most important day in the Jewish year. In fact, persons who observe little or nothing of their heritage year round often attend the synagogue this one day.

The explanation seems to be found deep in our most basic fears and superstitions. Irrespective of religious or cultural teachings, man instinctively fears reprisals for actions which he knows are harmful or hurtful to others. Regardless of any reverence for a particular deity, man has always intuited that there are powers in the universe greater than himself, and has responded with fear, awe, and the attempt in some way to propitiate these powers.

Origin and Evolution

The ancient Yom Kippur rituals were rooted in our ancestors' desires to rid themselves of the sins of the past year so as to begin the year anew. Leviticus 16 prescribes a complex methodology for evacuating the community's sins, culminating with the banishment into the desert of a goat laden with the collective wrongdoings of the past year.

Belief in the ability to transfer sins from human to animal was prevalent in ancient times; the Babylonians also celebrated a ten-day New Year festival, the fifth day of which was spent in a cleansing exercise called *Kuppuru,* wherein a ram was used to absorb the community sins.[1]

This kind of "transference" ritual provided a basis for the Jewish custom of kapparot, which apparently originated in Babylonia, and was widely practiced there by the tenth century. The custom spread, and kapparot was practiced for many centuries by Jews the world over. The kapparot—a fowl, usually a rooster for each male in the family and a hen for each female—was tied and then twirled around the head of its captor, whose chants were believed to transfer human transgressions to the captive. The fowl was then slaughtered, the sins presumably expiated with its death, and given to charity.

As with the scapegoat sent into the wilderness, the kapparot ceremony exemplified the deeply rooted belief that somehow sins can be transferred from human to animal, and with this transference, evil spirits that cause evil behavior frightened away. The practice of kapparot was long in dispute among rabbis, some of whom advised their followers against performing such rites.[2]

Over the centuries the custom of kapparot changed from the use of fowl to the use of coins; as the coins were twirled, chants relating to transgressions were recited, then the money was given to charity.

The penitential ceremonies involving first a scapegoat, later fowl, and finally coins are no longer a part of our Yom Kippur observances. However, a residual seems to remain in the form we moderns take of giving to charity through the pledge cards that are distributed in synagogues across the land on Yom Kippur.

Yom Kippur serves an important purpose within the total context of the Jewish year. It is a chance for a final reflection on the wrongs which one may have committed against one's friends, relatives, or neighbors, intentionally or not, during the past year. On Yom Kippur, Judaism provides the opportunity to attempt restitution as a community. The synagogue prayers are in the plural; nobody is exempt as the congregation prays for absolution for sins committed "knowingly and unknowingly."

Yom Kippur is a time unto itself; a day which differs from the usual work routine and from any other Jewish holiday. It is truly a fast between feasts; between Rosh Hashanah the week before, and the marvelous festival of Sukkot, which follows a few days later. When Yom Kippur is observed along with the many Shabbat and festival celebrations of the year, within the full rhythm of the Jewish festival cycle, it can be fully appreciated. But when the Day of Atonement is the one and only time that a person relates to his own heritage, then the beauty of multi-dimensional Judaism is lost. For what purpose is a fast without a feast to follow?

Preparation

On a spiritual level preparation for Yom Kippur takes place within the soul; on a practical level it takes place in the kitchen. No cooking is to be done on the day, yet a special meal is necessary before the Yom Kippur fast begins, and hungry fasters need good food afterward.

The tradition of eating a hearty meal before the fast stems back to Temple times when families ate a huge evening meal to fortify themselves for the next day. (The high priest, however, was fed sparingly lest he fall asleep during the prayers.)

In our family we have found that the practicalities of fasting necessitate that we plan enough time for a leisurely evening meal, and that nothing very salty or spicy is served lest we become too thirsty during the ensuing hours, since fasting means nothing to eat or drink from one sundown to the next. The mainstay of our Erev Yom Kippur menu is roast chicken, which my grandmother and mother always served. Actually, this food is customary with Jews the world over,[3] no doubt deriving from the chicken used in the kapparot ceremony.

Celebration

The word observance, rather than celebration, best describes Yom Kippur.

We gather with friends and family for the evening meal (to be completed before sunset when the new day and the fast begins).

Yom Kippur Eve

Because the holiday begins following the meal, we light the candles afterward, at sunset, and recite the Shehecheyanu.

The Blessing over the Candles

בָּרוּךְ אַתָּה יְיָ אֱלֹהֵינוּ מֶלֶךְ הָעוֹלָם · אֲשֶׁר קִדְּשָׁנוּ
בְּמִצְוֹתָיו וְצִוָּנוּ לְהַדְלִיק נֵר שֶׁל־ (שַׁבָּת וְ *On Friday add*)
יוֹם הַכִּפֻּרִים

Baruch ata adonai eloheynu melech ha-olam, asher kidshanu b'mitzvotav vitzivanu l'hadlik ner shel [On Friday add: Shabbat v'] Yom Ha-Kippurim.

Praised are You, O Lord our God, King of the universe, Who has sanctified us by Your laws and commanded us to kindle the light of the [On Friday add Shabbat and the] Day of Atonement.

Shehecheyanu—The Blessing for the New Season

בָּרוּךְ אַתָּה יְיָ אֱלֹהֵינוּ מֶלֶךְ הָעוֹלָם · שֶׁהֶחֱיָנוּ
וְקִיְּמָנוּ וְהִגִּיעָנוּ לַזְּמַן הַזֶּה :

Baruch ata adonai eloheynu melech ha-olam shehecheyanu v'ki-y'manu v'higianu la-zman hazeh.

Praised are You, O Lord our God, King of the universe, Who has kept us in life, and has preserved us, and enabled us to reach this season.

In keeping with the tradition that Yom Kippur represents one's "last chance" before the old year ends to seek forgiveness for any wrong committed against a friend, neighbor, or relative, some families use the Erev Yom Kippur meal as an opportunity for final reflection. Each family member wants to make sure to begin the new year without buried grudges toward another, so each takes a turn recalling hurts he believes he may knowingly or unknowingly have inflicted upon each of the others. Rather than to try to justify the words or acts, the person requests that his behavior be forgiven and forgotten.

After Erev Yom Kippur dinner we go to Kol Nidre services (the name comes from the Kol Nidre—"All Vows"—prayer sung at the beginning of the service). During the service in some congregations, the rabbi suggests that anyone in the room who wishes to apologize to, and ask forgiveness from, anyone else in the room do so at that time. No one sits. Everyone jumps up and goes first to one and then to another, talking, hugging, and kissing. These few minutes are in the truest spirit of Yom Kippur since Jewish theology holds that man cannot receive pardon from God for sins committed against his fellow man. That pardon must be sought and granted between man and man.

The next morning we go to services, then home for a stroll and/or a nap before returning to the synagogue for the Neilah (closing) service. Originally Neilah referred specifically to the "closing of the gates" of the Temple at the end of the day; now, however, many rabbis give it the connotation of the "closing of the heavenly gates"—that the mystical Book of Life is sealed on this day.

The Break-fast

After services, some families have a tradition of enjoying a big break-fast meal together in the home of friends or relatives; often this is a communal meal where each family brings one of the many courses.

We were once part of a small congregation which hosted its own break-fast meal. That way everyone could participate in Neilah services without having either to stay at home to prepare a meal for the other fasters, or having to come home and prepare a meal later. The menu was simple; everyone brought something the day before—juices, bagels, cream cheese, salads, cheeses, kichel, breads, and sweets. We used paper plates and cups. Everyone ate well and nobody left the synagogue hungry after Yom Kippur.

Nowadays, our family tradition is simply to go home after Neilah with the girls, and perhaps a friend or two, and have a quiet break-fast meal, which we have organized in advance of leaving for the late afternoon Neilah service.

I can't recall my grandma, my mother, or any of my aunts ever going to Neilah services; that was for the men. The women remained at home preparing the break-fast meal, while trying to remember not to taste anything as they arranged platters and heated food. I never stayed around to help but rather managed to leave with Daddy and Grandpa, returning with them a couple of hours later to a wonderful meal.

I still go to Neilah, nowadays with Dick and the girls, and still return home to delicious food—but now it takes a bit more doing on my part. My daughters, unlike their mother when she was their age, help prepare the break-fast table and meal before returning to the synagogue for Neilah.

It's traditional to break the fast with something sweet, both because it's symbolic of a sweet year to come and because it raises the blood sugar. It's also traditional to eat something salty to help replenish the body's lost salt.

The break-fast is almost always a dairy meal because it's light and easy to digest. In our home we break the fast with orange juice, coffee cake, and tea or coffee. Our favorite break-fast coffee cake is a simple one that Mother brought over one year at the end of the fast. We have been making it ever since.

Mother's Break-fast Coffee Cake

Batter: 1½ cups flour
½ cup sugar
2½ teaspoons baking powder
½ teaspoon salt
1 egg white
¼ cup corn oil
¾ cup skim milk

Topping: ½ cup tightly packed brown sugar
½ cup chopped nuts
2 teaspoons cinnamon
2 tablespoons flour
2 tablespoons corn oil

In a bowl mix together the flour, baking powder, salt, and sugar. In another bowl, beat the egg white; mix with the corn oil and milk. Add the egg-milk mixture to the dry ingredients. Mix topping ingredients together in a separate bowl. Grease an 8″×8″×2″ pan. Alternate batter with topping, in two layers, finishing with topping. Bake the cake in a 375°F. oven for 25 to 30 minutes until it is brown on top. Serves 8.

The rest of our menu often includes fresh fruit and salmon salad. (Most break-fast menus include some kind of salty fish. While our preference happens to be salmon, many families prefer herring.) Tuna or lox with bagels and cream cheese is another popular break-fast treat.

After our break-fast evening meal we go out to the back yard to begin erecting our sukkah frame. (This, we found out some years after we began doing so, is traditional, because a person is so anxious to begin putting up his sukkah that, after the Yom Kippur fast, he drives in at least one nail as a symbolic start.) Ours is indeed only a symbolic start because it's late, and dark, but it's nonetheless a beginning toward the festival of Sukkot, which arrives just four days later.

Sukkot

(Feast of Booths, Feast of Tabernacles, Feast of the Ingathering)

A Joyous Festival

The magnificent festival of Sukkot means several days of delightful preparation during which all family members are thoroughly immersed in sukkah construction and decoration, followed by eight days of shared celebration. This colorful, joyous festival also offers a variety of opportunities to invite literally all of one's relatives, friends, and neighbors to celebrate in the sukkah at some point during the holiday.

The first two days of Sukkot are stipulated in the Torah as days on which no work is to be done, except for the preparation and serving of meals. During the third through sixth days of the festival, work goes on as always, although the sukkah and the festival atmosphere make these days very different from ordinary workdays. The seventh day, called Hoshana Rabba, is characterized by the beating of willow branches during morning synagogue services. We like to gather willows to add to the sukkah decorations on this day. The final day of the festival, called Shemini Atzeret, is prescribed by the Torah as another day free from work. The rabbis have interpreted that one may eat but not sleep in the sukkah on this holiday. We enjoy meals, snacks, and visits with others in our temporary dwelling throughout the eight-day period. (In our climate this sometimes means we wear light clothing; other times jackets, sweaters, and scarves.)

Origin and Evolution

Sukkot provides us with the opportunity to re-enact our ties with the pre-Israelite ancients of thousands of years past, as well as to participate in the continuing drama of Judaism.

Centuries before Abraham there were fall harvest festivals in the ancient world. Although the dates varied from year to year according to the amount of rainfall, whenever the harvest was completed a thanksgiving celebration took place. The people gathered to thank their deities for the food they would eat during the coming months. As our Israelite ancestors became a separate people they addressed thanks for their crops to Yahweh, and celebrated with the harvest festival we call Sukkot.[1]

Long after the festival itself originated, a historical reason relating to the Exodus from Egypt became attached to Sukkot, as was the case with the spring harvest festivals of Pesach and Shavuot. But whereas the Bible ascribes a highly dramatic event as the reason for each of the spring festivals (for Pesach, the event is the Exodus itself; and for Shavuot, it is the receipt of the Torah at Sinai), the reason attached to Sukkot is simply that we dwell in booths (sukkot) to remember our ancestors' forty years of wandering in the desert after the Exodus.

Our forebears surely must have lived in tents rather than in booths.[2] However, recognizing ties with the nomadic life of old; recalling our wanderings both through the desert and the Diaspora; and realizing the impermanence of man, of our lives and location are all important today. And because of the highly participatory nature of Judaism we don't just remember and recognize in a vacuum—we relive the event each fall by building and using a temporary dwelling for eight days.

Sukkot in Temple Times

In Temple times the richly colorful week-long festival of Sukkot was known as *the festival* of the year. Even those pilgrims who couldn't leave their crops and fields for the spring pilgrimage festivals of Pesach and Shavuot journeyed to Jerusalem for the fall thanksgiving celebration. Jerusalem was filled with visiting families who constructed temporary leaf-and-fruit-covered booths and celebrated there for a week. The Temple was the center of all activities, with trumpets blowing, animal sacrifices, morning "water libation" ceremonies, and the nightly *Simchat Bet Hasho'evah,* a torch dance ceremony during which the lights from huge candelabras shone all over Jerusalem.[3]

Although the Temple is long gone, generations of our ancestors preserved Sukkot with the sukkah evolving as the outstanding feature of the festival. Therefore, thousands of years later we retain much of the festival's original fun and color, right in our own back yards, where we erect and decorate our own sukkah each fall, and celebrate with friends, family, and neighbors.

Preparation

Dick and I had no exposure to Sukkot during our childhoods or in the early years of our marriage. When we returned to Minneapolis fourteen years ago we met a number of friendly families, many of whom were also part of the university community. The year we moved in we were invited to join one family for an Ukrainian Easter celebration, and another for the Indian New Year.

Then one fall evening, Naomi, a recent acquaintance, called to ask, "Would Dick be able to drive over and help Ben put up the sukkah tonight?" "Sure," Dick said, glad to be helpful, but not knowing in the least to what he'd agreed.

Dick drove over to help Ben. The following night we were all invited to dinner in the sukkah—a wooden booth which Ben had attached to their home, roofed with cornstalks, and decorated with fall leaves and fruit. Later that week we were invited to "Open Sukkah" at Naomi and Ben's, where we drank wine and ate honey cake with their other friends and their neighbors.

Dick, preschoolers Miriam and Rachel, and I were charmed with the whole festival, and were particularly excited that we weren't only experiencing how other people celebrated a holiday—this holiday was *ours* if we wanted it. And, did we! The following fall, the Yom Kippur fast was barely over when we called Naomi and Ben and asked, "Will you all come and help us build a sukkah?" From then until their family moved out of state several years later, our families enjoyed helping one another right down to frantic last-minute calls back and forth—"Do you have extra gourds?"—and joint last-minute trips to a generous friend's farm, where we'd quickly cut down more cornstalks.

Our need for cornstalks derives from the rabbinic interpretation that the roof of the sukkah should be open enough so that the stars can be seen, yet covered with a particular kind of natural material called *sekhakh.* This material should: 1) grow from the earth; 2) be cut down, and no longer be connected to the ground (this means one should *not* build the sukkah under a huge tree using the hanging branches to serve as a roof); and 3) not be subject to ritual impurity as would be, for example, animal skins or cloth.[4] Materials that meet these specifications and are most frequently used are branches cut from trees or bushes, bamboo reeds, very narrow wood beams, or cornstalks, which happen to be the particular kind of sekhakh most readily available to us in Minnesota.

Luckily, several friends have large gardens to which we make trips each fall to cut sekhakh. The gathering of the sekhakh is an event to which our family has always greatly looked forward; and no wonder, for it's a means in modern times to experience the construction of our own dwelling.

Sukkah-building

Ben's sukkah was a collapsible, wooden structure which he reassembled each Sukkot and stored in the rafters of his garage. It consisted of three walls which were attached to the back wall of his house, so Naomi was able to open the kitchen window and pass the food through, saving many trips in and out of doors.

Our sukkah, which Dick built, consists of six square frames of 2″×4″s, made to fit together in the shape of a hexagon. We lay long thin strips of wood across the top to support the sekhakh. These strips and the six frames can be assembled and disassembled easily each year. The advantage is it's large and light; the disadvantage (if it is one) is that besides covering the roof with sekhakh we need to tie branches or cornstalks around all the sides to fill in the thin open beams.

Our sukkah frame is an example of putting one's own touches on an ancient tradition, for never before had we ever heard of, or seen anything but a rectangular sukkah. In fact, at first I was very self-conscious about our "different sukkah." Was it really all right? A couple of years after Dick designed ours, some friends built a similar but much more elaborate round sukkah.

Recently a new rabbi moved to town and both we and our friends invited him over during Sukkot. Afterward, he remarked, "How interesting, the Jews of Minnesota build round sukkot." This, I suspect, is how new interpretations of old customs are born!

Those interested in building their own sukkah for the first time can find some basic plans in *The Jewish Catalogue*[5] or can inquire at their local Jewish community center or synagogue. In some communities a prefabricated sukkah can be purchased and then easily erected.

Sukkah-decorating Party

Once we have the sukkah frame up and huge mounds of cornstalks fill one corner of the back yard, the real excitement begins. Each of our girls invites some friends to join us for a sukkah-decorating afternoon—one of the merriest of all our family traditions.

Each year I take renewed pleasure in seeing the way in which this shared event knows no age limits, and at how our daughters work together with fervor on the decorating festivities. A sukkah-decorating afternoon can mean, in addition to our family, another eight, ten, or twelve of the girls' friends joining in to help. Our brigade of sukkah decorators used to be composed of toddlers and grade-schoolers; now, it's college students, high-schoolers, and grade-schoolers, with an occasional toddler accompanying a sibling for the fun of it.

Rebecca's contemporary, Donna, was the first to arrive at a recent sukkah-decorating festivity, bringing with her some brightly colored fall leaves she'd picked along the way. Moments later a walking grapevine entered the back yard, which when untangled turned out to be propelled by Alicia, who's been helping us decorate since she and Miriam were seven years old. "We always go to our house to pick grapevines out of our garden for the sukkah roof anyway," Alicia said, "so this time I thought I'd bring the vine along when I came. As it turned out, the vine brought me." (In addition to the fact that using a grapevine on the roof of our sukkah has become our tradition because of Alicia's family's generosity in providing us with this form of decorating material, there is an older reason for its use: grapes and olives, for which Israel is still known, were part of the ancient Sukkot harvest celebrations.)

Within a few minutes some of Rachel's friends walked up the driveway, with a carload of Miriam's classmates pulling up behind them. Rebecca and Donna jumped up and down with excitement as two more grade-schoolers arrived; then, using heavy twine, we all began tying cornstalks around the sides of the sukkah.

Once we had the sukkah's sides completely "cornstalked," Dick and the tallest teen-agers placed stalks and grapevines on the top as roof covering, carefully arranging them so as to abide by the rabbinic injunction that one must be able to see the stars through the sukkah's roof but that the interior of the sukkah must have more shade than sun.

Meanwhile, the grade-school contingent went to the riverbank to hunt more brightly colored leaves, then rushed back thrilled with their finds—some whole fallen branches of flaming gold, orange, and brilliant red leaves—which they immediately attached to the doorway of the sukkah's frame.

Once the frame and roof were covered, we all vied for the largest and most beautiful of the gold, green, yellow, and orange gourds to tie around the inside of the sukkah.

Anything that is bright and plentiful, and that reflects the harvest of the geographical area, is appropriate sukkah-decorating material. Pomegranates, grapes, and other indigenous fresh fruit adorn the sukkot of Israel; however, we use gourds rather than fresh fruit since our Minnesota squirrels are oblivious to the rabbinical injunction that sukkah decorations are not to be eaten during the festival.

Miriam has tapes of Israeli music playing during the decorating activities and we sing and work along with them as background.[6] Among our favorites are "Artsa Alinu," which became popular during this century among the pioneers of modern Israel, and the spiritual folk tune "Yom Tov Lanu."

Artsa Alinu

We have come to our beloved land. We have plowed and planted but we have not yet harvested our crop.

אַרְצָה עָלִינוּ
כְּבָר חָרַשְׁנוּ וְגַם זָרַעְנוּ
אֲבָל עוֹד לֹא קָצַרְנוּ

Yom Tov Lanu

יוֹם טוֹב לָנוּ חַג שָׂמֵחַ יְלָדִים נָגִילָה
לְסֻכָּתֵנוּ בָּא אוֹרֵחַ אַבְרָהָם אָבִינוּ בָּרוּךְ הַבָּא
יַחַד הַחַג נָחוֹג בְּלוּלָב הֲדַס אֶתְרוֹג
הוֹי הֶאָח נִשְׂמַח מְאֹד וּבְמַעְגָּל נִרְקֹד

A holiday for us
A happy holiday children enjoy
Abraham, our father, visits our sukkah
Blessing upon him
Together we will celebrate the holiday with
lulav and etrog
We will dance in a circle.

Sukkot Foods

Each year while the decorating is progressing, Rachel, Rebecca, and I take turns going in to our kitchen to mix up a couple of loaves of zucchini bread, or to pull a batch of applesauce cookies from the oven. We bake a great deal on sukkah-decorating afternoon because hungry decorators consume plates of cookies, along with cups of hot cider sucked through cinnamon sticks; and in addition, as long as all the ingredients are out anyway, we bake for the freezer to ensure that we'll have cookies, bars, and breads to serve throughout the week-long festival.

We like ingredients that reflect the harvest season, so we include recipes that make use of available fruits and vegetables.

Among our favorites is *zucchini bread.* The recipe is from our good friend Sue, who baked and brought bread—made from her home-grown zucchini—to our sukkah for many years.

Zucchini Bread

3 eggs (I use 3 egg whites, 1 yolk)
1 cup oil
2 cups sugar
1 teaspoon vanilla
2 cups grated zucchini
1 teaspoon baking soda
1½ teaspoons baking powder
3 teaspoons cinnamon
½ cup nuts
3 cups flour

In a mixing bowl, beat together the eggs, oil, sugar, and vanilla for 1 minute. Add the zucchini and mix it with the other ingredients. Combine the baking soda, baking powder, cinnamon, nuts, and flour. Mix well and then blend into the zucchini mixture. Pour into two greased 9″×3″×3″ loaf pans. Bake at 325°F. until firm and golden brown, about 1 hour. Let cool before removing from pans. Makes two loaves.

Another favorite is, and has been, one of Rebecca's specialties since she was six years old. We aren't sure why but when she makes it the result is always moister and more delicious than when anyone else in our family tries. We've accused her of adding a secret ingredient or two, but she maintains that she follows this recipe:

Cinnamon-Molasses Cake

1 cup molasses
1½ cups water
1 teaspoon baking soda
1 cup corn oil
1 cup sugar
2 egg whites, slightly beaten
2¼ cups flour
1 teaspoon baking powder
1 teaspoon ground ginger
2 tablespoons cinnamon

In a large saucepan, combine the molasses, water, and baking soda and bring to a boil; boil for 1 minute. Let cool. In a bowl, mix together the corn oil, sugar, and egg whites; add to the molasses mixture. In a large mixing bowl, sift together the flour, baking powder, ginger, and cinnamon. To the dry ingredients, add the molasses mixture. With an electric mixer, on low speed, beat for 2 minutes. Pour into a greased 8″×8″× 2″ pan. Bake at 375°F. until firm, about 40 minutes. Makes 12 squares.

Celebration

Dinner in the Sukkah

Sukkot lends itself perfectly to celebration with other family groups, for the sukkah provides a delightfully informal atmosphere, and proves the point that one needn't have a fancy house in order to entertain one's friends. Besides that, the grass "floor" need not be vacuumed or swept; paper plates are most appropriate; fresh fruits and vegetables of the season abound, making cooking largely unnecessary, and what cooking is done, simple.

Some families eat every meal in the sukkah, others eat only their evening meals there, and still others eat there only when the weather permits. According to the Talmud one must eat the first meal of the festival in the sukkah—and, because we're always anxious to eat in the newly erected and decorated sukkah—this is a *mitzvah* ("commandment, precept, or religious duty") our family gladly fulfills.

We usually invite close friends to share the fun of the first night of Sukkot with us. As we gather in our newly gourd-squash-pumpkin-decorated, cornstalk-walled hut, we precede the meal with the lighting of the festival candles; the festival Kiddush; the Shehecheyanu; the blessing for the sukkah, *lulav* and *etrog;* and the blessing over the bread.

The Blessing over the Candles

בָּרוּךְ אַתָּה יְיָ אֱלֹהֵינוּ מֶלֶךְ הָעוֹלָם · אֲשֶׁר קִדְּשָׁנוּ
בְּמִצְוֹתָיו וְצִוָּנוּ לְהַדְלִיק נֵר שֶׁל (***on Friday add*** : שַׁבָּת וְ) יוֹם טוֹב :

Baruch ata adonai eloheynu melech ha-olam, asher kidshanu b'mitzvotav vitzivanu l'hadlik ner shel (on Friday add: Shabbat v') Yom Tov.

Praised are You, O Lord our God, King of the universe, Who has sanctified us by Your laws and commanded us to kindle the (on Friday add: Shabbat and) Festival light.

Kiddush—The Festival Blessing over the Wine

בָּרוּךְ אַתָּה יְיָ אֱלֹהֵינוּ מֶלֶךְ הָעוֹלָם · בּוֹרֵא פְּרִי הַגָּפֶן :

On* שַׁבָּת *add the words in brackets.

בָּרוּךְ אַתָּה יְיָ אֱלֹהֵינוּ מֶלֶךְ הָעוֹלָם · אֲשֶׁר בָּחַר־

בָנוּ מִכָּל־עָם וְרוֹמְמָנוּ מִכָּל־לָשׁוֹן וְקִדְּשָׁנוּ בְּמִצְוֹתָיו ·
וַתִּתֶּן־לָנוּ יְיָ אֱלֹהֵינוּ בְּאַהֲבָה [שַׁבָּתוֹת לִמְנוּחָה וּ]
מוֹעֲדִים לְשִׂמְחָה חַגִּים וּזְמַנִּים לְשָׂשׂוֹן · אֶת־יוֹם [הַשַּׁבָּת
הַזֶּה וְאֶת־יוֹם] — סֻכּוֹת: On חַג הַסֻּכּוֹת הַזֶּה · זְמַן שִׂמְחָתֵנוּ
[בְּאַהֲבָה] מִקְרָא קֹדֶשׁ זֵכֶר לִיצִיאַת מִצְרָיִם: כִּי בָנוּ
בָחַרְתָּ וְאוֹתָנוּ קִדַּשְׁתָּ מִכָּל־הָעַמִּים [וְשַׁבָּת וּ] מוֹעֲדֵי
קָדְשְׁךָ [בְּאַהֲבָה וּבְרָצוֹן] בְּשִׂמְחָה וּבְשָׂשׂוֹן הִנְחַלְתָּנוּ ·
בָּרוּךְ אַתָּה יְיָ · מְקַדֵּשׁ [הַשַּׁבָּת וְ] יִשְׂרָאֵל וְהַזְּמַנִּים:

Baruch ata adonai eloheynu melech ha-olam
borey p'ri ha-gafen.

(On Shabbat add the words in brackets)

Baruch ata adonai eloheynu melech ha-olam, asher bacharbanu mikol ha-amim v'romamanu mikol-lashon v'kidshanu b'mitzvotav, vatiten-lanu adonai eloheynu b'ahava [Shabbatot lim'nucha u']
mo'adim l'simcha chagim u'zmanim l'sason, et-Yom [ha-Shabbat hazeh v'et-Yom] Chag ha-Sukkot hazeh. Zman simchateynu [b'ahava] mikra kodesh zeycher litzi'at Mitzrayim. Ki vanu vacharta v'otanu kidashta mikol-ha-amim [v'Shabbat u'] mo'adey kodsh'cha [b'ahava uv'ratzon] b'simcha uv'sason hinchaltanu. Baruch ata adonai m'kadesh [ha-Shabbat v'] Yisrael v'ha-zmanim.

Praised are You, O Lord our God, King of the universe, Who creates the fruit of the vine.

(On Shabbat add the words in brackets)

Praised are You, O Lord our God, King of the universe, Who has chosen us from all peoples, and exalted us above all nations, and sanctified us by Your laws. And You have given us in love, O Lord our God [Shabbat for rest], holy festivals for gladness, and sacred seasons for joy: [this Shabbat day and] this day of the Feast of Tabernacles, the season of our Gladness [in love]; a holy convocation, as a memorial of the departure from Egypt; for You have chosen us, and sanctified us above all peoples, and Your holy [Shabbat and] festivals You have caused us to inherit [in love and favor] in joy and gladness. Praised are You, O Lord, who hallows [the Shabbat] Israel, and the festive Seasons.

Shehecheyanu—The Blessing for the New Season

בָּרוּךְ אַתָּה יְיָ אֱלֹהֵינוּ מֶלֶךְ הָעוֹלָם · שֶׁהֶחֱיָנוּ
וְקִיְּמָנוּ וְהִגִּיעָנוּ לַזְּמַן הַזֶּה:

Baruch ata adonai eloheynu melech ha-olam shehecheyanu v'ki-y'manu v'higianu la-zman hazeh.

Praised are You, O Lord our God, King of the universe, Who has kept us in life, and has preserved us, and enabled us to reach this season.

The Blessing in the Sukkah

בָּרוּךְ אַתָּה יְיָ אֱלֹהֵינוּ מֶלֶךְ הָעוֹלָם · אֲשֶׁר קִדְּשָׁנוּ
בְּמִצְוֹתָיו וְצִוָּנוּ לֵישֵׁב בַּסֻּכָּה:

Baruch ata adonai, eloheynu melech ha-olam, asher kidshanu b'mitzvotav vitzivanu leysheyv ba-sukka.

Praised are You, O Lord our God, King of the universe, Who has sanctified us by Your laws and has commanded us to dwell in the sukkah.

Following the sukkah blessing, we bless two other symbols of the festival: the lulav and the etrog.[7] The lulav, a palm branch, and etrog, a large lemon-like citron, along with myrtle and willow, comprise the four festival symbols called the Four Species, which some scholars believe in ancient times were probably a talisman for rain.

Later, numerous rabbinic interpretations became attached to these species, one of which is that they represent different facets of human brotherhood—the tall palm branch denoting those persons of power and influence; the aromatic etrog, persons of saintliness and learning; the myrtle, the average men and women of a community; and the willow, representing the poor and the lowly —each of them different, yet together mutually responsible for the welfare and good name of the whole.[8]

The Blessing over the Lulav and Etrog

בָּרוּךְ אַתָּה יְיָ אֱלֹהֵינוּ מֶלֶךְ הָעוֹלָם · אֲשֶׁר קִדְּשָׁנוּ
בְּמִצְוֹתָיו וְצִוָּנוּ עַל־נְטִילַת לוּלָב׃

Baruch ata adonai, eloheynu melech ha-olam, asher kidshanu b'mitzvotav vitzivanu al n'tilat lulav.

Praised are You, O Lord our God, King of the Universe, Who has sanctified us by Your laws and commanded us to take up the lulav.

If Sukkot begins on Friday evening, we postpone blessing the lulav and etrog until after Shabbat.

After passing the lulav and etrog from person to person, we bless the bread and sit down at our sukkah table.

Ha-Motzi—The Blessing over the Bread

בָּרוּךְ אַתָּה יְיָ אֱלֹהֵינוּ מֶלֶךְ הָעוֹלָם · הַמּוֹצִיא לֶחֶם
מִן הָאָרֶץ׃

Baruch ata adonai, eloheynu melech ha-olam, ha-motzi lechem min ha-aretz.

Praised are you, O Lord our God, King of the universe, Who brings forth bread from the earth.

Since our meals during this thanksgiving period are geared to the many available fall fruits and vegetables, our first night of Sukkot menu often consists of stuffed peppers, orange-squash casserole, a huge tossed salad, and baked apples for dessert. Both stuffed foods and round foods are customarily eaten on Sukkot by both Ashkenazic and Sephardic Jews. Our stuffed peppers and baked apples symbolize the "plenty" of the harvest.

Sukkot Stuffed Peppers

8 large green peppers, halved and seeded
2 pounds lean ground round steak
½ teaspoon ground cumin
1 cup cooked rice
¼ cup chili sauce
Salt and pepper to taste
2 (16-ounce) cans tomato sauce

In a large saucepan, parboil the peppers for 5 minutes in water to cover. Drain. In a large bowl, mix together the meat, cumin, rice, chili sauce, salt, and pepper. Fill the peppers with the mixture and place them in a large baking dish. Pour over tomato sauce. Cover with foil and bake for 45 minutes in a 400°F. oven. Serves 8.

Variation: A meatless version is also delicious. Fill the peppers with garbanzo beans and/or corn, pour over tomato sauce, and bake as directed above. When peppers are done, uncover the dish and top each pepper with a slice of mozzarella cheese. Place under the broiler until cheese melts, about 1 minute.

Orange-Squash Casserole

4 large butternut squash seeded and cut up
½ cup orange juice
¼ cup honey
½ teaspoon cinnamon

In a large pot, cook cut-up squash in water to cover for half an hour or until tender. Drain well. In a large bowl, mash the squash. Add the orange juice, honey, and cinnamon; blend well. Transfer the squash to a greased 8″×8″×2″ casserole dish. Bake covered, in a 350°F. oven for 20 minutes. Serves 6 to 8.

Sukkah Lunches

There is nothing so pleasant, relaxing, and otherworldly as having lunch in the sukkah. It's time out from the "real world"—very different from a back-yard picnic, as one is enclosed in a cozy little sun-heated hut, among cornstalks, grapevines, and gourds; certainly different from the usual peanutbutter sandwiches in the kitchen, or restaurant lunch routines.

Unless it's raining into the soup we always have the yom tov lunches in the sukkah. And whoever is home enjoys lunch there during the rest of the week, too. We invite friends, on a casual basis, to share these lunch times—any number from five to fifteen people may show up, as well as assorted squirrels, chipmunks, and crows.

Rebecca and I make a huge pot of soup at the beginning of the festival, and another midway through. We have several kinds of cheese on hand, crackers, and dark bread, a big basket of large red apples, a gallon jug of cider, and a carafe of wine.

This means that lunch can go from refrigerator to sukkah (with the soup going via the stove burner) in practically no time.

Soup of the Earth

3 (28-ounce) cans whole tomatoes
2 cups sliced carrots
1 cup sliced celery
3 medium onions, cut up
½ pound fresh spinach, washed and chopped
1 cup cut-up parsnips
1 large head cauliflower, broken into flowerets

1 cup cut-up fresh parsley
1 bay leaf
Salt and pepper to taste
1 (16-ounce) package egg noodles.

In a 4-quart saucepot, combine undrained tomatoes, vegetables, and seasonings. Bring to boil, lower heat, and simmer, covered, for 2 hours. Add noodles for the last 15 minutes of cooking time. Yields 16 servings.

Variation: Any additions to or subtractions from those vegetables listed above will produce an equally good soup.

Open Sukkah

On the Sunday afternoon of the holiday we have an Open Sukkah, also learned from Naomi and Ben, where entire families come for wine, cider, sweets, and most of all to visit with us and with one another. For us it is a perfect time to see not only those families with whom we ordinarily get together at other times during the year, but to keep in touch with those whom we, for one reason or another, don't see as often as we'd like. Also, since we live in a mobile community and meet new families each fall, our Open Sukkah is a wonderful time to introduce them to so many others that afterward, although the newcomers may not remember all the names, they know enough faces so they don't feel so new anymore.

We have particularly enjoyed sharing this holiday over the years with some of our non-Jewish neighbors, several of whom have become an integral part of the festival by helping us to decorate, and often bringing home-grown peppers, herbs, squash, and pumpkins to adorn the little booth. They and their families are among our annual celebrants at Open Sukkah time. In fact, two teen-age neighbors, who have been very involved and helpful sukkah decorators since they were six years old, used to plague their respective parents all fall with the incessant question: "Why can't we have a sukkah?"

Simchat Torah

(Day of Rejoicing in the Torah)

The "Ninth Day" of Sukkot

With the whole family in the swing of the festival season, eight days of Sukkot is really not quite enough merriment; or so our wise ancestors of the tenth century must have reasoned when they added Simchat Torah at the end of the existing Sukkot festival.

Although Simchat Torah is actually a holiday separate from Sukkot, and one which originated much later, we usually think of it as a kind of "ninth day" of the Sukkot festival. Simchat Torah celebrates the completion of the year's cycle of Torah readings, which culminate with the last chapters of Deuteronomy, the fifth of the Five Books of Moses. Although the custom of completing the cycle on this day was set down in Talmudic times, the festivities which mark Simchat Torah did not surround the practice, nor did the festival get its name, until centuries later.

Sometime after the twelfth century the custom of beginning the cycle of readings anew was added to Simchat Torah; therefore, the first section of the book of Genesis is also read at this time.

The process of continuity—of ending and rebeginning—is symbolized by the seven *hakafot* (ceremonial processional circuits) of congregants, many of them holding Torah scrolls, parading around and around the inside of the synagogue. In Temple times processionals were formed around the altar on each day of Sukkot. On the seventh day of the festival, seven processionals were formed. The Simchat Torah procession originated in the sixteenth century as a way of enabling children to feel closer to the Torah. Folklorists say that ceremonial circling was one of the oldest ways in which man used to try to propitiate the spirits—evil ones were thought to be kept out of the inside of the circle.

Preparation

When our three girls were younger, preparation for Simchat Torah at our house always consisted of their making special flags to wave during the hakafot. While Miriam and Rachel have long graduated from flag-making, this activity is still a source of fun for Rebecca, and is one in which I always enjoy joining her. We cut the flags from brightly colored construction paper into oblong shapes and glue the paper to sticks that we gather from the yard; then we decorate the flags with six-pointed stars and Torah scrolls. Rebecca gaily waves the flags during the evening Simchat Torah synagogue services.

Celebration

This festival asks to be celebrated within a community—in the synagogue or by dancing in the streets.

I have marvelous memories, which now reach back a decade and a half, of celebrating this holiday with my father, who discovered Simchat Torah in time for his young grandchildren, and introduced Dick and me to it as well. Going to Simchat Torah services with my father, enjoying the huge crowds of laughing, flag-waving mobs of children and the lively commotion of singing and dancing through the aisles during the seven hakafot, was one of our family's happiest annual events.

I think I loved our family Simchat Torah the more because Daddy, who was a pediatric resident in the days before the polio vaccine, believed that crowds were definitely unhealthy for young children. Under normal circumstances he was so cautious about exposing his grandchildren to germs that he wouldn't even take them into a grocery store in which there were a dozen people. So every year before we went to Simchat Torah services I'd call to tease him. "Do you think it's okay to take them? Won't they get sick?"

"Naw," he'd say, "not on Simchat Torah."

Some communities have Simchat Torah street dances where celebrants of all ages dance and sing. This has been especially popular since Simchat Torah was "rediscovered" by Russian Jewish students in the 1960s, when Jews who hadn't been allowed to practice their religion for years "came out" and danced in the streets on Simchat Torah night.

This happened primarily in the major cities of Russia—in synagogue areas of Moscow and Leningrad—and sent waves of response through Jewish communities of the world. There was reaction especially on campuses, from Jews in Israel, London, and the United States, often in the form of Simchat Torah rallies, marches, and street dances, which were intended as demonstrations of solidarity with our Soviet Jewish brethren.

A friend who recently emigrated here recalls participating in a Simchat Torah festival during her college days in Leningrad nearly twenty years ago. "What surprised me the most," she said, "was that there were thousands and thousands of people—they just kept coming and coming—who knew the Jewish songs and dances. Somehow the music had been kept in their families even though they didn't practice Judaism or ever attend a synagogue. I didn't have any Jewish background, and was amazed how many did. We kept dancing to frailickas . . . and after that night, though I'd never heard them before, I heard orchestras all over Russia playing those happy tunes."

After services on Simchat Torah day we have a festive lunch, frequently with friends. There are two constants on our Simchat Torah menu—a watermelon basket and Cottage Cheese Knish.

One of our favorite ways to serve fresh fruit is to halve a watermelon, remove the "meat," and cut it into wedges. We cut up other fresh fruits as well and fill the melon to overflowing with all colors and kinds of fruit, trimmed with purple and green grapes. Simchat Torah provides us with the chance to enjoy a watermelon basket before the fall melon harvest is gone. It is customary to eat round foods on Simchat Torah to symbolize the wholeness of the year; the fact that we don't stop, but continue. The end-of-harvest round watermelons are perfect for this occasion and the watermelon basket doubles as a centerpiece.

Cottage Cheese Knish, topped with sour cream, goes well with the fresh fruit.

Cottage Cheese Knish

Batter: 1¼ cups flour
½ cup vegetable oil
3 tablespoons sugar
2 eggs
⅔ cup milk
2 teaspoons baking powder
Pinch of salt.

Filling: 1 pound pressed cottage cheese (dry cottage cheese) or if available use 2 percent cottage cheese and omit sour cream
2 tablespoons butter or oil
2 egg whites
1 tablespoon sour cream
1 teaspoon vanilla
1 teaspoon sugar

In a large bowl, mix together all batter ingredients. Set aside. In another bowl, mix together all filling ingredients. Grease an 8″×8″×2″ pan. Pour half the batter in the bottom, then spread all the filling over the batter. Top with the rest of the batter. Bake in a 350°F. oven for 1 hour. This can be baked a day or two before the holiday, refrigerated, and reheated. It can also be made weeks ahead and frozen. Serves 6 to 8. Delicious with sour cream and strawberry jam.

Simchat Torah sunset draws the more than three-week fall holiday season to a close. The fall festivals are over for another year but the bright memories linger through the year to come.

The Ancient Winter Festivals

Hanukkah
Purim

Hanukkah

(Festival of Dedication)

Source of Light

By the time our family has disassembled the sukkah, disposed of the cornstalks, and raked up the last remaining gourd, two months have slipped by and it's time for Hanukkah. The Festival of Dedication, which celebrates Jewish refusal to assimilate into a majority culture, is considered a minor Jewish festival in that it is not prescribed in the Torah. However, for over 2,000 years, it has been a major source of light to Jewish families the world over during the long, dark winter.

Origin and Evolution

While the backgrounds of many of the older Jewish festivals are scant, with origins open to a variety of interpretations, Hanukkah commemorates a documented historical event: the rededication of the Second Temple in 165 B.C.E., when, against all odds, a small band of Jews overcame the mighty Syrian oppressors who sought to obliterate Jewish belief and convert all Jews to the ways of Hellenism.

The Syrian-Greek attempts at Jewish conversion did not occur overnight, but rather began with seduction and ended years later in violence. In the initial years some Jews—particularly those of the upper economic classes—were converted through their attraction to Greek culture and national life, of which the Greek religion was a part. Later, Syrian ruler Antiochus charged that those Jews who hadn't willingly become Hellenized would become so unwillingly. His targets were Jews who had clung tenaciously to Mosaic principles, refusing to substitute homage to Zeus and the pantheon for monotheism.

Those Jews, spurred into action first by Mattathias, and later organized by his son Judah Maccabee, though much fewer in number than the Syrians, successfully battled them and regained the Temple, which the Hellenizers had defiled.

The oldest source books dealing with Hanukkah are the Books of Maccabees, in which it is stated that after the Maccabeean victory, the warriors scrupulously cleansed the Temple, then rededicated it with a joyous celebration:

> And they kept eight days with gladness, as in the feast of the tabernacles, remembering that not long before they had held the feast of the tabernachles, when they wandered in the mountains and dens like beasts. Therefore, they bore branches, and fair boughs, and palms also, and sang psalms unto Him that had given them good success in cleansing His place. They ordained also by a common statute and decree, that every year those days should be kept of the whole nation of the Jews (Mac. II:10).

Some scholars have deduced from this passage that the first Hanukkah was actually a second, or delayed, Sukkot celebration. Since both the First and Second Temples were originally dedicated on Sukkot there was ample precedent for the eight-day Sukkot festival to be celebrated to rededicate the Second Temple after its desecration.

Candle-lighting

The main Hanukkah ceremony is candle-lighting; one flame is kindled each night for a total of eight nights. Because there is nothing about candle-lighting in the Books of Maccabees, and reference to light at Hanukkah does not appear in recorded literature until Josephus Flavius[1] almost two hundred years later, scholars have searched for a historical explanation for the custom.

According to folklorists, Hanukkah candle-lighting fits into the evolutionary scheme of festival development. (1) A nature celebration to do with the seasons—rain, moon, sun, or all of these—is present from early times. (2) Later, when a particular event occurs, the customs that had been part of the nature festival continue to be celebrated but they are imbued with a new meaning; one to do with the event. The event becomes historicized; soon we forget that a nature festival preceded it, and so we explain the customs attached to the event in terms of the event itself. (3) Thus, the custom persists while its meaning has changed and its origin is forgotten.

In interpreting Hanukkah candle-lighting along these lines, folklorists explain that for centuries prior to the Maccabees there must have been a winter festival to do with fire and light where people fearful of the long, dark winter days lit bonfires, not only for warmth, but to propitiate the sun to return to them. After the Maccabeean victory, when the celebration of Hanukkah began, the fire-lighting continued but in the form of the Hanukkah candle-lighting.

This evolutionary concept of the development of the candle-lighting custom doesn't wholly explain the Hanukkah lights. Because Hanukkah may originally have been celebrated as a delayed Sukkot, it's likely that the kindling of the lights was an integral part of the Hanukkah festival from the beginning, deriving from the lighting of the huge menorahs at the Temple courtyard during the evening Simchat Bet Hasho'evah part of the ancient Sukkot ritual.[2] In his classic *The Jewish Festivals,* Hayyim Schauss says that "great golden menorahs, set on bases that are fifty feet high" burned each night in the center of the court. Each menorah had four branches which held cups into which oil was poured, then lit, so that "the lights of these menorahs attain such intensity that all Jerusalem is lit up by them."[3]

In our own day such lights now blaze again in Jerusalem during Hanukkah, when huge *hanukiyot* (nine-cupped candleholders) top the Knesset (parliament) and other large buildings. These hanukiyot blaze with lights that attain such intensity that once again they illuminate all Jerusalem.

Whatever the origin of the Hanukkah candle-lighting custom, it has come to symbolize Jewish survival against all odds. The account given in the Gemara (Talmudic commentaries) maintains that when Judah Maccabee regained the Temple he found all the sacramental oil profaned, except for one sealed vial which held enough oil to burn in the Temple menorah for one day. (In Temple times the menorah was normally lit every day.) However, the oil miraculously lasted for eight days.

This story provides us with a two-fold metaphor: first, that the light of Judaism could not be extinguished, but rather burns—unaccountably by ordinary means—throughout even the darkest hours; second, that while the Maccabeeans were so outnumbered in forces that logically they should have been slain in a day, the belief and determination of those few overcame the brute strength of the many and Judaism was preserved. Thus we kindle the Hanukkah candles to recall this victory against assimilation and to recall the battle the Maccabees waged for Jews to remain separate from the dominant religion of the day.

Preparation

Hanukkah offers the opportunity for fun and gaiety in the preparation, as well as in the eight-day celebration. In our home, preparation for the evenings of get-togethers with family and friends includes making Hanukkah posters (so that one will be certain upon entering the house exactly what holiday it is), making hanukiyot, grocery shopping for all the special ingredients we'll need for on-the-spot cooking, and making gifts so that on one of the festival evenings members of our family unit can exchange small presents.

Decorating

As preschoolers our girls used to busy themselves for several days in advance of the holiday making "Happy Hanukkah" posters depicting various facets of the festival. As the girls have grown I miss seeing these all over the walls and woodwork and now ask Rachel and Rebecca if they'll each make a Hanukkah picture or two to hang during the holiday. (I failed to save the pictures from year to year, erroneously assuming there would be an infinite supply.)

Since Hanukkah may originally have been a delayed Sukkot celebration, we save certain reminders of Sukkot for Hanukkah. Our Hanukkah centerpiece is the same arrangement of orange crown squash and red, yellow, white, and green gourds that rested for eight days on the table in our sukkah. (All that's necessary to preserve the squash and gourds is to bring them into the house; no lacquer or preservative is required.) The lulav stands in a vase nearby, also a reminder, as we kindle the Hanukkah flames, that after successfully battling the Syrian Greeks, our ancestors rededicated the Temple and "kept eight days with gladness . . . as in the feast of tabernacles, they bore branches, and fair boughs . . ." (Mac. II:10) Thus, again we realize in Hanukkah the theme of continuity of the festivals perpetuated by the flame which refuses to be extinguished.

Making Hanukiyot

The hanukiyah is the nine-cupped oil lamp or candleholder used for the Hanukkah lights. Eight of the cups are for each night's light; the ninth is for the *shamash* (the servant light), which is used to light the others.

Most modern hanukiyot are made to hold candles, whereas in lamps of old, oil was used. The nine-cupped hanukiyah is different from the seven-pronged menorah dating to Solomon's Temple times, and on which the traditional synagogue menorah is patterned. However, the Hebrew word hanukiyah is only now gaining popular usage in this country, so the nine-cupped candelabra is still commonly referred to as the "Hanukkah menorah."

In earlier years our family used one of two hanukiyot—either the one that belonged to my grandparents, or the one that was a wedding present brought to Dick and me from Israel by close friends. But, our need for more hanukiyot increased as the family grew and it became clear that candlelighting was ever so much more fun when each child had her own candles to light. So we begin making our own hanukiyot in the weeks prior to Hanukkah. Recently, I was delighted to discover that there is historical precedent for this multi-hanukiyot concept long predating our American penchant for multi-everything per household. A commentary in the Mishnah states: "The precept of light on Hanukkah requires that one light be kindled in each house: the zealous require one light for each person; the extremely zealous add a light for each person each night."[4]

In our home we now use several hanukiyot each Hannukah as, in addition to lighting our own candles, we kindle lights for Soviet Jewish families who may not be free to do so themselves. So each year we utilize our many home-crafted hanukiyot, some of which have lasted but one season and some for many. One of our favorites is a painted flat board; glued to it are walnut shells, which serve as candleholders. We've also made some unusual hanukiyot of clay, similar to the simple clay oil lamps fashioned in Greco-Roman times.

A hanukiyah can be made of literally any material as long as it's constructed so that each candle flame will remain distinct rather than forming a single blaze. Some scholars say this rabbinic injunction was designed to ensure that the Hanukkah lights would in no way seem to be associated with the bonfires of surrounding "pagan" cultures.

Hanukkah Foods

While technically Hanukkah does not *require* any dietary changes, our family grocery list looks quite different during the winter festival from other times of the year. Generally we're so cholesterol-conscious that a dozen eggs lasts at least a month; but we use a couple of dozen eggs during Hanukkah week. And while a bottle of cooking oil ordinarily lasts for months, during Hanukkah the oil knows no miracles; thus we use two or three bottles that week. During all other weeks of the year we rarely fry food; but during Hanukkah week we put a special institutional-size frying pan into frequent use.

Two legends, both involving members of the Hasmonean (priestly) family as central figures, provide the rationale for our Hanukkah grocery list. The story of the Maccabees, Hasmoneans who discovered a day's supply of sacramental oil that miraculously lasted for eight days, gave rise to the custom of frying Hanukkah foods in oil. The heroine responsible for the particular kind of fried food—the *latke*—is another Hasmonean named Judith. According to the Book of Judith, set in about 350 B.C.E., the Israelites fought long and hard against Assyrian forces, and finally were ready to surrender when the wealthy young widow, Judith, stole into the enemy camp. There the military commander, Holofernes, attracted by her great beauty (and matching *ḥutzpah*), invited her to a feast. She fed him vast amounts of wine and cheese until he fell asleep and she relieved him of his head, which she then took home. Seeing evidence that the enemy commander was dead, the Israelites' morale soared, while the frightened enemy, deprived of its leader, fled.

One night, many centuries later, some of our ancestresses, tired of frying Hanukkah dinners in oil in memory of male Hasmonean heroism, decided on a heroine instead. So they made cheese pancakes to serve during Hanukkah, in honor of the cheese Judith served Holofernes before he lost his head. It was only much later (post-sixteenth century) in Eastern Europe, when pot cheese was either unavailable or terribly expensive, that the plentiful potato was substituted and the potato pancake (latke) became synonymous with the Hanukkah celebration. Whether it's made of cottage cheese or of potato, however, the cardinal feature of the latke is that it is fried in oil and thus integrally bound to Hanukkah.

In Israel, *sufganiyot*—doughnuts fried in oil—rival the latke. Another delicious Israeli Hanukkah food is the fresh-fruit fritter dipped in batter and fried in hot oil.

Because we want to try each of these delicious kinds of foods at least once during Hanukkah, our festival grocery list looks something like this:

Plenty of liquid vegetable oil

Dozens of eggs (for the various pancake and doughnut batters)

A 10-pound bag of potatoes, for all the potato latkes we'll eat

A 5-pound bag of flour

Yeast

Lots of fresh fruit for eatable centerpieces, both with the various kinds of latkes and as a dessert

Nuts in the shell (to use in playing the dreidl game—pages 99–100) to crack and eat while singing and visiting with friends

Gift-making

The custom of giving Hanukkah *gelt*—coins—to each child on one or all nights of Hanukkah is traceable at least to eighteenth-century Eastern Europe, and probably predates that by many centuries. There are some who argue that the giving of gifts rather than gelt at Hanukkah is also a very old custom, but it seems unlikely. We find in Nehemiah 8:10 directions to "give portions" on Tishri 1, implying that gift-giving was an original part of the Rosh Hashanah observance (it was a part of many New Year celebrations the world around; it still is a popular custom in Israel). We find in the scroll of Esther that "giving portions" is a necessary part of the Purim celebration, which is not surprising if, as some scholars assert, Purim customs were originally derived from the Persian New Year's festival.

Giving *tzedaka* (charity) is customary on Purim, Rosh Hashanah, and Yom Kippur, and in honor of a *yahrtzeit* (anniversary of a death), or a *simcha* (happy occasion), such as a bar mitzvah or wedding. So giving charitably on festivals as well as on other happy and sad occasions is an integral part of Jewish life.

However, there seems to be no historical precedent in Judaism for purchasing gifts to give all on one day to everybody within the nuclear and extended family, and to many, many friends and acquaintances. Rather this form of giving is particular to the Christian celebration of Christmas as it has been practiced in the United States, especially in the post-World War II years.

The American Jewish custom of giving Hanukkah gifts seems indeed to derive from the Christian custom of giving presents on Christmas (and if Christmas came in June we'd be giving gifts at Shavuot). However, there is nothing wrong with borrowing a good idea; in fact borrowing from the general culture in which we've lived has long been a part of the development of our customs and ceremonies.

What's important is what we do with the idea we borrow. If we join the throngs of December shoppers, rushing to get done the chore of buying for everyone on a massive shopping list, we have borrowed an empty habit, and one which many Christians who wish to cut down on the commercialization of Christmas deplore. If we borrow the idea of gift-giving and use it as a substitute for giving Hanukkah "gelt" to the children; and if we make or buy thoughtful gifts for someone we love, it can be very positive. We exchange small gifts within our immediate family on one night of the holiday—when we celebrate Hanukkah family night, a this-generation Cardozo tradition. We set the highest priority on gifts which are hand-crafted rather than purchased.

The children have made some memorable gifts for one another and for Dick and me over the years. It's amazing what imagination and scraps of cloth, colored thread, colored pens and pencils, staples, glue, and paper can yield. (All the more surprising to me because I only sew a button on under extreme duress and can rarely generate a craft idea, let alone execute it.) A few of the gifts the girls made for one another over the years include: Hanukkah *coloring books* (an older sister of eight or nine draws pictures depicting Hanukkah stories for her younger sister to color, then staples these into a "book," and makes a cover.) Hanukkah *bingo*—a bingo-like game but with letters and numbers written in Hebrew, and pennies used as circles to cover the appropriate squares. *Pencil holders*—made of clay.

The girls have made many ingenious gifts for Dick and me including some beautiful embroidered and crocheted kepot (skullcaps). One year, Miriam made Dick a blue velveteen tallit prayer shawl bag, embroidered in silver thread. Several years ago Rachel made me a magnificent Jewish calendar, with a picture on each page depicting some special facet of each month. The upper half of each page was picture, the lower half calendar; and although I didn't want to mar it with scribbled appointment times she insisted, rightly, "That is what a calendar is for!" Rebecca made us a most unusual Havdalah tablecloth the year she was six—a secret project, many weeks in the making. It is composed of several different remnants of calico and a variety of ribbons sewn on in various lengths and designs.

Needless to say, these gifts made with small hands and an abundance of love and happy anticipation are constant reminders of joyful Hanukkah times.

Since Dick and I lack our daughters' artistic talents, we have long used Hanukkah as a particular time of year for the purchase of Jewish children's books, most of which can be found in paperback. For only a few dollars a year we have built quite a library of excellent books. Each book has been begun by being read aloud for the first time on the Hanukkah night when it was acquired, then read and reread throughout the years.

Celebration

It would seem that an eight-day holiday would allow us enough time for both immediate and extended family celebrations, plus evenings to get together with close family friends. But, eight nights of Hanukkah never seem to be quite enough and we always wish there were more evenings to celebrate. We usually enjoy the first night of Hanukkah with one or two other families. No matter how many children are present a hush falls as each one (often aided by a parent) lights his or her shamash and from it kindles the flame of the candle for the first night of Hanukkah. Candles are inserted into the hanukiyah from right to left (as Hebrew is read), then kindled from left to right so that the "new" candle is kindled first each night.

As soon as the candles are lit we sing or recite the blessings.

Hanukkah Blessings

בָּרוּךְ אַתָּה יְיָ אֱלֹהֵינוּ מֶלֶךְ הָעוֹלָם אֲשֶׁר
קִדְּשָׁנוּ בְּמִצְוֹתָיו וְצִוָּנוּ לְהַדְלִיק נֵר שֶׁל חֲנֻכָּה.
בָּרוּךְ אַתָּה יְיָ אֱלֹהֵינוּ מֶלֶךְ הָעוֹלָם שֶׁעָשָׂה נִסִּים
לַאֲבוֹתֵינוּ בַּיָּמִים הָהֵם בַּזְּמַן הַזֶּה.

The Blessings over the Hanukkah Candles

בָּרוּךְ אַתָּה יְיָ אֱלֹהֵינוּ מֶלֶךְ הָעוֹלָם · אֲשֶׁר קִדְּשָׁנוּ
בְּמִצְוֹתָיו וְצִוָּנוּ לְהַדְלִיק נֵר שֶׁל חֲנֻכָּה :
בָּרוּךְ אַתָּה יְיָ אֱלֹהֵינוּ מֶלֶךְ הָעוֹלָם · שֶׁעָשָׂה נִסִּים
לַאֲבוֹתֵינוּ בַּיָּמִים הָהֵם בַּזְּמַן הַזֶּה :

Baruch ata adonai, eloheynu melech ha-olam asher kidshanu b'mitzvotav vitzivanu l'hadlik ner shel Hanukkah.

Baruch ata adonai, eloheynu melech ha-olam she-asa nisim la'avoteynu bayamim haheym ba-zman hazeh.

Praised are You, O Lord our God, King of the universe, Who has hallowed us by Your laws and commanded us to kindle the light of Hanukkah.

Praised are You, O Lord our God, King of the universe, Who worked miracles for our fathers in days of old, at this season.

On the first night of Hanukkah, we also recite the Shehecheyanu.

Shehecheyanu—The Blessing for the New Season

בָּרוּךְ אַתָּה יְיָ אֱלֹהֵינוּ מֶלֶךְ הָעוֹלָם · שֶׁהֶחֱיָנוּ וְקִיְּמָנוּ
וְהִגִּיעָנוּ לַזְּמַן הַזֶּה׃

Baruch ata adonai eloheynu melech ha-olam shehecheyanu v'ki-y'manu v'higianu la-zman hazeh.

Praised are You, O Lord our God, King of the universe, who has kept us in life, and has preserved us, and enabled us to reach this season.

Songs

Immediately after singing the blessing over the candles, while we stand near them watching the flames, on this and all other nights of the festival we sing two of our favorite Hanukkah songs, "Ma-oz Tsur" (Rock of Ages) and "Mi Y'Malel." The words of "Ma-oz Tsur," a song of praise and hope, written in thirteenth-century Germany by an otherwise unknown poet called Mordecai, have been set to a variety of tunes over the centuries, the most popular of which is the Western European Askenazic melody composed around the fifteenth century.[5]

Ma-oz Tsur

מָעוֹז צוּר יְשׁוּעָתִי לְךָ נָאֶה לְשַׁבֵּחַ
תִּכּוֹן בֵּית תְּפִילָתִי וְשָׁם תּוֹדָה נְזַבֵּחַ
לְעֵת תָּכִין מַטְבֵּחַ מִצָּר הַמְנַבֵּחַ
אָז אֶגְמוֹר בְּשִׁיר מִזְמוֹר חֲנֻכַּת הַמִּזְבֵּחַ

Rock of ages let our song
Praise thy saving power
Thou amidst the raging foes
Wast our sheltering tower
Furious they assailed us
But thine arm availed us
And thy word broke their sword
When our own strength failed us.

"Mi Y'Malel," sung as a round, speaks of freedom past and future.

Mi Y'Malel

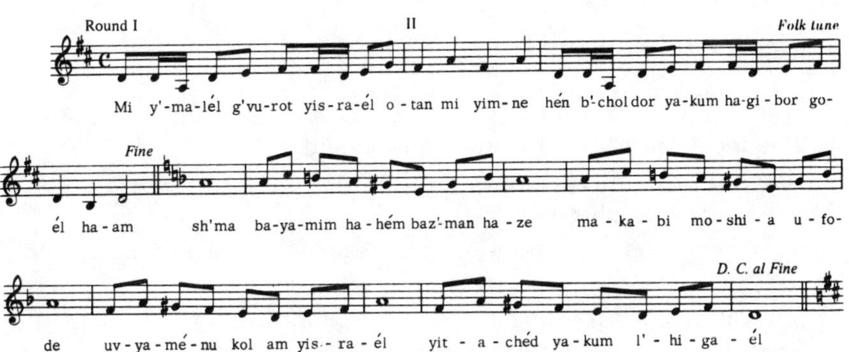

מִי יְמַלֵּל גְבוּרוֹת יִשְׂרָאֵל אוֹתָן מִי יִמְנֶה
הֵן בְּכָל דּוֹר יָקוּם הַגִּבּוֹר גּוֹאֵל הָעָם
שְׁמַע! בַּיָּמִים הָהֵם בַּזְּמַן הַזֶּה
מַכַּבִּי מוֹשִׁיעַ וּפוֹדֶה —
וּבְיָמֵינוּ כָּל עַם יִשְׂרָאֵל יִתְאַחֵד יָקוּם וְיִגָּאֵל

Who can retell the things that befell us?
Who can count them?
In ev'ry age a hero or sage rose to our aid.
Hark! In days of yore in Israel's ancient land
Brave Maccabeus led the faithful band.
But now all Israel must as one arise
Redeem itself through deed and sacrifice.

Hanukkah Dinners

A typical menu at our house for the first night of Hanukkah might be:

Fruited pot roast
Rice or baked potatoes to absorb the ample meat-fruit-sauce
Tossed salad—several different greens and bright cherry tomatoes
Fresh fruit
Sufganiyot

Fruited Pot Roast

1 (4- to 5-pound) chuck roast
1 (24-ounce) can whole tomatoes, with liquid
1 (16-ounce) can pitted apricots, with syrup
2 medium onions, sliced
1 cup mixed dried fruit (prunes, raisins, apricots, peaches, pears, etc.)

Place meat in small roasting pan. In a large mixing bowl, combine the undrained tomatoes and apricots with the onions and dried fruit. Blend well. Pour the mixture over the meat. Bake, covered, in a 325°F. oven for 4 hours, or until roast is fork-tender. Remove the pan from the oven; let the meat cool, and then refrigerate. When the meat-fruit sauce has jelled, skim off all the fat. Reheat and serve immediately. Or the pot roast can be prepared weeks ahead and frozen. Serves 8 to 10.

Note: To serve, slice meat and place on serving platter, topped with onions and fruit. Pour liquid into gravy boat and pass separately.

Sufganiyot

Sufganiyot are a traditional Hanukkah food in Israel. These doughnuts have been a family favorite in our home since Rebecca, at age six, discovered a recipe for them and made the batter before I realized what was happening. After supper the whole family gathered together and dipped the sufganiyot into the hot oil and fried the doughnuts.

¾ cup orange juice or water
¼ pound margarine
4 tablespoons sugar
2 packages dry yeast
3 cups flour

2 eggs, beaten
Dash of salt
Oil for frying

In a small saucepan, combine the juice, margarine, and sugar. Heat until the margarine melts and ingredients are blended. Cool the mixture until it is lukewarm. Then add the yeast to the saucepan and stir until it is dissolved. In a large bowl, combine the flour, eggs, and salt and add the juice-yeast mixture. Mix well. Knead the dough for a few minutes until smooth. Place the dough in a greased bowl, cover with a cloth, and let it rise in a warm place for ½ hour. Punch down. Place the dough on a bread board or counter. Take small balls of dough and with your hands roll them into 3″ or 4″ long strips. Form each strip into a circle. When all the dough has been formed into these doughnut shapes, cover and let rise for another ½ hour. Fry in hot oil, a few at a time, until golden. Drain well on paper towels. Makes about 16 doughnuts.

Variation: Pour 1 cup sugar and 1 tablespoon cinnamon into a plastic bag and shake well. Then add fried doughnuts, a few at a time, and shake until each is coated with the sugar and cinnamon mixture.

Undoubtedly, some of the best Hanukkah memories our children will have are of going to their grandmother's and to their great-aunt's homes for potato latkes. Both my mother and my Aunt Minnie always serve a full-course fish, chicken, or meat meal in addition, but it's latkes like theirs which must have inspired the folk proverb "Hanukkah latkes teach us that man cannot live by miracles alone."

For years, we made potato latkes at our house on at least two nights of the festival. On one memorable occasion we had invited two families for Hanukkah supper, and unlike Mother's and Aunt Minnie's Hanukkah meals, for which the latkes are additional, our menu was dependent on the latkes. Unhappily, our potato pancakes turned out soggy and besides that, none too plentiful, as somehow in doubling the recipe we must have divided some of the ingredients. Anyway, one of our friends—who had learned super latke-making from his father—jumped up from the table and offered to rescue the situation, which in short order he did. In our family this friend is affectionately known as Aunt Tissy, a name he acquired the day before Miriam's Bat Mitzvah when he did an improvization of a nonexistent visiting relative's hyperbolic compliments.

Ever since that Hanukkah night several years ago when he rolled up his sleeves and made batch after batch of latkes for fourteen of us, whenever our girls see me getting the grater and potatoes out their recommendation is: "Call Aunt Tis and find out if he'll come over and do it."

I do and he does. Thus has developed a most delightful annual event when Aunt Tissy's family and ours gather in the kitchen to peel, scrape, grate, and then consume a triple recipe of latkes, singing between batches.

Aunt Tissy's Latkes

6 potatoes
1 onion
2 eggs, beaten
¼ teaspoon baking powder
¼ teaspoon pepper
½ teaspoon salt
3 tablespoons flour (to thicken)
Oil for frying

Peel and grate the potatoes and onion. Add the beaten eggs to the grated vegetables. Add the rest of the ingredients except the oil and mix well. Drop by tablespoons onto hot oil. Shape the potato mixture into round, flat pancakes. In hot oil, fry on both sides a few at a time until they are crisp. Drain well on paper towels. Makes about 12 latkes.

On one night of the festival, which we plan long enough in advance to ensure that all sewing, embroidery, drawing, etc., are completed, our family unit has a Hanukkah party, at which the girls present the gifts they have made for one another and for Dick and me.

The menu for this party has varied over the years, but more times than not we have Judith's Latkes which Miriam says are just an inside-out blintz. Basically, she's right—with a blintz the pancake is folded around a cottage cheese filling; with Judith's latkes the cottage cheese is part of the pancake batter.

Like Holofernes, we tend to overdose on these addictive pancakes, which, when served with a fresh fruit salad, make a most filling meal. After dinner we sit around the fireplace, open and exclaim over each hand-crafted gift, pop popcorn, and sing.

Judith's Latkes

3 egg whites
2 egg yolks
1 cup dry or 1 per cent cottage cheese
1 cup milk
1 cup flour
1 teaspoon baking powder
Oil for frying

In a large mixing bowl, beat the egg whites and yolks together. Add the cottage cheese and milk, and stir well. Into a separate bowl, sift the flour and baking powder; add the sifted dry ingredients to the egg-cottage cheese mixture. Blend well. Shape the batter into flat pancakes. In hot oil, a few at a time, fry until they are brown on both sides. Drain well on paper towels. Makes about 12 pancakes.

Dinner is not the only time for Hanukkah festivities. It's fun, particularly on the weekend days of Hanukkah, to get together with other families for sledding, winter hiking, or cross-country skiing, then to gather inside for singing, games, dancing, cookies, and cocoa. When the sun sets, we culminate the festivities with candle-lighting.

The Dreidl Game

One Hanukkah, following an afternoon of sledding, we returned with friends to their house for candle-lighting, songs, and Hanukkah games. This was the first time our two-year-old Rebecca and our friends' two-year-old, Jonathan, had played the "put" and "take" game of dreidl, and both toddlers were quite admirable, even when they spun *shin* and they had to put the large walnuts being used as "chips" back into the pot.

The dreidl is a spinning top with the Hebrew letters

Nun נ Gimel ג Hey ה Shin ש

These letters, each of which appears on one of four sides of the dreidl, were originally the initials of the Judaeo-German words meaning "nothing," "all," "half," and "put," which were later interpreted to stand for the Hebrew words *Nes Gadol Haya Sham,* "A Great Miracle Happened There."

Rules for the dreidl game (borrowed from the German gambling game called Trendle) are as follows:

> Everyone starts with an equal number of pennies, nuts, or wrapped hard candies.
> Each player puts one of these in the middle of the playing surface (at our house it is usually the floor).
> The first player spins the dreidl. If it lands on . . .
>
> Gimel—the player takes everything that is in the middle.
>
> Hey—the player takes half of everything in the middle.
>
> Shin—the player puts one in the middle.
>
> Nun—the player neither takes nor receives anything.
>
> Before the next player spins the dreidl, everyone puts another piece in the middle.

Dreidl is the Yiddish name for the spinning top; in Hebrew it is called *s'vivon.*

We all sang "S'vivon," while Rebecca and Jonathan played. It amuses me to see that now, many years later, Rebecca never plays the game without either humming or singing "S'vivon" as she spins the dreidl.

S'vivon

סְבִיבוֹן סֹב סֹב סֹב חֲנֻכָּה הוּא חַג טוֹב
חֲנֻכָּה הוּא חַג טוֹב סְבִיבוֹן סֹב סֹב סֹב
חַג שִׂמְחָה הוּא לָעָם נֵס גָּדוֹל הָיָה שָׁם
נֵס גָּדוֹל הָיָה שָׁם, חַג שִׂמְחָה הוּא לָעָם

Spin, top, spin.
Hanukkah is a good holiday
A joyous holiday for the nation
A great miracle happened there.

Each year, as we look at the hanukiyot filled with blazing lights on the last night of Hanukkah, I am glad that when the two sages, Rabbis Hillel and Shammai, disagreed over the method of lighting the Hanukkah lights, Hillel won. Shammai wanted all lights to be kindled on the first night of the festival, then one less on each night of the holiday to symbolize the bullock offering of the Sukkot festival.[6] Hillel, however, argued for the reverse, which has resulted in having the shamash plus eight flames blazing on the last night of Hanukkah, each one a reminder of a joyous and special evening.

Purim

This merriest of all the Jewish festivals, which celebrates a time in Jewish history without persecution, arrives with the last days of winter, heralding news that spring is all but here. Purim is a delightful time for family members of all ages to don costumes, play-act, and eat *hamantaschen.*

Origin and Evolution

The source of the Purim story is the Book of Esther, which tells a tale set in the fifth century B.C.E. Many historians, however, believe most of the Purim customs to be associated with the ancient Persian New Year's festival, which far predates that book. Whatever their origins, for well over 2,000 years the Purim customs have been imbued with particular Jewish meaning because Purim celebrates a time when the theme of Jewish persecution was reversed—a time which may have been, a time which may be.

Persecution has been part of our Hebrew-Jewish heritage since Joseph entered Egypt. Ever since, our people have suffered at the hands of kings, governors, and dictators who wished to annihilate us in various countries, in many generations. At such times, some Jews have managed physical survival by converting—or by pretending to convert—to the oppressors' religions, often practicing Judaism in secret.

Purim, which celebrates a reversal of this Jewish persecution theme is based on the Book of Esther, whose author is unknown. It talks of a time when a secular king who ruled most of the known world married a Jewess, killed his Jew-hating prime minister, appointed a Jew instead, and decreed that all Jews in his huge domain should annihilate those who sought their destruction (and plunder their property for good measure). This edict so terrified non-Jews that many converted to Judaism in the hope of avoiding death. The story is set in Persia, where the king called Ahasuerus (whom many historians assume to be Xerxes) has banished his queen and is in search of a replacement. Of all the beautiful maidens brought for his approval, he chooses Esther, of whose Judaism he is unaware.

Esther's relative Mordecai, who works in the palace, is an enemy of Haman, the king's Grand Vizier. Haman, antagonized by Mordecai's refusal to bow before him, gets the king's permission to decree the murder of not only Mordecai, the Jew, but of all of Mordecai's people. Esther, asked by Mordecai to intervene, fasts, and then invites both the king and Haman to two successive banquets—at the second of which she tells the king of Haman's plans to kill her and all of her people. The infuriated king orders that Haman be hanged on the gallows he had erected for Mordecai. The king appoints Mordecai to be Grand Vizier and amends the royal edict to kill the Jews to read instead that the Jews in every city should:

> . . . gather themselves together, and stand for their life, to slay, and to cause to perish, all the forces of the people and province that would assault them, their little ones and women, and to take the spoil of them for a prey, upon one day in all the provinces of King Ahasuerus, namely upon the thirteenth day of the twelfth month, which is the month of Adar (Esther 8:11–12).

So charged by the king, and aided and abetted by many of the king's men (governors of the provinces ordered by the Grand Vizier to help the Jews overcome their foes), the Jews throughout

Ahasuerus' one hundred and twenty-seven provinces killed those men who would have murdered them.

This story perpetuates a theme of hope for a day yet to come to a people who time and again have been oppressed and murdered. For the Book of Esther need not stand as a book about a time that was, but rather can be interpreted as a wish for a time that will be: ". . . in the day that the enemies of the Jews hoped to have rule of them; whereas it was turned to the contrary, that the Jews had rule over them that hated them" (Esther 9:1).

The majority view of historians seems to be that neither the story nor its variations as related in the Book of Esther could have happened. The reasons cited include the lack of recorded evidence that any of the Persian kings named Xerxes had a wife named Esther; the fact that such a king could not have married, unaware, a Jewish woman, because the Persian king could marry only from among the seven leading families of the country whose lineage would be well known; the absence of any Persian records about a Grand Vizier named Haman or about any Jewish revolt wherein many thousands of the populace were killed.

A minority view is that the Book of Esther is rooted in some kind of historical fact. This view includes the possibilities that a historical incident similar to that related in the Book of Esther really occurred; that the king was not Xerxes but Artaxerxes II, who reigned almost a century after Xerxes; that the other protagonists bore different names; that the reasons for Haman's hatred of Mordecai were far deeper and more complex than related in the Book of Esther; and that had there been a Jewish revolt it wouldn't have been anything the Persians would have wanted recorded for posterity.

Whether or not they agree on the accuracy of the Book of Esther, many historians do seem to feel that the celebration of Purim began in Persia and that most of the Purim customs were originally customs of the Persian New Year's celebration.[1] The ancient Iranian year began at the vernal equinox, and Purim, too, usually occurs near that time.

The calendar in Persia and throughout the ancient world often included "interim days," which fell between the close of the old year and the beginning of the new year. During these days—which were not reckoned as ordinary time—it was customary for the usual to be inverted. For instance, a commoner would be mock king, and the laws of the land would be reversed.

While it seems highly unlikely that during such interim days Persian Jews, who were a minority in the empire, actually became rulers and reversed laws so as to kill their enemies, it is much more probable that at this time of year Persian Jewry celebrated—through party and masquerade—their own version of the reversal theme.

According to the Megillah (Scroll of Esther) the festival derives its name from the Hebrew word *pur,* which means "lot" and relates to the lots which Haman cast to determine the date of Jewish destruction.

The celebration of Purim takes place on Adar 14, (the day when the Book of Esther relates that Jews avoided destruction by annihilating the enemy), except in Jerusalem, which is a walled city. The Purim celebration occurs a day later there because of the extra day's battle that the Book of Esther relates took place in the walled city of Shushan.

Purim Katan

In addition to the annual celebration of Purim, the theme of which pertains to world Jewry, there are numerous Purim Katan celebrations. These are the little or minor Purims celebrated by various Jewish communities throughout the world commemorating a particular incident when individuals, families, or entire communities were threatened with extermination by various Hamans, yet escaped unharmed. Often, afterward, a scroll is written (as was the Megillah) and read at the annual Purim Katan celebration. Among the Purim Katan celebrations are:

The Purim Taka ("Window Purim") celebrated annually since 1741 by the Sephardic Jews of Hebron on the occasion of the anniversary of their deliverance from payment of an intolerable tax—with failure to do so punished by death or slavery.[2]

The Plum Jam Purim Katan celebration in Jung-Bunzlau, Bohemia, to commemorate the deliverance of the David Brandeis family from jail and possible death in 1731 for the supposed poisoning of a non-Jew with plum jam made by Mrs. Brandeis and sold in their little store. Actually the Brandeises were framed by an important citizen of the town, who hoped to see all the Jews driven out, and who, when the truth came to light, was exiled in their stead.[3]

Preparation

Purim preparation at our house begins well in advance of the festival with the making of hamantaschen. Hamantaschen, also known as *mohntaschen,* "mohn" meaning poppy seed, and "taschen" meaning pockets, are thought to have originated in Germany where the word mohntaschen also referred to a dough-filled cookie. When the poppy seed-filled cookies became associated with the festival of Purim the name gradually changed to hamantaschen, referring to the hat Haman supposedly wore.[4] The first written mention of the poppy seed-honey mixture in connection with Purim is found in a medieval poem by Abraham ibn Ezra, who lived in the early part of the twelfth century and who mentions the mixture as a Purim delicacy.[5]

Although our kitchen equipment is more sophisticated than was Abraham ibn Ezra's, I doubt that making hamantaschen took his family any more time than it does ours. For us, making and baking hamantaschen is an off and on (mostly on) evening and weekend project which begins at least a week prior to the holiday. We make several batches of hamantaschen for a variety of reasons: because the baking is a happy experience which keeps holiday spirit high; because we like to give portions of the delicious sweet to friends and neighbors; and because we never have just the right proportion of dough to filling, or filling to dough. So, we either have to make more dough so the filling doesn't go to waste, or more filling to go with "all that extra dough."

On the first evening of our hamantaschen marathon we make batches of dough and filling. A tip my grandma passed on gives our dough a distinctive tartness to offset the sweetness of the filling: include grated orange rind and fresh lemon juice in the recipe.

Hamantaschen

Dough: ½ cup vegetable oil
3 eggs
½ cup cold water
Juice of 2 lemons
1½ cups sugar
Pinch of salt
Rind of 1 orange, grated
3 teaspoons baking powder
6 cups flour

In large mixing bowl, mix together oil, eggs, water, lemon juice, sugar, salt, and orange rind. Into another bowl, sift together baking powder and flour. Add the dry ingredients to the oil-egg mixture slowly, kneading flour in a cup or so at a time. Chill dough for several hours or overnight. This is enough dough for approximately 36 small or 24 medium-size hamantaschen.

We like a fruit filling that can either be chopped or blended, so we usually make some batches one way, and other batches, another.

Filling: 1 cup dried prunes
1 cup dark raisins
½ cup dates
1 cup figs
1 cup dried apricots
¼ cup coconut
⅛ cup jam or honey

Chopped: The dried fruit can either be chopped with a sharp knife or in a food processor, mixed together thoroughly, and then moistened with the jam or honey.

Blended: Place the fruit in a large saucepan, add 1 cup water, and cook over low heat for ½ hour as for stewing fruit. Then it's soft and can easily be puréed in a blender. Blend for a minute or so.

Filling the Dough: Roll dough out on a floured surface until thin. Cut into circles with the top of a coffee cup. Put a heaping teaspoon of the filling into the center of each circle. Fold over into triangular shapes. Place the triangles on greased cookie sheets. Bake in 350°F. oven for 20 to 30 minutes, until light brown.

Another one of our favorite fillings is a combination of fairly equal amounts of raisins, carob chips, crushed walnuts, and a little jam to moisten. These are so tempting that the girls have to hide them from me, lest I eat them all before the holiday.

We make several more batches of hamantaschen on subsequent afternoons, or evenings, singing much of the while. Songs are frequently punctuated, however, by such interjections as, "The hamantaschen are supposed to be three-cornered, like Haman's hat"—"No, they're not, they're three-cornered like his ears"—"his hat"—"his ears"—"Who said they had to be three-cornered? Mine's round and look how good it looks."

Each of our daughters has made hamantaschen since she's been old enough to sit at the table to do it—and I must say we've had all shapes of hats, some of which would have served Haman right!

One of our favorite "bake-along" songs is the folk song "Utsu Étsa."

Utsu Étsa

עֻצוּ עֵצָה וְתֻפָר
דַּבְּרוּ דָבָר וְלֹא יָקוּם
כִּי עִמָּנוּ אֵ־ל

You can scheme all you want
But your plotting won't work
Because God is with us!

Making Masks

Mask-making is a joyful Purim preparation activity that, when our girls were younger, kept their creative fingers occupied for many minutes, even hours. Nowadays Rachel and I help Rebecca, whose supplies for the event include paper bags, white or colored paper, crayons and colored pens, and elastic thread. We then make all manner of masks including those of wicked Haman, beautiful Esther, childlike Ahasuerus, and happy Mordecai.

Making Games

Rebecca likes to make "Pin the Crown on Esther," and "Pin the Hat on Haman" games but somehow these never last from year to year. So there is the fun of making new ones every Purim season. She has found that heavy poster board or poster paper works best for the drawing of the chosen face, with lightweight paper for the crown or hat.

Celebration

Our Purim celebration includes masquerading, feasting, enjoying the custom of *shalach mones* (giving gifts of food) participating in a Purimspiel (Purim play), going to the synagogue for the Megillah reading, and participating while there in commotion and noisemaking with groggers.

Purim Eve

Masquerade

Those who contend Purim has its roots in the ancient Persian New Year's festival believe that the masquerade has been a part of the festival since its beginning. (Masquerading on New Year's festivals was characteristic of many ancient societies, its purpose, some scholars say, to fool the evil spirits.)

Purim masquerading became very popular in the sixteenth century under the influence of the Roman carnival. It reached its greatest heights in the nineteenth-century European communities where the festival was known as "the day of the students" because Yeshivah students would don costumes, assume the roles of entertainers, and go from household to household parodying their teachers, the rabbis. One student would take the part of King Solomon and debate whether women were superior to cholent (warm food); another would play Moses and explain that he'd returned to earth in search of his Torah, "which has been hidden away under a heap of explanation, commentary and supercommentary."[6] Today, masquerade and carnival are much a part of synagogue and community Purim festivities the world over; the most exciting and spirited is held in Tel Aviv where the Adlyada is a city-wide celebration. (Adlyada translates from Hebrew as "till he knows not," and refers to the saying that on Purim one may drink "till he knows not Mordecai from Haman." An Israeli friend says she's always understood it to mean "until Ahasuerus knows not Esther from Vashti.")

Masquerade is a part of our Purim home celebration, too. Although our older girls no longer participate in the Queen Esther contest, there were years when every girl at our house dressed as Queen Esther for our Erev Purim supper, and Dick judged the contest. I must say he was a clever judge, reserving the right to define his own categories and awarding a prize to each daughter on the basis of such things as most original costume (best use of my old nightgowns), best make-up job (whoever did not have lipstick on her forehead), and cleverest crown (the one that fell off the fewest times during dinner).

Purim-partying and Shalach Mones

In recent years, Miriam and Rachel have staged Purim parties for Rebecca and her friends. The children come in costume on Erev Purim afternoon, play the Pin the Crown or Hat game and Hide the Hamantaschen, a takeoff on hiding the Pesach afikoman devised by Rebecca. The prize is wrapped candy; the child who has the most candy when the final whistle blows is the winner.

After games, and eating hamantaschen, the costume-clad children make up baskets of fruit and hamantaschen; each child takes two baskets and brings them to neighbors. This observation of the custom of sending "portions" called *mishlo'ach manot* (Hebrew) or *shalach mones* (Yiddish) to friends on Purim, as well as the injunction to give gifts to the poor, derives from the Book of Esther (9:22) ". . . and they should make them days of feasting and gladness, and of sending portions one to another . . ."

Sending "portions" at Purim is not meant to be limited to children. Shalach mones is a custom that has become lost to many of us in this country as Jewish communities have dispersed, but it was very much a part of European Purim for countless centuries. There women spent days prior to the holiday baking hamantaschen and many other delicacies, which they sent to neighbors—under a white napkin—on Purim day.

The custom of shalach mones still lives in some areas of our country. In fact, a woman who moved recently from an assimilated New York City suburb to a predominantly Jewish one found she had more than realized her dream of a stronger community when Purim arrived and with it dozens of white-napkined plates of sweets.

Purim Eve Services

The sun is barely down when we go to services for an evening of fun rivaled only by Simchat Torah. Our synagogue, like many others, holds special children's Megillah (Scroll of Esther) readings the evening of Purim, when delighted, costumed children turn groggers or stomp their feet every time Haman's name is mentioned. (The purpose of this is to "erase" Haman's name, and the custom, as old as the Megillah reading, derives from the injunction in Deuteronomy 25:19 "to erase" the name of Amalek, who supposedly was a direct ancestor of Haman's and the first enemy of the Jews after the Exodus from Egypt.) The practice of using the grogger—a combination of two primitive percussion instruments, the "bull-roarer" and the "scraper"—at the mention of Haman's name originated in thirteenth-century France and Germany.[7] Since the use of noisemakers to ward off evil spirits at the turn of the seasons was an ancient custom, the adaptation of the grogger to use at the mention of Haman's name is ingeniously appropriate!

Purim Day

Purim Se'udah

Technically, Purim is not a full holiday; school is in session and work goes on as usual. Like many other families, we arrange to have a Purim Se'udah (festive meal) in the late afternoon of Purim day. The meal begins while it is still officially Purim and lasts on into the evening.

We usually enjoy our Purim Se'udah with several other families. Everyone wears costumes of characters in the Esther story for this joyful—sometimes riotous occasion.

Our Purim menu is such a simple one that by the standards of many of our foremothers it wouldn't deserve the name "feast" at all. For in times past the Purim feast was an opportunity for preparation of such many and diverse dishes that Kalonymus ben Kalonymus, the fourteenth-century Jewish parodist, wrote in his Massekhet Purim of more than twenty-four meat, poultry, and pastry dishes which were "told to Moses on Mount Sinai, all of which one must prepare on Purim."

With all due respect to Kalonymus ben Kalonymus I would rather have a one-course meal of our magnificent Shushan Eggplant—a dish Esther must surely have served the king—than twenty-four courses of such foods as the turtledoves and swan mentioned by ben Kalonymus.

Shushan Eggplant

4 medium eggplant
½ cup seasoned bread crumbs
2 onions, sliced
1 cup sliced mushrooms
1 cup sliced black pitted olives
1 (28-ounce) can tomato sauce
2 (8-ounce) cans tomato purée
1 teaspoon pizza seasoning
10 slices mozzarella cheese
½ cup Parmesan cheese

Peel and cut eggplant into slices. Place half the slices in a greased 9″×13″ baking dish. Sprinkle half of the bread crumbs over the eggplant. Mix together the sliced onions, mushrooms, and olives. Place half of the mixture over the eggplant, and reserve the rest. Mix together the tomato sauce, tomato purée, and pizza seasoning and pour half over the eggplant. Cover with half of the mozzarella cheese. Repeat the layers. Cover the baking dish with foil and bake for 2 hours in a 400°F. oven. Remove the baking dish from the oven, sprinkle Parmesan cheese over the top, and replace in the oven for 5 minutes. Serves 8 to 10.

This eggplant dish is our adaptation of the custom of eating a meatless meal on Purim. Cooked salted chick-peas, usually called *Nahit* or *bub* have long been eaten on Purim because Esther supposedly ate only beans and peas while she was in the palace so as not to violate the dietary laws. We like the idea of a vegetarian meal for this occasion but prefer eggplant to beans. (After all, Esther was in a palace, not a prison.)

Our Shushan Eggplant is accompanied by a large tossed salad, with plenty of hamantaschen for dessert. Beverages consist of grape juice for the children and wine for the adults, as Purim gives license for one to drink to the point where one isn't sure whether he is cursing Haman or praising Mordecai.

Purimspiel

Families of mid-sixteenth-century Europe waited at their dinner tables for the Purimspielers—groups of traveling players who went from home to home presenting, in exchange for coins, short plays often based on the story of Esther. The Purimspiel, which was patterned after the German play of the Reformation period, became so popular by the eighteenth century that they were performed in theaters and were widely attended by Christians as well as Jews.

Like the families of old Europe, we enjoy a Purimspiel in our home; but unlike them we do our own. While our original Purimspiel is no rival for those of the European theater, it certainly is one of the highlights of our Purim celebration.

Sometimes we perform our Purimspiel while sitting at the table. Other times the stage is the living room floor. The audience (those of us not on stage at the moment) sits on chairs and couches surrounding the performers. We often devise costumes—long dresses for Esther and Vashti, construction-paper crowns, and jewelry borrowed from the girls' old costume boxes, now housed in our attic. Ahasuerus and Haman wear large hats for the occasion and sometimes don bathrobes fashioned into capes.

A variety of themes were chosen for Purimspiels throughout the ages. Some of the most frequently performed were biblical spiels—Josephspiels, Danielspiels, and, of course, Estherspiels. Sometimes actors added touches of the popular culture in whatever age and country they lived and performed. True to custom, our family favorite is an Estherspiel merged with a bit of contemporary Americana (we sing some of the lines to the familiar tune of "Oh! Susanna" for no reason other than that the words fit).

Since we often have a dozen or more in attendance, there are usually several "performances" of the play each Purim so that each person gets to read a part of his or her selection. Of course the play lends itself to modification by other families. When there is a small group, some persons may take more than one part. That in itself can lend much hilarity to the occasion.

Our Purimspiel

CHARACTERS

Ahasuerus, the king
Vashti
Mordecai
Esther
Haman
Crowd

SCENE I

The Palace.

The King Ahasuerus and his cronies are drinking loudly and noisily.

KING: My wife is the most beautiful woman in the kingdom.

CROWD: Let us see her, Your Majesty.

KING: Vashti, Vashti, come here.

(VASHTI enters wearing a veil over her face.)

KING: Vashti, remove your veil and let everyone see your beauty.

VASHTI: Anything else for my king, but not that.

KING: Remove your veil at once.

VASHTI: No, Your Highness.

KING: Take it off.

VASHTI: No, no, no, nonononononono (Runs off stage).

KING: Now what do I do?

CROWD: Off with her head!

KING: Not her head.

CROWD: Yes, otherwise our wives will defy us, too.

KING: Haman, Haman *(Calls to Haman who is off-stage).* Banish Vashti from the palace this very night.

SCENE II

The king sits unhappily on his throne.

KING (to the tune of "Oh! Susanna," he sings):

Oh, I want a queen, a pretty queen
To rule this land with me.
And I want my queen to
Love me true, and stay eternally.

KING: What shall I do, what shall I do? Haman, tell me.

HAMAN: Let's have a Queen Contest, Your Majesty. The winner will be Miss Persia, and you're the prize, Your Majesty.

KING: Haman, you're a genius. Announce it at once. Tomorrow we'll decide.

SCENE III

The next day.

(All verses to the tune of "Oh! Susanna.")
One by one each female parades past the king.

KING *(Singing):* Oh, I've seen a hundred maids or more
They look the same to me.
None of them is right it seems
For my queen to be.

(Esther enters and slowly walks past him.)
KING *(Singing):* Oh, you are sweet and lovely, too
A regal queen you'd be
Oh, Esther, dear, I'll love you true
Will you marry me?

The king places the crown on Esther's head.
ESTHER (Singing): I'll be yours, I truly will
Loyal by your side

If my uncle Mordecai
Will let me be your bride.

SCENE IV

Mordecai and Esther are talking in the garden.

ESTHER: Uncle Mordecai, there must be some mistake, Haman couldn't convince the king to murder all the Jews.

MORDECAI: Haman can convince the king of anything! Esther, remember when the news of the Queen Contest was posted and you didn't want to enter? "What would a nice Jewish girl like me be doing in the Persian palace?" you asked. Well, now you know! Remember, I told you that sooner or later our people would be in great danger and with you in the palace we'd have a chance?

ESTHER: Yes, Uncle.

MORDECAI: Well, this is our chance. You've got to get to the king, and fast.

ESTHER: Fast. That's just what I'll do. I'll fast for three days, and pray. Then, I'll have the courage to go talk to the king about this.

SCENE V

Three days later.

ESTHER: *(Walking toward the throne room):* I'm so afraid. The king and Haman are always together in the throne room, making important decisions. I'm afraid to go in. The king has killed people for intruding upon him there. Well, it's now or never *(Opens door).* If he puts his scepter out it's all right; if it's his sword, I die.

KING *(Holding out golden scepter):* Well, well, my dear, what brings you here?

ESTHER: Good morning, Your Majesty. I'm giving a party tonight in my chambers and I came to invite you. And, you too, Haman.

KING: We'll be delighted.

SCENE VI

Party in Esther's Room.

KING: This was terrific. Esther, you give the best parties of any woman I've ever known.

ESTHER: Then, will you both come back tomorrow? Same time, same place?

KING: We'll be here.

SCENE VII

Esther's Room.

KING: I'm still filled with food and wine from last night's party, and now, look, you've put on another feast.

ESTHER: Nothing but the finest for you, my king.

KING: Esther, this is all even more delicious than last night's feast.

ESTHER: I'm glad to please you, Your Majesty, to do whatever you like.

KING: I like whatever you do. Esther, what can I do to make you as happy as you have made me?

ESTHER: Do you really want to know?

KING: Tell me. I'll do anything you ask.

ESTHER: Then abandon the plan to murder all the Jews.

KING: Murder the Jews? Who's going to murder the Jews?

ESTHER *(Singing to the tune of "Oh! Susanna"):*

Oh, here there is a cruel man
And Haman he is called
He plans to murder all the Jews
Oh, it must be forestalled!

KING: Haman, is this so?

HAMAN: Well, sir, the thing is, sir, I . . .

ESTHER: It's true, sir; look out the window at the gallows Haman ordered built to hang Mordecai the Jew. Then he plans to kill all of our people.

KING *(Looks out, then back to Haman):* Guards, guards *(Enter guards).* Take him away, at once! He shall be hanged right there on the gallows he has built. And, now, Esther, I shall have to find a new prime minister.

ESTHER: I know just the man, Your Majesty, my uncle Mordecai.

KING: Mordecai, you say? Guard, bring me the Palace Record. Now let's see, is there anything in the record to prevent Mordecai from becoming prime minister? Hm-m-m. No offenses, no misdemeanors, no . . . look! It is recorded that Mordecai once reported a plot to kill me. To kill *me*?

ESTHER: Yes, Your Majesty. It was shortly after we were married and my uncle Mordecai was coming to visit me at the palace gates. I was late, and while he waited he heard two of the guards talking about a plan to kill you that very night. He ran and reported them to the chief magistrate, and they were banished from the palace immediately.

KING: A man of such loyalty to me should indeed be prime minister. Guard, go find Mordecai and bring him at once.

SCENE VII

ESTHER: Just think, Mordecai, yesterday was the day Haman was to have killed you, and all our people. And, now, today, Haman is dead and you are prime minister. We must celebrate at once!

MORDECAI: Let's make today a holiday. We'll call it Purim.
Esther and Mordecai lead everyone in singing the familiar "Hag Purim."

Hag Purim

חַג פּוּרִים חַג גָּדוֹל הוּא לַיְּהוּדִים
מַסֵּכוֹת רַעֲשָׁנִים זְמִירוֹת וְרִיקוּדִים
הָבָה נַרְעִישָׁה רַשׁ רַשׁ רַשׁ בָּרַעֲשָׁנִים

This is probably the most popular *Purim* song: "The holiday of *Purim* is a great day for the Jews. There are masks, groggers, songs and dances. Come, let's make noise with our groggers."

After our Purimspiel what do we do for an encore? Why, drink more wine, sing more songs, and eat more hamantaschen, of course!

The Ancient Spring Festivals

Passover Shavuot

The Ancient Spring Festivals

The spring festival season provides Jewish families with a time to recall the two most significant events in the drama of our peoplehood: the Exodus from Egypt, which we commemorate at the Passover Seder; and the receipt of the Torah at Mount Sinai, which we celebrate on Shavuot.

Commemoration of these major historical moments has been superimposed upon the simple agricultural celebrations of our ancient Near Eastern predecessors. Our Passover Seder derives from the ancient Pesah meal and is thought to have been a "firstling festival" celebrating the first-born of the herds. The week following the Seder derives from the Feast of the Unleavened Bread and recalls a time when our ancestors planted their barley.

The seven weeks between the Pesah meal and Shavuot is a time of the "counting of the Omer," which refers to an ancient custom of waving a barley sheaf while counting the days until the harvest. This custom probably originated in the ancient Near East, before the Hebrews, as sympathetic magic wherein the ceremony was performed to encourage new crops. With the exception of the thirty-third day, called Lag B'Omer, the days of the Omer count are ones of semi-mourning, perhaps because in ancient times the days between the planting and the reaping of the harvest were days when the entire community lived in a state of uncertainty. Shavuot comes seven weeks after the Omer count begins and commemorates the spring wheat harvest.

No longer actively concerned about the welfare of the crops, our contemporary families are free to experience the spring festivals on a different level—for us it's a time to celebrate who we are, from whence we came, and our purpose in being here.

Passover

At Passover, we celebrate the planting of our 3,500-year-old family tree. Regardless of how many miles separate parents from children and grandchildren, many families make every effort to have a Passover reunion so that the entire extended family can sit down at one table to recall our roots—the deliverance of our ancestors from slavery in Egypt, the conception of our peoplehood, and with it the birth of an unparalleled sociological phenomenon: our survival. No other belief system of the ancient Near Eastern world has survived intact. Had only the religion lasted it would have been extraordinary. But that the beliefs, practices, and sense of peoplehood have survived in complete dispersion for over thousands of years, despite all odds—including Pharoahs, czars, kings, Hamans, and Hitlers of every variety—is nothing short of miraculous. Thus, at Passover, we celebrate a freedom we have repeatedly fought to maintain at all costs at all times in all generations.

The first night of the Passover festival (first two nights for Orthodox and Conservative Diaspora Jews) is marked by the *Seder,* a special meal and home service. Outside of Israel the festival lasts eight days for Conservative and Orthodox Jews, seven days for Reform Jews. In Israel, Passover lasts seven days. For those who observe a seven-day festival, the first and last days are holidays on which no work is done; for those who observe eight days, the first two days and last two days are complete holidays. The *hol hamo'ed—intermediate days*—are half holidays during which work goes on as usual.

Origin and Evolution

Passover is an amalgamation of two ancient Near Eastern agricultural celebrations: (1) a family celebration called the Pesah meal, dating back to desert days, from which our Seder night(s) developed, and (2) the week-long Feast of the Unleavened Bread, which developed later as the Hebrews became farmers in the Promised Land and from which the rest of the week of Passover evolved. Over centuries, the ancient Pesah meal and the Feast of Unleavened Bread came to be celebrated concurrently, and both rose from their agricultural origins to be imbued with new and higher meaning: the commemoration of the Exodus from Egypt.

Each festival grew to represent a different aspect of the Exodus. The Pesah meal became the occasion for the Passover Seder, during which the historic, emotional, and spiritual aspects of the Exodus are recalled through an evening-long ceremony of stories, prayers, foods, and songs. The week-long Feast of Unleavened Bread came to symbolize the practical aspects of the Exodus and is celebrated as a rememberance of the Hebrews' hasty departure from Egypt, before the bread could rise.

Many scholars believe that the Pesah meal celebration predated the entrance of the Hebrews into Egypt; that it was a "firstling festival" and as such represented a sacrifice of the first-born lambs or goats. On the eve of the full moon (fourteenth) of Nisan, family groups gathered to celebrate this Pesah meal, at which each family roasted a new lamb, smeared its blood on the doorposts of their homes, then hastily ate the animal together with unleavened bread and bitter herbs. They consumed the meal in the middle of the night, and burned any of the uneaten roasted animal before daybreak. The head of each household conducted this family ritual.

Although unleavened bread (a bread usually connected with sacrifices and/or used when a meal was prepared in haste) was one of the three necessary components of this ancient Pesah meal, many scholars believe that the week-long Feast of the Unleavened Bread was not originally tied to the Pesah meal but rather was a later-occurring and separate holiday celebrating the beginning of the barley harvest.

The major features of the Feast of the Unleavened Bread were: (1) removal of any leaven from the premises during the period of the beginning of the cutting of the grain, and (2) avoidance of eating any leaven during that first week. Some folklorists maintain that the basis of this practice was the ancient belief that leaven contained impurities; that evil spirits lurked there.

There are many divergent theories as to when and how the festivals of the Pesah meal and Feast of Unleavened Bread merged and became imbued with the Exodus story, but for our purposes these are of less significance than the fact that the "rite of spring" theme of these festivals was replaced by a theme of a different kind of birth. For thousands of years the Pesah meal and the Feast of Unleavened Bread have been known as Passover, the festival which commemorates the beginnings of the Jewish peoplehood through the Exodus of the Hebrews from Egypt, and their deliverance from forced slavery to freedom in a promised land.

Ashkenazic Jews no longer refer to the Pesah meal but rather call the special meal and attendant ceremony of the first night of Passover the Seder, a Hebrew word meaning "order," referring to the order of the home ceremony. (Sephardic Jews refer to this first night of the Passover celebration as the *haggadah,* which means "the telling," while Ashkenazic Jews call the *book* used for the Seder service the haggadah.) Most American Jews are accustomed to using the Ashkenazic terms, Seder for the home ceremony and haggadah for the book used during that ceremony.

The Seder is rooted in the ancient Pesah meal, and retains some of its basic features; we still celebrate it as a family holiday on the fourteenth of the Hebrew month of Nisan, the original date of the ancient festival, and we still eat unleavened bread and bitter herbs. But instead of slaughtering and eating a new lamb we place a shank bone on the table in recollection of this aspect of the original Pesah evening. The head of the household, who once conducted the ancient ritual, now conducts the Seder service.

Families of Temple times celebrated the Pesah meal publicly rather than in the private units of pre-Temple times. Each lamb was slaughtered, as in pre-Temple times, by the individual head of a household, then everyone gathered around the Temple site to eat. In Greco-Roman times, after the destruction of the Temple and the dispersion, exiled families gathered privately once again for the Pesah meal, eating it in their own homes, remembering life in Israel. It was in exile that the retelling of the Exodus story developed in a form similar to that which we know today. Now living in Roman lands, exiled Jews patterned the form of the Seder service on the Greco-Roman "talk-feast," a meal during which the assembled participated in an evening-long discussion on a topic of mutual interest.[1]

To their Pesah meal, Jewish families added a ceremonial discussion based on the biblical injunctions that we must retell the story of our liberation from slavery to our children so that every generation will remember it (Exod. 12:26; 13:8; 13:14; and Deut. 6:20).

In addition to the retelling of their ancestors' exodus from Egypt, the exiled Jews told of the deliverance to the Promised Land, and recalled the generations during which their families lived there. Thus, the retelling of the deliverance from Egypt developed from the standpoint of those who found themselves in a new and unwelcome exile from the land that had been promised to them, and in which they had dwelt happily.[2] Combined with the retelling of the story of the Exodus from Egypt, which took place over 1,000 years before, was the hope of return to the Promised Land—a hope still uttered at the conclusion of the Seder of Diaspora Jews in our own day—*"L'Shana Haba-a B-yerushalayim!"* ("Next Year in Jerusalem!").

Preparation

Because of its dual origin, Passover requires preparation for two festivals. The first part of this dual preparation, deriving from the Feast of the Unleavened Bread, involves cleansing the home of all leavening and leavened products, and, depending upon one's level of observance, changing all dishes and utensils used during the rest of the year because of their contact with leavening. The second part of the preparation involves getting ready for the Seder.

Since ancient times, ridding one's home of leaven has been a necessary prelude to the Passover festivities. If, as many scholars argue, Passover was once a New Year's festival, then cleaning out the old year fits the pattern of ancient Near Eastern New Year's preparations. Rabbinic interpretation of this cleansing of one's premises is that leaven symbolizes our impurities and evil impulses, and by ridding the house of leaven one can begin anew, feeling a sense of "rebirth."

On the night before the Passover Seder, after their mothers had spent days cleansing their homes of leaven, Jewish children of Eastern Europe delighted in taking candles from room to room, looking behind furniture, under beds, in every nook and crevice, searching for any remaining crumbs of bread or other food that contained leaven. In addition to ridding their homes of leaven, this certainly ensured a thorough spring cleaning.

While the candlelight search for leaven is still practiced in some homes today, our family's version of this custom is to rid the kitchen of leaven through an annual event that includes putting into large cardboard boxes all canisters and packages containing leavening agents and leavened products—flour, baking powder, regular cereals, etc. We also observe a long-standing Ashkenazie custom to abstain from eating kitniyot (the collective name for the seven grains from which bread could be made) and therefore put aside such items as corn and corn products, peas, soybeans.

Removing Leaven and Selling Chametz

The basic rule that underlies the special dietary laws of Pesach is that for eight days a Jew must not eat, own, or derive any benefit from *chametz* or from *s'or.* The term chametz refers to products made of naturally or artificially fermented wheat, rye, barley, oats, or malt. S'or refers to yeast and yeast-like products that *cause* or *accelerate* the fermentation of these grains. It is fermented grain products that are forbidden, not all fermented food. For instance wine, made of fermented grapes, is permissible.

Since provision had to be made for the food that remained on the kitchen shelves on the day before Passover, the rabbis developed a procedure for technically ridding the home of all chametz while not wasting the food. The solution is that our leavened products can be kept out of the kitchen (yet on the premises) but "sold" to a non-Jew for the duration of the holiday, then "repurchased" at the end of the eight days. Most synagogues take care of these transactions for their congregants.

Changing of the Diet, Dishes, and Utensils

Rabbinic interpretation of biblical prohibitions against eating leavened bread mandates that during the festival of Passover we eat no leavening, no flour (except matzah meal), and none of the seven forbidden grains out of which bread could presumably be made. In addition, any possible contamination with leavening is to be avoided; even canned fruits and vegetables are to bear the "kosher for Passover" label.

When in doubt about a product one can check with a local rabbi. (In our home we observe the absention from leavening, forbidden grains, and so on, and also abstain from buying the very costly Pesach canned goods by using primarily fresh fruits and vegetables and fresh fish, meats, and poultry throughout the festival.)

It is also rabbinically mandated that every dish and utensil in the kitchen be changed to Pesach dishes. While strictly observant Jews change dishes without question, others—who do abide by the Passover dietary restrictions—do not consider changing dishes necessary.

In any event, the *actual* need—or lack of it—for changing dishes and utensils is only part of the story. Just as we use a special challah cover, table settings, and candlesticks for Friday night to separate Friday from the rest of the week, use the hanukiyah for Hanukkah, and erect the sukkah on Sukkot, it is meaningful to mark Passover as the week different from all weeks—virtually and actually to separate it from the rest of the year—not only by eating different foods but by serving them on dishes different from those on which we ordinarily eat.

We have a set of Passover dishes that my mother used, and my grandma before her, to which my earliest childhood memories are attached. From the time our daughters were very young, they have loved the ritual of getting the boxes of Passover dishes out of their basement storage place, unwrapping them, washing them by hand (Mother has convinced them that the dishwasher will harm the dishes' gold rims; and as products of the machine age our girls enjoy the "treat" of washing these dishes by hand as their great-grandmother did), packing up the rest-of-the-year dishes, and putting the Passover dishes on the shelf instead. Each year, as I join them in this process, I realize how much children love custom; how much the rituals of holiday preparation and celebration are an integral part of them, and of their security; and how much richer their futures will be for the memories of the past, which these treasured moments so shortly become.

Once this part of Passover preparation is completed, it is time to begin the preparation for the Seder.

We always have, or attend, two Sedarim. One is always at home; however, even when both of them are at home there doesn't seem to be much more preparation for two than for one. Regardless of the number of Sedarim, there are essentially two categories of Seder preparation: preparing the food and setting the table; and reviewing the haggadah.

Food and Table Preparation

We've finally found that the ease with which we prepare for the Sedarim corresponds directly to the completeness of our grocery list. Without a complete list we always forget this, then that—requiring multiple last-minute trips to the grocery store. This frenzy does not lend itself to a relaxed preparation for events to come. Hence, our personal redemption is a well-thought-out advance list including the symbolic foods necessary for the Seder plate, foods to be eaten prior to the meal, and foods to be used for the meal itself.

Shopping List for Symbolic and Ceremonial Foods

First on the list are the foods symbolic of the festival, which will be placed on a plate on the Seder table in front of Dick, who leads our service. Explanations for the use of these particular foods are given on pages 135–6 as part of the description of the Seder plate.

horseradish

neck of turkey or chicken, shank bone of lamb (since we serve turkey as the main course, we roast and use that turkey neck)

egg—to be roasted

parsley, celery, or lettuce greens

haroset ingredients—nuts, apples, cinnamon, honey, and wine

A plate or basket of three matzah will also be placed on the table, to be used during the ceremony. In addition to the above items we add to the list, of course, enough matzah to last eight days. Once the symbolic festival foods are listed, we then add the groceries necessary for the Seder meal itself.

Grocery List for Seder Meal

eggs—to be used hard-boiled as first course

jars of gefilte fish—also to be used as first course

large turkey

new potatoes

fresh asparagus

lots of fresh vegetables: carrots, celery, radishes, green pepper, cherry tomatoes, lettuce

frozen strawberries and cans of frozen orange juice—to be used for dessert fruit ices

Seder Meal Preparation

For the first few years of our marriage we lived within a twenty-minute drive of my parents' house and thus my contribution to the Seder was the same as it had been all the while I was growing up:

to arrive on time. When we moved to Boston and it was suddenly incumbent upon me to "assume the duties of a Jewish homemaker" by preparing a Seder, it seemed an overwhelming task. I placed numerous calls from Boston to Minneapolis—"what goes into the haroset, anyway?" "How do you *roast* an egg?"—and developed an overnight appreciation of my mother's Sedarim, which previously seemed just to have happened.

Nowadays our Sedarim do just happen, as a result of what Dick's superior in the Army used to call "good prior planning." First, we plan Seder grocery shopping for a time when it will be convenient to prepare much of the food immediately, which saves putting everything away, then getting it all out again.

Second, because our festival menu is based on our love for the Seder service and our reluctance to be in the kitchen while any part of the reading and singing is in process, we plan foods that can be cooked ahead of time. By the afternoon of the Seder day the table is set, the food is all ready except for reheating, and we can shower, rest, and come to the table as guests at our own Seder.

PREPARATION OF SYMBOLIC FOOD

ROASTED EGG: Cook egg as for hard-boiling but do so in TEA; this cooks the egg, while giving it a deep brownish color.

HAROSET: This recipe for haroset yields more than enough for a dozen guests, provided my husband is not among them. Because of his appetite for haroset, and because we usually have many guests to both Sedarim, I usually quadruple the recipe. Our non-quadrupled recipe for 12 servings of haroset, which can be made a couple of days in advance, follows:

Peel half a dozen Winesap or Delicious apples and cut into small chunks. Sprinkle generously with cinnamon. Add several ounces of crushed walnuts, and a generous handful of dark raisins. Pour in 1/4 cup Passover wine, 1/2 cup honey. Mix together thoroughly and cover. Serve cold.

The other symbols (described on pages 135–6) require only to be put on the Seder plate at the time it is arranged.

FIRST-COURSE PREPARATION: SALAD, EGGS, FISH

CARROTS, celery, green pepper, radishes: Can be peeled several days in advance, sliced, and stored in salt water to keep crisp until arranged on serving platter, with cherry tomatoes in the center, the morning of the Seder or even the day before. (Covered with plastic wrap, the salad will retain crispness.)

EGGS: Can be hard-boiled several days in advance, rinsed under cold water, and peeled immediately, since the peel comes off easily when they are still hot; eggs can then be stored in an air-tight plastic bag to prevent their turning colors, and will keep very well this way for days.

FISH: On Seder day, on a tray, we arrange slices of gefilte fish (several good brands are on the market) on a bed of lettuce, and surround the fish with hard-boiled eggs cut in half.

Like the symbolic foods of the Seder plate, the foods of the first course are also imbued with symbolism: The fresh vegetables celebrate the new season; the fish, fertility; the eggs, the rebirth of spring, a reminder that they were served as a first course at the Sedarim of almost 2,000 years ago, as well as a reminder of the destruction of the Temple.

MAIN-COURSE PREPARATION

TURKEY: 1 (12–14-pound) turkey
Salt
Paprika
3 cups white wine
2 cups water

Place the turkey in a roasting pan and sprinkle it with salt and paprika. Pour wine and water over it. Cover the pan and roast the turkey for 4 hours. Uncover the pan and continue roasting another 30 minutes, just long enough to brown. The wine, water, and covering keep the turkey very moist. Turkey can be roasted during the afternoon of the Seder, removed from the oven just before the Seder begins, to give it time to cool a bit, then sliced just before it's eaten. Juices are poured into a separate container, reheated, and poured over the turkey slices before serving. Serves 12 to 16.

POTATOES: In a large saucepan, boil new potatoes (2 or 3 per person) in their jackets in water to cover until tender. Drain and store in a covered bowl in the refrigerator until serving time. To reheat, put in kettle on stove with small amount of water in the bottom, cover, and cook over medium heat for a few minutes.

FRESH ASPARAGUS: Clean asparagus ahead of time. Boil quickly for a few minutes in a small amount of water. Serve immediately.

FRUIT ICE DESSERT: 3 cups fresh orange juice
3 cups water
4 pints clean, hulled strawberries
¼ cup sugar

VARIATION: Add other fruit as desired: for instance,
1 cup fresh pineapple slices
1 cup drained frozen peaches

Whirl all the ingredients in a blender until frothy. Then pour mixture in cupcake tins into which paper cupcake holders have been placed. Freeze. Individual ices can be removed by putting the bottoms of the cupcake tins in hot water for a few seconds. Then the ices can be placed on a stainless steel serving tray and kept in the freezer until serving time. Yields 24 ices.

Aside from the time it takes for the turkey to cook in the oven, the rest of the Seder food preparation doesn't add up to more than a couple of hours, yet the food is all good, and when arranged beautifully and served at the sparkling Seder table, the results are as spectacular as if we'd slaved in our kitchen for a week.

Friends and relatives who attend our Seder often ask what they may bring, and for this there is an open slot in the menu: a baked dessert to augment the fruit ices. This enables guests to feel a part of the preparation, provides us with baked goods for the Seder—usually more complicated recipes than we'd have used—and doesn't require heating last minute casserole dishes.

I have memories of the need for an additional stove, which always arose at my mother's and Aunt Minnie's Sedarim, when our family unit and theirs traditionally joined for the second night of Passover, and when whoever was not having the Seder would make "a little extra" and thus would arrive at an already completely laden table bearing another full meal.

Setting the Seder Table

Everybody needs a daughter like Rachel, preferably every day, but at least on the day of Seder preparation. Rachel, who has been our official table setter for the past several years learned it from her older sister, Miriam, who used to beg to be allowed to "set the table alone." So for years Rachel watched and waited. Now Rachel insists on setting it alone while Rebecca argues to help but winds up waiting in the wings.

In addition to setting the table in the usual way, at least two forks apiece are necessary, one for the first course, one for the main course. We use two plates, a salad plate for first courses, and a dinner plate for the main course. The dessert plates, utensils, and cups and saucers for tea or coffee are kept in reserve on another table. Of course a wineglass is necessary at each place.

Rachel puts pitchers of salt water (symbolic of the tears we shed when we were slaves in Egypt) on the table—one for every six guests. She puts a plastic disposable "plague bowl" (into which wine will be spilled as we recount each of the ten plagues visited upon the Pharoah when he refused to release the Israelites) at each place—as well as a paper plate with a green vegetable and some haroset and horseradish (bitter herbs) on it. She covers each paper plate with clear plastic wrap until we're ready. (In the years when I set the table, it was done the quick and easy way. We had one "plague bowl" for every several guests, and one platter of green vegetables, which was passed around, followed by the bowl of horseradish and the bowl of haroset.)

ARRANGING THE SEDER PLATE (K'ARAH) This plate goes in front of the leader so that when the time comes he can explain the symbols. There are usually six compartments on the Seder plate (a plate made especially for this purpose can be purchased in synagogue gift shops, or any plate can be used and the six items placed on it): shank bone (neck of chicken or turkey); roasted egg; bitter herb (horseradish); parsley, celery, or lettuce; salt water; haroset.

This list of symbolic foods is in fact a "mini-history" of the development of the Seder. The bitter herbs and roasted bone derive from the ancient Pesah meal. Some culinary historians believe that the haroset, too, was an ancient condiment, perhaps used at the Pesah meal of old. The roasted egg and greens come from Greco-Roman times where the customs of the people among whom the Jews then lived included eating hors d'oeuvres of fresh greens dipped in salt water, and a first course of hard-boiled eggs. The haroset derives at least from these times when a fruit nut condiment was popular.

By the Greco-Roman period, each of the symbols was imbued with a meaning pertaining to either the Exodus from Egypt or the new exile from the Promised Land. The bitter herbs were said to be reminiscent of the bitterness felt by the Hebrews when they were slaves of Pharoah in Egypt; the haroset symbolized the mortar and bricks used by the Hebrews for the heavy labor they performed there; the roasted bone and egg became symbols pertaining to the destroyed Second Temple, reminiscent of the sacrifices offered there; the egg both recalls the mourning for that lost holy place and also symbolizes rebirth. The greens are not only symbolic of the new season but for Jews celebrating Passover today in a free land are a symbol, too, of the brightness and good fortune which we enjoy, and a reminder to appreciate this period in Jewish history rather than simply to accept it.

In addition to the symbolic food of the Seder plate, we place these other symbols on or near the table.

Matzah Plate—three matzot, covered by a napkin are on plate in front of the leader

Elijah's Cup—large goblet to be filled when door is opened for the prophet Elijah, who it is hoped will come to announce the Messianic Age

Leader's Pillow—so that the leader can "recline" to symbolize that on this night we are not slaves but can relax in freedom

Reviewing the Haggadah

We usually review the haggadah a night or two before the first Seder to decide who will lead which parts. (Dick is the head leader, and as a good administrator, delegates much to many.)

There are literally hundreds of haggadot on the market, and while different versions vary in composition, the common denominator is the presentation of the fifteen parts—or core structure—of the ceremony, a structure which has been operative at least since the third century of the common era and probably for centuries before that. Most haggadot number each of the fifteen parts, and if they are not already numbered it is helpful to gain a fuller appreciation of the Seder to go through and do so.

Since, from the very beginning, Passover has been first and foremost a family holiday, we interpret the haggadah as a script for an evening-long drama in which we are all the participants. Children take part in all aspects of the service, whose order itself was adapted with them in mind. Nearly every one of the fifteen parts in the haggadah involves the specific participation of the children.

Following is a summary of the structure of the traditional haggadah, which is, in turn, the script for the Seder evening: the *Prologue* (which prepares those assembled for the common activity to come), Section I (the commemoration of the past), Section II (celebration of the present), and Section III (the future), followed by an *Epilogue* of familiar songs.

Prologue—Points 1–4

This brief ceremonial period serves to join the group in common activity as well as to gain the interest and excitement of the children.

The first cup of wine is poured:

Prologue:

1. Kaddesh—Kiddush (blessing) is made over the first cup of wine and the blessing for having reached this season (Shehecheyanu) is recited.

2. Urchatz—ceremonial hand-washing, performed since ancient times for hygienic reasons.

3. Karpas—A green vegetable is dipped into salt water. (The vegetable symbolizes the rebirth of the season; the salt water the tears shed by the enslaved Hebrews in Egypt.)

4. Yachatz—The middle matzah from the matzoh plate is broken. The children pay keen attention, as the larger half of the broken matzah will serve as the afikoman (the piece they will hide and then ransom before completion of the evening service). The smaller half of the matzah will be used for the Ha-Motzi (blessing) just before the meal begins.

Drink the first cup of wine, pour the second cup.

Section I—Our Past

5. The maggid is the heart of the Seder service, during which the story of the Exodus from Egypt is retold and songs are sung. Everyone present takes part.

The maggid section of the haggadah includes:

- An offering of hospitality and a prayer that next year we may be in Israel and that all men will be free.
- The Four Questions, which are asked by the youngest child present, about why this night differs from all other nights.
- The Parable of the Four Sons.
- The "pouring out" of the ten plagues suffered by the Egyptians until the Hebrew slaves were finally let go. (A small amount of wine is poured into a small bowl as each plague is called out; a part of the ceremony enjoyed by children of all ages.)
- The singing of "Dayenu"—recounting the many miracles and wonders of Jewish history that bring us to this day; children love this song's repetitive syllables and delightfully catchy tune.

Drink the second cup of wine.

Section II—Our Present

Everything that goes on during Section II pertains to the meal: Points 6–10 consist of a series of preliminary blessings; point 11 is the meal itself; point 12, the afikoman; point 13, the Birkat Ha Mazon (blessing after the meal).

6. Rachatz—For ceremonial reasons, wash hands prior to the beginning of the meal. With the leader and others leaving the table, this usually is the opportunity giggling children seize to snatch the afikoman, collaborate on a hiding place, and decide on a ransom.

7. Ha-Motzi—Blessing before the meal.

8. Matzah—Blessing over the unleavened bread.

9. Bless and eat the bitter herbs—since the bitter herb is symbolic of bondage it is not eaten in a reclining position. The bitter herbs are dipped in haroset to sweeten them, as a symbol that sweeter days follow those of bondage.

10. Korekh—Eat a matzah and maror (bitter herb) sandwich, referred to as the "Hillel sandwich." We eat the bread of poverty with the bitter herbs just prior to our present-day festive meal as the remembrance of the poverty and bitterness of life and diet of the enslaved Hebrews in Egypt.

11. Shulhan Orekh—the festival meal.

12. Tazfun—Ritual dessert. Eat the afikoman, the piece of matzah symbolic of the Pascal lamb, which in Temple times was the final food of the Seder feast.

The leader must now ransom the afikoman back from the children in order to complete the Seder.

The word afikoman is a popularization of the Greek words *epikomas* and *epikomios,* which refer to reveling and carousing with music and dancing. The prohibition against eating or drinking (except for the prescribed two cups of ceremonial wine) after eating the afikoman is apparently to prevent emulation of the Greek late-night custom of roaming from party to party eating and drinking.[3] An invitee who is one of a limited number of participants at a Seder is to remain with his own group, and not roam around town with other groups.

13. Barekh—The Birkat Ha Mazon (the blessing after the meal). Drink the third cup of wine.

Section III—The Future Hope

The door is opened and a special cup of wine is filled, for Elijah the Prophet, who may enter to announce the coming of the Messianic age.

14. Hallel—Psalms of praise and thanksgiving. On the second night of Passover, between the Hallel and the conclusion of the Seder, comes the ancient custom of the Counting of the Omer, which harks back to the time of the agricultural festival when each year the Israelites brought to the sanctuary a measure (Omer) of their first barley harvest. We count the Omer today as a tie between Shavuot, which comes seven weeks after the second Seder, and Passover. Every night of those weeks represents one day less between the time we were released from bondage in Egypt to our receipt of the Law which governs that freedom—the Torah at Sinai. We count from the present toward the future.

15. Nirtzah—Conclusion of the Seder. Traditionally, the Seder concludes with the hope—"L'Shana Haba-a B'Yerushalayim" ("Next Year in Jerusalem!").

Epilogue—Songs from the Haggadah

Such favorite songs as "Ehod Mi Yode 'a," "Had Gadya," and "Addir Hu" are sung upon the Seder's conclusion.

Celebration

Why is the Seder night different from all other nights of the Jewish year? Because no other night requires so much thought, care, and preparation; and no other night's celebration provides for each and every family member to participate so actively.

The sense of anticipation heightens as the time draws near for the start of the Seder. Family and friends begin arriving, greeting one another and embracing. Some bring baked goods to the kitchen; one of the guests carries a burst of spring jonquils. The search for a vase ends successfully just in time for the call to the table.

The Four Questions

One of the most beautiful of all Seder sights is the sparkling eyes of the younger children as they anticipate the asking of the Four Questions. The questions ask why on this night we: (1) eat matzah; (2) eat bitter herbs; (3) dip twice—first dip the parsley in salt water, then dip the horseradish in haroset; (4) and recline when we eat? The reason each of the questions assumes a knowledge of the ceremonies to follow is that these questions were originally asked *following the dinner,* then moved up to precede the meal when it was found that the young children were too tired to participate after eating.

According to the earliest Mishnah texts (the collection of Jewish oral laws and ethics compiled in the third century that forms the basis of the Talmud), there were originally only three questions.

They were: Why on all other nights do we eat seasoned food once but on this night twice? Why on this night do we eat only unleavened bread? and, Why on this night do we eat only meat that is roasted?

The last question was dropped following the destruction of the Temple, when roasting an animal sacrifice was no longer relevant. The questions about seasoned foods (bitter herbs) and the unleavened bread remained and are among the Four Questions that we ask today. The other questions, about dipping parsley and horseradish, and about reclining, were added as centuries passed. Apparently, the compilers of the Mishnah intended the questions as samples of the kinds to be asked, but somewhere along the line particular questions—the two originally included in the Mishnah, and the two that arose along the way—"froze" and became the traditional Four Questions.[4]

It was our family's custom that the youngest child present at the Seder ask the questions until we attended a Seder in the home of friends several years ago where the number of children in their extended family totaled twelve. There, the youngest child from each household was invited in turn to ask the Four Questions. We promptly borrowed this lovely custom for all our subsequent Sedarim.

After the youngest child from each household has asked her or his question at our Seder, the older children volunteer the answers. This is a natural prelude to the retelling of the Exodus story and sometimes leads one of the adults to opine that there are indeed four kinds of sons (and daughters).

The Four Sons

The Torah says four times, in four different places (Exod. 12:26; 13:8; 13:14; and Deut. 6:20) that a father should tell his son the story of the Passover. The rabbis interpreted this to mean that the Torah speaks of four types of children: one who is wise, one who is rebellious, one who is simple, and one who does not know how to ask. Another interpretation is there are four kinds of children of Israel—all four of whom may be in attendance at a Seder—and that each son represents them, as well.

A few years ago friends brought to our Seder a new song called the "Ballad of the Four Sons," and led us in its singing to the tune of the familiar miner's song "Clementine." We were delighted with it and it immediately became a part of our Seder repertoire with one addition: We have all the men sing the words of the fathers, women sing the words of the narrator, and various children sing the words of the children.

Ballad of the Four Sons
(Tune: "Clementine," words: B. Aronin)

(Note: Future generations interpreting this twentieth-century rendition should be forewarned: this tune has absolutely no relationship to the Exodus from Egypt or symbolic significance thereto; it was selected because it fit the words.)

MOTHERS: Said the father to his children

FATHERS: At the Seder you will dine
You will eat your fill of matzah
You will drink four cups of wine.

MOTHERS: Now this father had no daughters
But his sons they numbered four;
One was wise and one a rebel
One was simple and no more.

And the fourth was sweet and winsome
He was young and he was small
While his brothers asked the questions
He could hardly speak at all.

Said the wise son to his father

WISE SON: Would you please explain the laws
and the custom of the Seder
Will you please explain the cause?

MOTHERS: And the father proudly answered

FATHERS: As our fathers ate in speed
At the Paschal lamb ere midnight
And from slavery were freed

So we follow their example
And ere midnight must complete
All the Seder, and we should not
After twelve remain to eat.

MOTHERS: Then did sneer the son, the rebel

REBELLIOUS SON: What does all this mean to you?

MOTHERS: And the father's voice was bitter
And his grief and anger grew

FATHERS: If yourself you don't consider
as a son of Israel
Then for you this has no meaning
You could be a slave as well.

MOTHERS: Then the simple son said simply

SIMPLE SON: What is this?

MOTHERS: And quietly
the good father told his offspring

FATHERS: We were freed from slavery.

MOTHERS: But the youngest son was silent
For he could not ask at all
His eyes were bright with wonder
As his parents told him all.

FATHERS: Now, dear children, heed the lesson
And remember evermore
What the father told his children
Told his sons that numbered four.

The way in which, within a few years, this song has become a "hit" at Sedarim around the country most certainly exemplifies how a new custom takes shape. Something has "always" been there (the Parable of the Four Sons has been part of the Seder evening since Greek times); someone takes the concepts and puts them into song; a familiar tune of the general culture fits the words, people are taken with the effect, and a tradition is born.

Retelling of the Exodus from Egypt

The heart of the Seder is the retelling of the story of the Exodus from Egypt. The story begins with the biblical narrative about Jacob and his twelve sons set forth in Genesis. The setting is Canaan, sometime between 1700 and 1450 B.C.E. Jacob's older sons sold their younger half-brother Joseph to Midianites, who took him into Egypt.

While imprisoned in Egypt on false charges, Joseph became known for his accurate interpretations of dreams, was ultimately called upon to interpret dreams of the Pharoah, and rose to wealth and power as his adviser. Joseph's predictions included that Egypt would enjoy seven years of plenty followed by seven years of famine. During the plentiful years, the Egyptians, under Joseph's supervision, stored crops which they sold to all the surrounding countries during the famine. Among those who came to buy corn were Joseph's brothers, whom Joseph forgave, and invited to join him in Egypt, where they all lived happily, and "multiplied exceedingly."

The biblical narrative tells us that the Hebrews lived well for several generations, then fortunes changed when there rose a new Pharoah over Egypt "who knew not Joseph" (Exod. 1:8) and set forth this edict:

> Behold, the people of the children of Israel are too many and too mighty for us. Come, let us deal wisely with them, lest they multiply and it come to pass that when there befalls us any war, they also join themselves unto our enemies and fight against us, and get them up out of the land (Exod. 1:9–10).

From the time of that royal proclamation, the life of the Hebrews in Egypt was no longer of peace and plenty but rather of sorrow and hardship.

The new Pharoah made the Hebrews' lives "bitter with hard service, in mortar and in brick" (Exod. 1:14). He ordered the midwives to kill all the Hebrew sons at birth, but they failed to do so. The Pharoah's daughter found a Hebrew baby in the bulrushes, called him Moses, meaning "to draw out," took him home and raised him. Although he grew up as a prince in the palace Moses did not forget his people, but rather saw their burdens and hated the way they were treated. Once Moses saw an Egyptian beating a Hebrew. He killed the Egyptian, then fled to Midian.

The Book of Exodus relates that one day when Moses was out tending sheep, God appeared to him in a burning bush and told him:

> I have surely seen the affliction of My people that are in Egypt and have heard their cry by reason of their taskmasters; for I know their pains and am come down to deliver them out of the hands of the Egyptians and to bring them out of that land unto a . . . land flowing with milk and honey (Exod. 4:7–8).

Moses tried to intercede with the new Pharoah, to let his people go, but the Pharoah refused. As life became worse for the Hebrews, God visited terrible plagues on the Egyptians. Yet after each plague the Pharoah hardened his heart and refused to let the Hebrews go. Finally, God wrought the worse plague of all—the smiting of the first-born.

> For I will go through the land of Egypt . . . and will smite all the first-born in the land of Egypt, both man and beast; and against all the gods of Egypt I will execute judgments; I am the Lord (Exod. 12:12).

On that night, according to the biblical narrative, the Lord smote the first-born from Egypt but passed over the houses of the Hebrews. Meanwhile the Hebrews escaped from Egypt, pursued by the Egyptians. At the shores of the Red Sea, The Book of Exodus relates:

> The Lord commanded Moses to lift up thy rod, and stretch out thy hand over the sea, and divide it, and the children of Israel shall go into the midst of the sea on dry ground (Exod. 14:16).

When the Egyptian army pursued, they were drowned.

> But the children of Israel walked upon dry land in the midst of the sea; and waters were a wall unto them on their right hand and on their left. Thus the Lord saved Israel that day out of the hand of the Egyptians . . . and Israel believed in the Lord (Exod. 14:29–31).

There are several ways in which the Exodus story can be retold at the Seder. The traditional way is to go through the haggadah as it is written, with Seder participants asking questions and giving answers and opinions at various points. This method can make understanding the story difficult, however, particularly when young children take part because the traditional haggadah does not recount the story sequentially. Instead, it uses selected biblical verses embellished with much rabbinic comment as a means of telling the story and as a springboard for discussion. The traditional haggadah developed out of a clash in ninth-century Babylonia between a sect of Karaites and the powerful rabbis about what material was to be selected to be part of the "official" Seder.

The rabbis favored the rabbinic commentary method—thus, the highly respected Rabbi Amram ben Sheshnah included in his praybook (siddur) the material now in the haggadah. The Amram Siddur, including the haggadot portion, was rich with rabbinic commentary (only in the thirteenth century did the haggadah become a separate book). The Karaites objected because they wanted to stick more closely to the biblical text. They were, however, overruled in that the Amram version, now that it was *written,* not oral, and was stamped with rabbinic approval, became generally used, and with little change still is the haggadah of today.[5]

Had our family lived in the ninth century, I'm not sure we'd have been Karaites, but we probably would have argued for a sequential telling of the Exodus story to make it more comprehensible (with side-by-side rabbinic commentary infinitely more meaningful once one has the full sequence of the story in mind.).

One alternative to the traditional haggadah is having each participant take a turn at telling part of the story in his or her own words, and discussing questions as they arise. Another alternative is to let each participant take the part of one or more characters from the biblical story, and then ad-lib each part. We began doing this several years ago after Rachel, who was then nine, said, "You know it would be a lot easier for Becka to understand if we acted the story out." Not only was it easier for then four-year-old Rebecca to comprehend, but we found it delightful to participate in the drama of the story.

However the story is retold, the discussion that it generates about slavery and freedom is as important as the recounting itself. We were fortunate to have Russian Jewish friends, recent immigrants to the United States, with us for a Seder last year. Their young son—only three when he left Russia—immediately grasped the similarity between their danger-fraught exodus from Russia, and the story we related. His recollections were a firsthand testimony to our children that we haven't seen the last of the Pharaohs.

As our own family retells the Exodus story at the Seder table, we integrate songs that are central to the story's theme. We begin with "Avadim Hayinu" (we were once slaves, now we are free men).

Avadim Hayinu

We were slaves;
Now we are free.

We intersperse verses of "Go Down Moses" ("Let My People Go") at appropriate points throughout the retelling. The person taking the part of Moses calls out, "Let My People Go," as those assembled name each plague and Pharaoh answers, "No, no, no, no, no . . ."

As the children of Israel all cross the sea in safety, we sing "Hal'luya," then follow with the all-time Seder favorite, "Dayénu."

Hal'luya

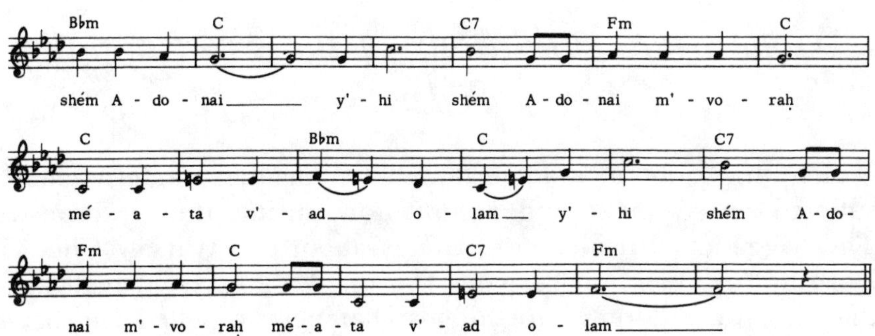

הַלְלוּיָהּ; הַלְלוּ, עַבְדֵי יְיָ, הַלְלוּ אֶת שֵׁם יְיָ. יְהִי שֵׁם יְיָ
מְבֹרָךְ, מֵעַתָּה וְעַד עוֹלָם.

Workers of the Lord
Let us praise his name now and forever.

Dayénu

אִלּוּ הוֹצִיאָנוּ מִמִּצְרָיִם, דַּיֵּנוּ.

If he had only brought us
out of Egypt it would have been sufficient.

Modern-day Additions to the Traditional Seder

Many haggadot include sections recalling that modern Jewry suffered enslavement and annihilation during the Holocaust. The haggadot also include readings about the Warsaw Ghetto Uprising (in which, on Passover Eve in 1943, the Jews, realizing that they were doomed to the gas chambers, rebelled and battled the Nazis for over a month). In recalling the Holocaust, and the Ghetto Passover Eve uprising, many families conclude their Seder with a special reading—now included in most haggadot—in recognition of the fact that Jews everywhere are not yet free.

Favorite Seder Songs

In addition to the songs we sing as we re-enact the story of the Exodus, we sing throughout the Seder as well.

After we eat our meal and sing Birkat Ha Mazon we open the door for Elijah the Prophet, and sing "Eliyahu Ha-navi," as we do at the Shabbat Havdalah ceremony. This symbolizes our hope for the coming of an age of freedom and peace for all mankind. (For Eliyahu Ha-navi" see page 31.)

Among our favorite concluding (Seder) songs is "Ehod Mi Yode'a," a delightfully spirited thirteen-verse rendition of various aspects of Jewish history. The singing gets faster and faster as the verses get longer and longer, with everyone trying to sing each verse in one breath.

We also sing "Ha Gadya" and "Addir Hu," both of which have their origins in medieval Germany and are among the oldest Jewish songs in popular usage. These songs are part of almost every haggadah and are therefore not included here.

Our Seder officially concludes with the song of hope, "L'Shana Haba-a B'Yerushalayim" ("Next Year in Jerusalem"), which has unified Diaspora Jewry for centuries the world over. No longer an abstract longing as it was for generations of our predecessors, L'Shana Haba-a B'Yerushalayim is now a possibility for every Jew. As Israeli friends of ours (who have no need to sing this song at their Seder in Israel) say: So, why not?

Next Year in Jerusalem!

Hol Hamo'ed: Intermediate Days of Passover

The first two nights of Passover get the whole family into the swing of a whole week that is different from every other week because we eat matzah as a constant reminder of what the celebration is all about—freedom from affliction.

The only problem is that matzah can become a pretty tasty affliction, so that after a week of Matzah Brei breakfasts we're sorry to see the festival end.

Matzah Brei—Grandma Bess's Way

6 sheets matzah
½ cup boiling water
6 eggs
½ cup milk
Salt to taste
Vegetable oil (for cooking eggs)

Break the matzah into pieces and put into a mixing bowl. Cover with boiling water to soften. Drain excess water. In a separate bowl, beat the eggs, add the milk and the softened matzah, and mix thoroughly. Add the salt. Heat oil in frying pan. Cook the matzah-egg mixture as for scrambled eggs. Serve hot with jam or syrup to 6 persons.

Instead of the usual school lunches there are Passover Popovers filled with delicious Seder leftovers. Dick has haroset "popover-wiches"; the girls take turkey until it's gone, then switch to sliced hard-cooked egg and lettuce.

Passover Popovers

½ cup vegetable oil
1 cup water
¼ teaspoon salt
1 teaspoon sugar
1 cup Passover matzah meal
4 eggs

In a large saucepan, bring to a boil the oil, water, salt, and sugar; add the matzah meal, stir it in, then let cool. After the mixture is cooled, beat in the eggs, one at a time. Grease a cookie sheet and place rounded balls of popover mixture, spaced well apart, on the sheet. (For 16 small popovers, form the mixture into meatball-sized balls. For 8 sandwich-sized popovers, make them larger.) Bake popovers in a 375°F. oven for 20 minutes, then lower heat to 325°F. and bake for another 30 minutes until they are golden brown.

One of the cornerstones of Jewish survival through the ages has been adaptability. While other small groups went by the wayside absorbed by larger or conquering cultures, we Jews have always managed to adapt to the host culture while preserving our unique Jewish identity by finding a new way to do the same thing.

Passover gives every Jew an annual opportunity to practice this ability, because never is the need for adaptability more apparent than when it comes time for Passover baking. For without flour or leavening can one bake anything, much less anything good?

Now, of course, the Passover cake-mix people have taken over some of the adapting so that for a price all one needs to do is to add two eggs to their efforts. But, there are still those of us who like to bake from scratch from time to time during the holidays, to avoid buying the package goods, to utilize our grandmothers' recipes, or to exercise our own abilities to create and adapt.

To me, Passover baking is synonymous with Esther Knight, mother of my girlhood friend Diana. In the days when relatively few girls went to afterschool Hebrew School. Mr. and Mrs. Knight saw to it that both of their daughters, Sharon and Diana, not only attended but graduated from the high school division. On those occasions the Knights opened their home to all their friends, relatives, neighbors, their daughters' classmates and classmates' families for a huge reception. The dining-room table was laden with large trays of scores of varieties of delicious kamish bread, strudel, cookies, and cakes, all baked by Esther Knight. And, since graduation traditionally fell during Passover it was all *"Pesadikah."*

Remembering her hospitality, I asked Diana and Sharon if they would be willing to share any of their mother's recipes. As generous as their mother was, they have.

Esther Knight's Pesach Toffee Bars

1 cup butter or margarine
1 cup sugar
1 egg
¼ teaspoon salt
1 cup Passover cake meal
1 teaspoon orange juice
1 (8-ounce) Passover chocolate candy bar, broken into squares

In a large mixing bowl, cream the butter and sugar until light and fluffy. Add the egg and beat well. In another bowl, sift together the salt and cake meal; add to the butter-sugar mixture. Mix well. Add the orange juice and blend thoroughly. Spread the mixture in a greased jelly-roll pan. Bake in a preheated 350°F. oven for 20 minutes. As soon as the pan is removed from the oven, place the chocolate squares on top. Spread the chocolate when it's melted and soft. When cool, cut into 12 to 16 bars.

Esther Knight's Apricot Bars

Pastry: ½ pound butter or margarine, softened
2 egg yolks
Pinch of salt
1 cup sugar
2 cups sifted Passover cake meal
2 teaspoons grated lemon rind

Filling: 1 1-pound jar apricot preserves
¼ to ½ cup lemon juice
½ cup chopped nuts

In a large bowl, combine all the pastry ingredients and mix together thoroughly. Spread three fourths of the dough on the bottom of a greased 9″×13″ pan and refrigerate the remaining dough. Bake in a preheated 325°F. oven for 20 minutes. While the dough is baking, prepare the filling. In a bowl, mix together the preserves, lemon juice, and nuts. Set aside. When the crust is baked, spread the preserve mixture over it while it is still hot. Crumble reserved, refrigerated dough on top of the preserve mixture. Bake at 325°F. for another 30 minutes. Cool before cutting into 16 bars.

It is the distinct dietary changes that keep the intermediate days of Passover special. And the spirit of the holiday, begun at the Sedarim, extends during the week as we continue to sing songs of the Seder when we're together at lunch and dinner enjoying the splendid foods. We find these days good opportunities to have a meal and sing some Passover songs with friends and relatives with whom we were not able to share a Seder.

The final days of Passover are *yamim tovim*—days free from work, for synagogue and celebration. We say *yizkor* (memorial prayers) in the synagogue on the final day of the Pesach festival to remind us of our departed loved ones and so that we remember, in the midst of our most spirited holidays, that we too are mortal.

The entire Passover festival leaves our families realizing more clearly than ever our close ties with our ancient heritage. It also emphasizes what we frequently take for granted—our good fortune to celebrate that heritage as free persons in a free land.

Shavuot

Origin and Evolution

Shavuot actually begins on the eve of the last day of the seventh week of the counting of the Omer (a sheaf of new barley, offered at the Temple on the second day of Passover). The counting of the Omer refers to the counting of the days between that offering and the first day of Shavuot.

Orthodox and Conservative Jews celebrate Shavuot for two days; Reform Jews for one. In Israel the holiday is one day. The biblical names for this holiday are "Hag ha Shavuot" (Feast of Weeks), Yom-ha-Bikkurim (Day of the First Fruits), and "Hag Ha-Kazir" (the Harvest Feast). According to Leviticus: (23:15–16.)

> And from the day after the Sabbath, the day that you bring the sheaf of wave-offering you shall count fifty days, until the day after the seventh week; then you shall bring an offering of new grain to the Lord.

Because of the interpretation "you shall bring an offering of new grain to the Lord," in Temple times two loaves made of the finest wheat were offered to the Lord along with the bikkurim, the first ripe fruits.

The reference in the biblical quotation to the day, or morrow, after the Sabbath created controversy as to when the Omer count should begin, and thus, when Shavuot would actually fall. Mainstream Jewry has settled on the interpretation that the Sabbath refers to the first day of Pesach; however, some sects assume that it meant the Shabbat of Passover week; and, therefore begin the Omer count several days later, and celebrate Shavuot correspondingly later.

The Book of Ruth, which draws together the two reasons for the festival, is read in the synagogue on Shavuot. Set against the background of the barley festival, it tells of a non-Jewish woman who became one of the Jewish people and thus symbolizes both the ingathering of the harvest and the gathering in of the people to accept the Law.

Preparation

Decorating

Shavuot ushers in summertime. The main Shavuot preparation activity in our home is decorating. The girls do this by picking fresh flowers and ferns and turning the house into an indoor garden. The white, lavender, and deep purple lilacs that flourish on bushes in our back yard become lavish dining room, porch, and kitchen-table centerpieces so that whether we're at breakfast, lunch, or dinner we're aware that a special season has arrived.

Rebecca makes dandelion and lily-of-the-valley bouquets to adorn small tables and other surfaces. Rachel chooses various leaves and ferns with which to decorate our mantel.

The first time we ever bought flowers for Shavuot was as apartment-dwellers in Jerusalem; we and everyone else in town crowded into the flower markets, which, during the days preceding Shavuot, overflowed with ferns and flowers. By two o'clock on the afternoon before the holiday began, flower markets were so empty that one could scarcely believe greenery had ever been sold there. Apartments and homes all looked and smelled like gardens; summer had officially arrived in Jerusalem!

Nobody is sure where or why the Shavuot custom of decorating one's premises with greens originated, but it has long been associated with this festival. Our ancestors probably wanted to capture the first sign of summer and bring it into their dwellings for the same reasons we do: because it looks and feels so wonderful.

Making Cheese Blintzes

The afternoon before Shavuot is a time of happy preparation in our kitchen, for it is the occasion of our annual blintz-making. We make and eat this delicious food in keeping with the Shavuot custom of eating dairy meals.

There are almost as many reasons suggested for this custom as there are dairy dishes: after Sinai people were hungry and ate dairy foods, which were quicker than meat to prepare; the Israelites waited so long at the foot of Sinai that by the time they got back to their tents the milk had all soured and had to be made into cheese; when celebrating the receipt of the Torah meat might have served as a reminder of the incident of the golden calf; dairy products remind us that the land of milk and honey was the Israelites' destination after receipt of the Torah. Yet another explanation is that Shavuot was originally both a pastoral and an agricultural festival, and churning and cheese-making are commonly associated with harvest festivals in many parts of the world.[1]

I learned blintz-making from Dick's grandma Bess, when she was eighty-five. Dick's cousin, Sis, and I, both newlyweds, prevailed upon Grandma to teach us how she made her delicious blintzes; so she tried. The problem was that Sis and I, fresh from college, arrived with our notebooks and pencils ready to record each thing Grandma did. But Grandma's hands were much quicker than our eyes. "Wait a minute, Grandma . . ." "Now what was that spice you just added?" "Exactly *how* much did you put in?"

"Well, darling dears, it was just a touch of cinnamon"—or "now that was just a dash of vanilla, I don't know how much—just enough to give it the right flavor . . ." And so went our lesson. But the real shocker came when it was time to put the blintzes in the oven. "What temperature?" we asked. "This old oven doesn't have such a thing as a temperature gauge," Grandma replied. "Besides you can't rely on them anyway. Here, just put your hand in . . .

there . . . when the oven feels about that hot it's just right for the blintzes."

This is my rendition of Grandma's "a little bit of this; a little touch of that" blintzes. And, although I set the temperature gauge at 350°F. to bake them, I never put blintzes in the oven without first putting in my hand to test the heat.

Since a cheese blintz is simply a crepe or pancake with a cottage cheese filling, the trick is in making the crepe. It's hard to go wrong on the filling.

Cheese Blintzes

Crepe Batter: 3 eggs
2 tablespoons oil—plus additional oil for frying
1¼ cups milk
1 cup flour
1½ tablespoons sugar
Dash of salt

Filling Mixture: 1 pound dry cottage cheese
¼ cup sour cream
1 egg white, beaten
Dash of cinnamon
½ teaspoon vanilla flavoring

In a large bowl, mix together the eggs, oil, and milk. Stir in the flour, sugar, and salt. In a 7″ frying pan heat a very small amount of oil. Pour in just enough batter to cover the bottom of the pan lightly. Fry for 1 minute, until the bottom of the crepe is light brown. Remove the crepe from the pan onto a paper towel. Repeat frying process until all the batter is used. Makes about 12 crepes.

In a large bowl, mix together the filling ingredients. Place a tablespoon of filling in the center of each crepe . . . on the brown side, since the other side will become brown when the crepes are baked. Wrap the crepe around the filling like a jelly roll, then fold sides in so that the filling won't fall out. Bake on a greased cookie sheet in a preheated 350°F. oven for 30 minutes. Serve hot with sour cream and jam or let cool, freeze, then reheat and serve weeks later.

Celebration

Shavuot Dinner

Our Erev Shavuot dinner is the first meal of the season that we eat on our screened porch. Rachel sees to it that the table is beautifully adorned with fresh flowers. We usually have blintzes with jam and sour cream accompanied by a large fresh-fruit platter including fresh strawberries and whatever other fruits are plentiful.

We recite the blessing over the candles, the festival Kiddush, the Shehecheyanu, and the blessing over the bread.

The Blessing over the Candles

בָּרוּךְ אַתָּה יְיָ אֱלֹהֵינוּ מֶלֶךְ הָעוֹלָם · אֲשֶׁר קִדְּשָׁנוּ
בְּמִצְוֹתָיו וְצִוָּנוּ לְהַדְלִיק נֵר שֶׁל (*on Friday add*: שַׁבָּת וְ) יוֹם טוֹב :

Baruch ata adonai eloheynu melech ha-olam asher kidshanu b'mitzvotav vitzivanu l'hadlik ner shel (On Friday add: Shabbat v') Yom Tov.

Praised are You, O Lord our God, King of the universe, Who has sanctified us by Your laws and commanded us to kindle the (On Friday add: Shabbat and) Festival light.

Kiddush—The Festival Blessing over the Wine

בָּרוּךְ אַתָּה יְיָ אֱלֹהֵינוּ מֶלֶךְ הָעוֹלָם · בּוֹרֵא פְּרִי הַגָּפֶן :

On* שַׁבָּת *add the words in brackets.

בָּרוּךְ אַתָּה יְיָ אֱלֹהֵינוּ מֶלֶךְ הָעוֹלָם · אֲשֶׁר בָּחַר־

בָּנוּ מִכָּל־עָם וְרוֹמְמָנוּ מִכָּל־לָשׁוֹן וְקִדְּשָׁנוּ בְּמִצְוֹתָיו ·
וַתִּתֶּן־לָנוּ יְיָ אֱלֹהֵינוּ בְּאַהֲבָה [שַׁבָּתוֹת לִמְנוּחָה וּ]
מוֹעֲדִים לְשִׂמְחָה חַגִּים וּזְמַנִּים לְשָׂשׂוֹן · אֶת־יוֹם [הַשַּׁבָּת
הַזֶּה וְאֶת־יוֹם] חַג הַשָּׁבֻעוֹת הַזֶּה · זְמַן מַתַּן תּוֹרָתֵנוּ
[בְּאַהֲבָה] מִקְרָא קֹדֶשׁ זֵכֶר לִיצִיאַת מִצְרָיִם : כִּי בָנוּ
בָחַרְתָּ וְאוֹתָנוּ קִדַּשְׁתָּ מִכָּל־הָעַמִּים [וְשַׁבָּת וּ] מוֹעֲדֵי
קָדְשֶׁךָ [בְּאַהֲבָה וּבְרָצוֹן] בְּשִׂמְחָה וּבְשָׂשׂוֹן הִנְחַלְתָּנוּ ·
בָּרוּךְ אַתָּה יְיָ · מְקַדֵּשׁ [הַשַּׁבָּת וְ] יִשְׂרָאֵל וְהַזְּמַנִּים :

Baruch ata adonai eloheynu melech ha-olam borey p'ri ha-gafen.

(On Shabbat add the words in brackets)

Baruch ata adonai eloheynu melech ha-olam, asher bacharbanu mikol ha-amim v'romamanu mikol-lashon vi'kidshanu
b'mitzvotav,
vatiten-lanu adonai eloheynu b'ahava [Shabbatot lim'nucha u']
mo'adim l'simcha chagim u'zmanim l'sason, et-Yom [ha-Shabbat
hazeh v'et-Yom] Chag ha-Shavuot hazeh. Zman matan Torateynu
[b'ahava] mikra kodesh zeycher litzi'at Mitzrayim.
Ki vanu vacharta v'otanu kidashta mikol-ha-amim [v'Shabbat u']
mo'adey kodsh'cha [b'ahava uv'ratzon] b'simcha uv'sason hinchaltanu.
Baruch ata adonai m'kadesh [ha-Shabbat v'] Yisrael v'ha-zmanim.

Praised are You, O Lord our God, King of the universe, Who creates the fruit of the vine.

(On Shabbat add the words in brackets)

Praised are You, O Lord our God, King of the universe, who has chosen us from all peoples and exalted us above all nations, and sanctified us by Your laws. And You have given us in love, O Lord our God, [Shabbats for rest,] holy festival for gladness, and sacred seasons for joy: [this Shabbat day and] this day of Shavuot the Feast of Weeks, the season of the Giving of our Torah [in love]; a holy convocation, as a memorial of the departure from Egypt; for You have chosen us, and sanctified us above all peoples, and Your holy [Shabbat and] festivals You have caused us to inherit [in love and favor] in joy and gladness. Praised are You, O Lord who hallows [the Shabbat,] Israel, and the festive Seasons.

Shehecheyanu—The Blessing for the New Season

בָּרוּךְ אַתָּה יְיָ אֱלֹהֵינוּ מֶלֶךְ הָעוֹלָם · שֶׁהֶחֱיָנוּ
וְקִיְּמָנוּ וְהִגִּיעָנוּ לַזְּמַן הַזֶּה׃

Baruch ata adonai eloheynu melech ha-olam shehecheyanu v'ki-y'manu v'higianu la-zman hazeh.

Praised are You, O Lord our God, King of the universe, Who has kept us in life, and has preserved us, and enabled us to reach this season.

Ha-Motzi—The Blessing over the Bread

בָּרוּךְ אַתָּה יְיָ אֱלֹהֵינוּ מֶלֶךְ הָעוֹלָם · הַמּוֹצִיא לֶחֶם
מִן הָאָרֶץ׃

Baruch ata adonai eloheynu melech ha-olam ha-motzi lechem min ha-aretz.

Praised are You, O Lord our God, King of the universe, Who brings forth bread from the earth.

One of our fondest memories is of spending Erev Shavuot in Jerusalem, a time when Israeli families sit around the table, singing for hours. Balcony windows are all open, and the strains of one family's songs joins with another until the whole street is filled with music. In fact, a family in one apartment may start a song, and families in other neighboring apartments join in so that many persons who may never really socialize with one another end up singing together.

Under Kabbalistic influences, Shavuot became a time when some men stayed up all night reading selected passages from Jewish classics. A less frequently observed custom was that of staying up all night reading the Book of Psalms because of the Shavuot connection with David. (Ruth was an ancestor of David's.) Yizkor is recited in the synagogue during services on the second day of the festival.

In some medieval Jewish communities the children were introduced to their religious schooling on Shavuot because it commemorates the receipt of the Torah. The youngsters were given their lesson, then treated to sweets of all kinds so that they would associate learning and sweetness. In Reform and Conservative synagogues in this country, today, Shavuot has become the time for confirmation, which ironically all too often marks the end of a person's Jewish education.

Our family custom on Shavuot days is to go to morning services, then have a picnic lunch. We follow this with a stroll (hiking is for every day, strolling for holidays) by the water, and then with a relaxed afternoon of visiting in the welcome sunshine.

The Modern Spring Festivals

Yom Hasho'ah
Yom Ha'atzma'ut

The Modern Spring Festivals

We are a historical people. We remember our past, and utilize it in our present to ensure our future. Our entire calendar year is filled with historical events, which are kept vividly alive in our memories, generation after generation, through celebrations. In modern times two events occurred of such magnitude that we instituted new holidays to recognize them: Yom Hasho'ah, which commemorates the Holocaust, and Yom Ha-atzma'ut, Israel Independence Day.

It is both exciting and humbling to realize that those of us living during the infancy of these two holidays bear the responsibility for creating ways in which these events will be remembered by future generations.

When our families comprehend the relevance of our past to our present and futures, contemporary events take on a very personal meaning, for we see ourselves as participants in the continuing drama of our peoplehood. We look at the impact of the Holocaust on our lives and at our obligation to transmit to our families the understanding that Jews the world over are one people and that we each need to work to ensure that never again can we allow tyrants to trample us.

We realize through Israel our connection with the whole of the Jewish peoplehood—past, the country where our people began; present, the Diaspora where we lived for 2,000 years; and future, in both the Diaspora homes we have created and in Israel, our first and enduring home.

Yom Hasho'ah

(Holocaust Day of Remembrance)

Origin

Yom Hasho'ah—Day of Catastrophe—is the Holocaust Day of Remembrance. Shortly after Israel proclaimed statehood, Yom Hasho'ah was established by the Israeli Knesset (parliament) on the twenty-seventh day of the month of Nisan. That date falls on the fourteenth day after the beginning of Passover, during the counting of the Omer, which is a traditional time of mourning.

Yom Hasho'ah is intended as a day to remember the totality of the Holocaust, on which we honor those who suffered and died. It is also the day on which we pay special tribute to those who participated in the Warsaw Ghetto Uprising.

The word Holocaust literally means "sacrificial offering which is consumed by fire," and refers to the period from Hilter's rise to power in 1933 to the end of World War II during which time six million European Jews died. Three overlapping yet definite stages of Jewish persecution, deportation, and finally annihilation comprise that period. The first, from 1933 through 1939, consisted of Jewish persecution within Germany, during which time Jews were beaten, robbed, and their businesses destroyed or confiscated. By November 1938, public schools were closed to Jewish school children. On *Kristallnacht* (the Night of the Broken Glass), November 9, 1938, thousands of Jewish homes, businesses, and synagogues throughout Germany were burned; over a hundred Jews were killed and thousands injured.

The second phase began in the fall of 1939 when Germany

invaded Poland and two million Polish Jews came under German domination. Two years later, with the invasion of Russia, three million more Jews were under German rule. From 1939 to 1942, as Germany raged through Europe occupying more and more territory, European Jews were expelled from their homes and crammed into specially created ghetto areas where they endured tremendous hardships.

The last phase, the Final Solution, began in late 1941 with the erection of the first of many death camps where thousands of Jews were gassed to death on a daily basis. By 1942, Nazis were heavily involved in two major wars: their battle against the Allies and their war against the Jews.

Germany often diverted troops, machinery, and manpower from the military war to use in the war against the Jews. Even when the railroads were needed for troops and munitions they were instead used to transport Jews to concentration camps. In Polish war industry plants, skilled Jewish workers were removed from their jobs and "resettled" in concentration camps.[1]

While neither persecution nor expulsion were new techniques for dealing with "undesirables," annihilation in the gas chambers represented a tremendous technological advance in the dehumanization of mankind. Historians estimate that well over half of the six million Jews who perished during the Holocaust did so in the gas chambers in Hitler's nearly successful attempt to find the Final Solution to the Jewish question.

Events of the Holocaust are well documented from German records. In 1945, the National Archives in Washington, D.C., microfilmed fifteen million pages of official Nazi documents. The United States used the most relevant of that material as evidence before the International Military Tribunal at Nuremberg against Nazi war criminals.[2]

The Holocaust is taught as part of World War II history at universities throughout the country as well as in specific Holocaust courses in universities, colleges, and seminaries throughout the world. It is also documented in nonfiction books written by concentration camp survivors, and has recently become the subject of television dramas and documentaries.

A number of Holocaust memorials have been built in various parts of the world. Two of the best known are Yad Vashem in Jerusalem and the Anne Frank House in Amsterdam.

The Yad Vashem complex is comprised of a museum, library, synagogue memorial hall, and a research institute, which houses more than twenty-five million documentary pages on the Holocaust, as well as thousands of microfilms and tapes and testimonies of survivors. Markers along a street called the Avenue of the Righteous Gentiles, which borders the entire complex, pay tribute to documented cases of heroic non-Jews who risked their lives to save their Jewish brethren.

Our family was invited to Yad Vashem one morning on the occasion of the honoring of an eighty-year-old former mayor of a small French village, who was responsible for saving the lives of dozens of Jews. When asked what had motivated him to risk his own life as well as that of his family's, he replied, "Well, what else could I have done?"

Whereas at Yad Vashem we realized the tremendous magnitude of the Holocaust, in the Anne Frank House we felt its depth. It was as if we were going to visit a friend or relative. Every room was as we knew it would be; even the pictures of Anne's favorite movie stars pasted on the wall were as she herself described them in her diary. I never felt a more interchangeable part of the Jewish whole than when we stood in Anne Frank's bedroom and I realized that since the Holocaust we Jews are united in the knowledge that except for the accident of geography any one of us could have perished in Auschwitz.

Commemoration

Secular Observances in the United States

The Holocaust is presently commemorated in this country in both secular and in religious settings. Many of the secular programs are sponsored by the United States Holocaust Memorial Council, which was established by Congress in 1978. The council then named one week each year (during which Yom Hasho'ah falls) as National Days of Remembrance. Commemoration activities include a civic program in Washington, D.C., with the participation of national leaders, government-sponsored ceremonies in capitol buildings in over half of the states of the union, as well as various city-sponsored Days of Remembrance events. In addition, hundreds of colleges and universities, churches and synagogues, and local community centers observe Days of Remembrance in programs individually designed by various groups.

Religious Observances in the United States

Because lasting rituals take centuries to develop, there is as yet no uniformity in Yom Hasho'ah liturgy in synagogue services. Rather, modern Judaism is in a period of experimentation as various congregations develop services comprised of prayers and readings. Among the Yom Hasho'ah services we have attended in recent years was a beautiful synagogue service written by the youth of the congregation, in which children and teens read their original poems and essays, then closed the service with a reading from the Book of Ezekiel and a special memorial prayer.

The United States Holocaust Memorial Council has published an excellent guide for services which can be held within communities, synagogues, or homes called *A Holocaust Commemoration for Days of Remembrance.*[3] It begins with the lighting of six memorial candles, one for each million Jews who perished, and continues with prayers, readings, and poems. It's structured loosely enough so that parts can be added or deleted, according to the size of the group and preference of the participants.

An increasing number of churches hold Day of Remembrance commemorations each year. One service that I attended with a Christian friend was divided into six parts, each symbolizing the death of one million Jews. During the service a child read a poem composed by a boy who died during the Holocaust, and a young woman read a part of Anne Frank's diary. Throughout the service each congregant held an unlit candle. At the conclusion, one person lit his candle, then the person next to him received the light from his candle, and so on, until everyone held a flame in memory of those who perished.

The National Conference of Christians and Jews has developed an outstanding Day of Remembrance service called the "Miracle of Denmark,"[4] which can be used in synagogues, churches, or interdenominational services. The service beautifully details the way in which King Christian of Denmark led his people in resisting the Nazis. It describes the Danes' unprecedented and heroic attempts to warn and hide Jewish citizens. As a result, only 500 out of 8,000 Jews were finally apprehended by the Nazis and carted off to concentration camps. The Danes protested continuously until, a year and a half after the Jews were taken, almost all Danish Jews were returned. Huge crowds turned out to welcome them home with candy, cigars, and love when they arrived. While we frequently recall that most countries of Europe, when overrun by the Nazis, complied with German regulations, ghettoized their Jews, and ultimately handed them over, this "Miracle of Denmark" service enables us to remember and honor those who refused to do so.

Home Observances

Yom Hasho'ah home observances vary according to the ages of the children and the backgrounds of the parents. In families of actual survivors, Yom Hasho'ah is a day of personal family mourning when yahrzeit (remembrance) candles are lit for deceased relatives, and memorial prayers are recited.

Many of us who are "empathetic" survivors relate to the Holocaust as we do to the biblical passage that states that we were once slaves in Egypt. Thus, we make Yom Hasho'ah, like Pesach, a time to retell the story so that the generations to come will never forget it. The difference is that with Pesach we're 3,500 years down the road and therefore can afford the luxury of encapsulating the events of the Exodus from Egypt into an evening's retelling. The Holocaust, however, is so recent and influential in shaping our lives as Jews today that we discuss its various aspects within our families throughout the year.

However, on Yom Hasho'ah, some families like our own retell the Holocaust story in a particular way—in terms of three basic questions: How? Why? and How Not? We discuss "how" it happened in light of the historical material available—knowledge of the factors that enabled the Nazis to rise to power, and information from their own records of what they did once they achieved that autonomy.

We try to answer "why," in terms of the documented attitudes toward Jews within Germany and other countries before and during the time of the Holocaust. Every year, as historians make new discoveries, more light is shed on the means by which the Final Solution was devised and implemented. Each year we learn more about what the free world did and did not know at the time, and about what was and was not done to help the Jews.

We attempt to answer "how not" with an analysis of ways in which we might participate in creating a kind of society in which such acts as were perpetrated during the Holocaust could not be repeated.

As yet no universal Yom Hasho'ah meal—or lack of it—surrounds the retelling of the story of the Holocaust. In our family we have a sparse Erev Yom Hasho'ah meal consisting of hard-cooked eggs, symbolic of mourning since the days of the Temple's destruction, and toast, to remember that our brethren in the concentration camps received only a tiny bread ration as their entire meal for the day. We drink only small amounts of water, to recall that they had nothing else to drink except a little water each day; and of course, we eat nothing sweet. On Yom Hasho'ah day we eat as usual, except that we omit anything with sugar or honey so that we are conscious all day of the lack of sweetness.

Yom Hasho'ah Observance in Israel

Ceremonies are held at Yad Vashem Erev Yom Hasho'ah and again the next morning. School children from all over the city place wreaths of flowers outside the building, which memorializes the six million victims. Representatives of various Israeli organizations, many of whom are concentration camp survivors, also lay wreaths. A military band plays somber music; there are a few short speeches. Everyone then goes into the chapel to recite memorial prayers in front of an eternal flame that burns day and night in memory of those who perished.

A two-minute-long siren sounds thoughout the State of Israel at eight o'clock on Yom Hasho'ah morning. The moment the siren begins, everything comes to an immediate halt. Those walking stop in their tracks. Cars and buses stop wherever they are. All commerce ceases. For two minutes the siren literally brings to a halt the lives of those now living to symbolize what the Nazis did to those millions now dead. Then, as quickly as it began, the siren stops and life resumes, symbolic of the fact that the Jewish people now continue in their own land.[5]

Yom Ha'atzma'ut

(Israel Independence Day)

Origin

Yom Ha'atzma'ut, Israel Independence Day, falls on the fifth day of the Hebrew month of Iyar and celebrates the day on which modern Israel became an independent state. The date is May 14, 1948, on the secular calendar.

Although Yom Ha'atzma'ut is young, it is rooted in 3,500 years of history, for it celebrates the fulfillment of the world's oldest recorded promise.[1] The Book of Genesis relates that God promised Abraham, "I give all the land that you see to you and your offspring forever . . . walk about the land, through its length and its breadth, for I give it to you" (Gen. 13:15–17). Historians estimate that the children of Israel entered the Promised Land in about 1250 B.C.E. Since that time there is no period in recorded history when the land was without Jews.

However, for nearly 1,900 years after the destruction of the Second Temple in 70 C.E., most of the world's Jews lived in dispersion outside of the Promised Land. Israel was under a succession of dominations—Roman, Muslim, British—until 1948 when it was returned to those who, according to the Bible, hold the title deed.

Modern Israel is the fulfillment of a long-felt Zionist need. The root of the term Zionism is the word "Zion," which for nearly 2,000 years has been synonymous with Jerusalem. (The modern word Zionism first appeared at the end of the nineteenth century, was coined by Nathan Birnbaum, and referred to the movement whose goal was the return of the Jewish people to Israel.)

Theodor Herzl, as visionary and charismatic as any of the ancient prophets, first felt the need for a modern Jewish homeland when, as a young journalist from a highly assimilated Jewish family, he witnessed an anti-Jewish incident in France. From that time, he worked fervently to bring the Jewish homeland about. Like Moses, he never made it to the Promised Land (although he was reburied there after the creation of the State), but he saw it clearly when he convened the First International Jewish Congress in 1897 and said, "At Basle I created the Jewish State. In five years, perhaps, and certainly in fifty everyone will see it." Fifty-one years later the State of Israel was proclaimed.

For at least several decades before Herzl became involved, there were waves of Jewish migration to Palestine and heavy interest in the establishment of a Jewish homeland. Herzl, though, is most often credited as the driving force who succeeded in interesting Lord Balfour, England's Prime Minister, in the need for Israel (then called Palestine and under Turkish domination) to become a Jewish homeland. Although Herzl died in 1904 and Lord Balfour was out of power for over a decade, Chaim Weizmann continued negotiations with the British to establish a British-Zionist connection in Palestine.

In 1917 British troops, aided by a number of Jewish platoons, defeated the Turks. The British issued the Balfour Declaration stating that Palestine would become "A national home for the Jewish people." However, politics, including the British closing the doors of Palestine to Jewish immigration in 1939, delayed the return of Israel for over thirty years, during which time six million Jews died in the Holocaust.

At the end of World War II, when the concentration camps were liberated and the entire world saw the havoc Hitler had wrought, Palestine was still not open to surviving Jews. Rather, it took three more years and continual negotiations on the part of Chaim Weizmann and other Zionists to bring the United Nations finally to partition Palestine and thereby to create the Jewish state.

The day after Israel proclaimed statehood, large, much better equipped Arab armies from surrounding countries attacked her. Yet, with few arms and a tiny army she fought against all odds to win the War of Independence. To maintain that independence, Israel has had to defend herself in three subsequent major, full-scale wars: the Sinai War in 1956, the Six Day War in June 1967, and the Yom Kippur War in 1973.

Each year as we celebrate the birthday of modern Israel we also mark one more year that she has battled attackers, withstood pressures to give up her land, and refused to succumb to terrorism. Israel today is the living reality of the flame that will not be extinguished.

Celebration

Commemoration in the United States

In this country Israel Independence Day celebrations include rallies, fairs, dances, and other kinds of public gatherings usually sponsored by synagogues or community centers and held on or around May 14, or Iyar 5.

The programs and locations vary from year to year. One year our Jewish community sponsored a huge, week-long Israel Independence Day celebration at a local shopping center. Hundreds of thousands of people of all backgrounds came to enjoy the Israeli foods, browse through Israeli books and brochures, and to watch and take part in Israeli singing and dancing. Many colleges and universities throughout the country are sites of Israel Independence Day celebrations. Usually sponsored by Jewish student associations, the events enable Jewish students to share their traditions with friends of varying backgrounds.

Most Jewish religious schools hold Yom Ha'atzma'ut celebrations. Rebecca attends a two-afternoons-per-week Hebrew school that holds an annual outdoor Yom Ha'atzma'ut program. The children tell the story of the establishment of the Jewish state, sometimes through original plays, other times through readings, then sing and enjoy Israeli dancing. Home celebrations commemorating Israel Independence Day are becoming more popular every year. Often they take the form of an expanded family dinner where many friends are invited to one home. Sometimes such a celebration is patterned on an Israeli-style potluck cookout. A *kumsitz*—an Israel style sing-a-long—makes a wonderful Yom Ha' atzma'ut celebration.

At one kumsitz we attended, adults and children—toddlers through teens—sat around a bonfire singing, playing the guitar, and eating Middle Eastern food. Among the foods served were falafel and pita, hot corn on the cob (a favorite Israeli snack food), assorted dried fruits and nuts, and two kinds of cake with birthday candles (Israeli hostesses never serve only one variety of cake).

This spice cake with sabra liqueur sauce icing is a delicious and simple-to-create cake for Israel's birthday.

Sabra Spice Cake

1 (18½-ounce) package spice cake mix (made with vegetable shortening)
1 (3-ounce) package instant butterscotch pudding mix
½ cup oil
1 cup water
4 eggs
½ cup raisins
¼ cup Sabra liqueur
¼ cup orange juice
Powdered sugar
Grapes and orange slices for garnish

In a large mixing bowl, blend together the cake mix, pudding mix, oil, water, eggs, and raisins. Beat with an electric mixer on medium speed for 2 minutes. Greast a 10½" bundt cake pan generously with oil, pour in the batter, and bake about 50 minutes in a 350°F. preheated oven until cake feels firm to the touch, but not hard or crusty. Mix together the liqueur and orange juice, then add enough powdered sugar to reach the icing consistency preferred. (Some people like a thick icing, others prefer a thin icing that melts into the cake.)

While the cake is still warm, turn it out onto a plate. Poke holes in the top of the cake with a fork and then cover the cake with the icing. Fill the center of the cake with green grapes; garnish the sides and top with sprigs of grapes and fresh orange slices. Yields 12 large slices, 24 medium-size slices.

Although there are several good falafel mixes on the market, using a food processor one can make falafel from scratch almost as easily, and can adjust the seasonings to taste.

Falafel

1 pound garbanzo beans
2 teaspoons baking soda
2 quarts water
2 slices whole wheat bread
4 cloves garlic, peeled
¼ cup chopped fresh parsley
1 cup cracked wheat
1 cup hot water
2 tablespoons seasoned bread crumbs
1 teaspoon cumin
1 teaspoon coriander
1 teaspoon paprika
1 teaspoon salt
½ teaspoon pepper
Oil for frying

Soak the garbanzo beans overnight in baking soda and water. In a colander, rinse the beans and pour off the water. Grind the beans in a food processor. Transfer the bean purée to a large mixing bowl. Wet the bread with a little water. Add the bread, garlic, and parsley to the puréed garbanzos, and mix together. Soak the cracked wheat in hot water for 10 minutes; drain and add to the bean mixture. Then add the rest of the ingredients, except the oil, mix well, and form into small balls as for meatballs. In a frying pan, heat with plenty of oil and fry balls until golden brown. Drain well on paper towels. Place the balls on cookie sheets in a 250°F. oven to keep hot until all balls are fried. Serve inside pita bread. This makes about 6 dozen small falafel balls which can be served immediately or frozen and reheated on cookie sheets.

Commemoration in Israel

Being in Israel for the celebration of Yom Ha'atzma'ut is one of our family's most memorable experiences. There, the jubilant Independence Day celebration is preceded by a day of solemnity, a twenty-four-hour memorial period called Yom Hazikkaron, honoring all of those who died in the War of Independence and in the subsequent wars. Almost every Israeli has lost someone in the wars—if not a husband, father, brother, or son—a lifelong friend, or childhood playmate. Therefore, Yom Hazikkaron is a time for visiting the graves of those whose lives and deaths made possible the celebration to follow.

This day is more significant to many Israelis than is Yom Hasho'ah, for Israelis feel keenly the death of their soldiers, while Diaspora Jewry (which barely takes note of Yom Hazikkaron) identifies strongly with Jews murdered in a host culture.

The entire mood of the country changes as the sun sets, Yom Hazikkaron ends, and Yom Ha'atzma'ut begins. In Jerusalem we could not believe the spirit with which Israelis wholeheartedly celebrate Yom Ha'atzma'ut. By about nine o'clock Erev Yom Ha' atzma'ut nobody was home. The main streets in downtown Jerusalem, where everyone was out strolling, laughing, singing, and dancing, were all closed to traffic. Celebrants from ages two to eighty-two batted one another over the head with lightweight plastic hammers called *patishim.* (The patisch is reminiscent of the Maccabees—which means hammer—who, like modern Israelis, refused to be overcome in their determination to preserve our heritage.) Music was piped out of store windows. There were only a few fireworks. The whole incredibly happy celebration was conducted on a minimum budget. And, as one of our daughters, thinking of Fourth of July celebrations in the States, commented, "Nobody is drinking; everyone is high on the holiday itself!"

While many danced in the streets until dawn, others left the crowds for private parties, which began about midnight. We attended one in a friend's apartment, typical of the parties going on throughout the country, where people ate, sang, and danced. With everyone "high on the holiday," nobody drank anything stronger than soft drinks.

The next day was a full holiday, so people slept late. Yom Ha'atzma'ut is one of the few holidays that the entire country can celebrate on the road. (Most other festivals are ones on which the Orthodox do not ride.) By late morning almost every family who had a car was driving to meet friends for a picnic. We attended a large potluck picnic where each of the twenty or more families involved brought something. We all roasted hamburgers, ate salads, hot dishes, and desserts, hiked and played ball games throughout the afternoon.

Yom Ha'atzma'ut is an excellent focal point for a family visit to Israel (although visiting there is wonderful at any time of the year). One of our first discoveries on our initial visit to Israel was that a number of other American families, from varying income groups and walks of life, were living there at the same time. They weren't all retired businessmen, independently wealthy, or professors on sabbatical but were people from various backgrounds, interested in experiencing Israel firsthand, with their entire families. (Among them were an Illinois insurance salesman, his wife and two gradeschoolers; a physician who donated several weeks of his time to Hadassah hospital in exchange for learning their particular research and teaching techniques, his wife, and three children; and a husband-wife social worker team and their teenage sons.)

Those families, like our own, rented apartments in Jerusalem, (obtained through English language Israeli papers, or rental agents), bought groceries in the colorful markets, and participated in the city's many exciting activities.

Israelis—accustomed to immigrants and visitors from all over the world—instantly welcome and absorb newcomers into the culture. Our experiences are typical. A professor I telephoned with a research question immediately invited Dick and me to a social gathering in his home; a businessman Dick met casually invited us all to spend a Shabbat with him and his family. A woman I called with regards from a friend of hers insisted that our whole family come for dinner. And so it went. Although Dick and I speak little Hebrew, the language was never a barrier in the smallest shops or in the largest social gatherings, for most Israelis, who begin learning English in grade school, speak and understand it.

We were delighted to find the Israeli school system receptive to accepting short-term students. On our last visit, our older girls attended an *ulpan*—an intensive Hebrew language school for new immigrants and visitors. There, they met young people from throughout the world and communicated with them in Hebrew, the only language common to them all.

Rebecca attended fourth grade in a regular school where she arrived one April morning frightened and knowing absolutely no one. She skipped home at noon, however, with a new friend on each arm, excited about her experiences and about the teachers and children who helped her with her struggle to understand Hebrew. By the end of our visit, Rebecca's Hebrew was fairly fluent, her friends' English had improved, and she and they shed many tears at her departure.

A family interested in traveling to Israel can obtain much helpful information from Israeli representatives based in most large cities, who are usually affiliated with Jewish community centers. In addition, we've found Israelis temporarily living in the States, as students or on other short-term projects, to be marvelously helpful in providing us with information about accommodations and travel within the country.

In Israel our family realizes more than ever the rhythm of the week, and of the Jewish calendar year. Nothing has ever made us appreciate our link in the chain of Jewish history like spending Shabbat and festivals in the land in which they originated.

Life-cycle Ceremonies

Birth
Death
Bar Mitzvah, Bat Mitzvah
Weddings

Life-cycle Ceremonies

Ceremonies of birth, death, coming of age, and marriage are observed in some way in almost every society. Many of these rituals, called rites of passage, developed in ancient times and survived, fairly intact, for millennia. Others changed over time.

Our Hebrew-Jewish rites of passage are no exception. Some date back to the very beginning of our peoplehood. Some were no doubt borrowed from ancient Canaanite rituals that predate the Hebrews' entrance into Egypt, were absorbed, reworked, and made unmistakably Jewish. Others developed later in the tradition and changed as Jews lived in various host cultures throughout the ages. The origins of some rituals are not always traceable so we must rely on the speculations of archaeologists and folklorists. Other customs clearly originated in a specific time and place in our long and varied history.

In the chapters that follow four major Jewish life-cycle ceremonies will be discussed:—the natural passages of birth and death, and the social passages of Bar Mitzvah, Bat Mitzvah, and weddings.

Birth and death are the natural passages that ancient myth sought to explain, that modern science claims to understand, and that nonetheless still retain their mystery.

Bar Mitzvah and Bat Mitzvah mark a transition from childhood to adulthood. However, they signal a social rather than a biological transition in that the child's actual physiological changes may take place earlier or later than the time of the ceremony.

The wedding marks the establishment of a new household with the promise of a new family, thereby ensuring the continuity of the generations. The Bar Mitzvah and Bat Mitzvah and the wedding are ceremonies that enable the celebrants to pass from one stage to another of life development within the context both of the immediate family and the framework of a caring community.

Each rite of passage is composed of two parts: the ceremony and the meal that follows. The custom of a meal-attendant-to-the-ceremony is not particular to Jewish life-cycle ceremonies but rather appears throughout various cultures of the world. In Judaism, however, the meal following such ceremonies as the *brit, pidyon ha-ben,* Bar Mitzvah, and wedding is called a *se'udat mitzvah* (meal of the commandment). According to the Talmud participation in such a meal is not merely for enjoyment but rather it is a religious obligation.

A se'udat mitzvah can be held in the morning (as at the brit), afternoon, or evening and can take the form of a full meal or a reception. Sometimes, when the numbers of people are large, as at a Bar Mitzvah or Bat Mitzvah where the entire congregation is present, an abbreviated meal, called a kiddush, is served. Kiddush means "sanctification" and pertains to the prayer said over the wine on Shabbat and festivals. However, in popular usage it is extended to the blessing said over the wine whenever wine is served. So, when wine and sweets are served following a special ceremony, we refer to it as "the kiddush."

Birth

One wail ushers in a new generation. The birth of a baby is an exciting event in the life of every family. Particular ceremonies incorporate each new baby into the totality of the family and of the Jewish people.

These ceremonies include the synagogue naming service for a baby daughter soon after her birth, circumcision of the baby boy at eight days, and the pidyon ha-ben ceremony for the first-born male at thirty-one days. But before those ceremonies take place the family must make a critical decision—naming the baby.

The ancients believed that one's entire identity was bound up in a name. It was bad luck to discuss a proposed name for the baby for fear that the evil spirits would know the name, and the baby would die either before or at birth.[1] While we no longer attribute neonatal problems to demons, subconsciously many moderns must still have the notion that the entire being is merged with the baby's name. Otherwise why do prospective parents, of whatever heritage and religion, spend so many hours discussing, debating, and sometimes arguing heatedly over the name of their anticipated progeny?

Although daughters and sons are named in different ceremonies —a daughter in a special synagogue or home service, a son as part of his circumcision rite—the history of Jewish name selection applies equally to girls and boys.

In biblical times a newborn was named for a particular idea or event, or after plants and animals (such as Rachel, which means ewe; or Tamar, which means palm tree). Apparently it was hoped that the child would develop characteristics of the plant or animal the parents admired. It was also customary to merge the child's name with either El (the general name for God), as in Ezekial, or with Jah (the name of the God of Israel), as with Jeremiah.[2]

The still-popular custom of naming a child after a deceased relative originated after the Babylonian Exile when Jews adopted the ancient Egyptian and Greek custom of naming a son for a deceased grandparent. Naming a child for the deceased in other ancient cultures was frequently done in an attempt to "reincarnate" the dead and bring him back to life in new form. However, in Judaism this custom presumably had nothing to do with reincarnation but rather was intended as a means to honor that person, and to have his or her life serve as a model for the new child.

By the Middle Ages, Azhkenazic Jews attached such importance to the naming of a child after the deceased that it became almost a religious duty, while the naming after the living was regarded as an un-Jewish thing to do. Sephardic Jews did not name children for the deceased but rather did just the opposite and named their children after the living. The sentiment, however, was presumably the same.

Jews, particularly those who were more assimilated, began giving their babies secular rather than Hebrew names as far back as Greek and Roman times. However, the custom of giving a child both a Hebrew and a secular name isn't documented until the thirteenth century[3] when a civic name was used for all of a man's non-Jewish business and a Hebrew name was used when he was called to the Torah.

By the late Middle Ages, Jewish children were given two secular and two Jewish names, a custom which is still popular today. (For instance a child may bear the English name Helen Louise and the Hebrew, Hadassah Leah). The main reason for the use of double names was to enable a couple to honor more than one deceased relative. In time, a kind of protocol was developed to help reduce arguments: it was usual that a name from the father's side of the family was given first to the oldest child.[4] The mother chose the name of the second child, and so forth. Rather than using a civic name for ordinary life and reserving a Hebrew name for specific Jewish occasions, as we Diaspora Jews merge our Jewish and secular identities we often give our children Hebrew names to carry through all walks of life.

Sometimes in Jewish history the name of a child was not a matter of parental free choice. The Austrian Edict of 1787 limited Jews to biblical first names. In August 1938, Hitler's government stipulated 185 permissible forenames for Jewish males, 91 for Jewish females (many with negative connotations), which from that day forward were to be used by Jews.[5]

The State of Israel has brought with it a whole new era in baby-naming. Sometimes modern Israelis revive seldom-used biblical names (for example, Gera from the Book of Judges). Other times they create their own names from words in current Hebrew usage (for example, Orali—"my light"). This revival of ancient Hebrew names, as well as the creation of new ones, is also becoming more and more popular in the Western world.

Naming a Daughter

Historically, the only ceremony observed in connection with the birth of a baby girl was that she be named in the synagogue within the text of a prayer asking for her health and blessings. The father generally performed this ceremony on the Shabbat, Monday, or Thursday nearest her birth since those are mornings on which Torah is read. Sometimes this was deferred for a month until the mother could also attend the service.

Ceremony and Celebration

Today, as in times past, it is still appropriate either for the father to name his new daughter, or for the couple to participate jointly. For many families the question of who does the naming may be decided on the basis of how soon after birth the family wants their daughter named. If the family doesn't consider the timing crucial, they may wait until the mother is out of the hospital and ready to participate in the ceremony. If they feel the baby should be named immediately, the father names her.

Some people feel haste is important because in biblical times a new baby was named immediately. Later, it became customary to wait and announce a new boy's name at the time of his circumcision. Nonetheless, deep in our folklore lurked the belief that a name conferred protection against malevolent spirits; immediate naming was therefore considered "good luck."

My father, who was a psychiatrist, did not close his ears to people's superstitions. When he attended his usual daily synagogue services the morning after Miriam's birth and excitedly told the octogenarians of the congregation about his first grandchild, they replied, "How fortunate that it's Monday. You must name her immediately."

"I can't do that," he said. "We have to wait for her parents to name her."

"Never mind," they told him. "It's fine for you to do it. You're already here and she's already born. Better that she be named right away. She'll be safer that way."

Daddy was promptly called to the Torah where his granddaughter officially became Miriam Chai (the name he knew we had chosen)—Miriam, for Dick's mother, who had died several years before; and Chai, Hebrew for life, in honor of my grandfather Chaim.

When Rachel arrived three years later, Daddy convinced Dick (who normally scoffs at all superstition) that maybe it would be better to name the baby right away; so why take a chance? They named her on the Shabbat two days after her birth.

I wanted to participate in the naming of at least one of our daughters but neglected to mention it to Dick in the hectic rush to the hospital in the early hours of the Thursday morning of Rebecca's birth. Dick left the hospital while I rested after her delivery. As soon as he returned I told him how lovely I thought it would be for the whole family to name her. But, even before he spoke, I knew from his expression that he and Daddy had hurried off to services that morning and our newest daughter was already safely named!

Many couples today name their baby girl together in the synagogue on a convenient Sabbath sometime within the first month after the baby's birth. Often entire families participate in the ceremony. In some congregations the baby is named during the end of Shabbat synagogue services late Saturday afternoon or in the early evening. Often the family invites friends and relatives on the occasion of the naming of their daughter, and sponsors a kiddush following the services. Some families name their daughters in the synagogue, then have a kiddush at home that afternoon or evening, where wine, sweets, coffee, and tea are served.

A new custom of naming a daughter in a home ceremony developed during the past few years. Various forms of the ceremony have been created within different congregations and families, the common denominator being the presence of a rabbi, the parents, and the baby. In addition, some ceremonies include special parts to be read by the grandparents and siblings.

The baby is named during the course of the short service. Her parents give her name, and the reason they chose it. Her name is then used throughout the service wherein prayers and readings are recited in her honor.

Friends and relatives are invited to share in the service, and a festive kiddush or meal is served afterward. We attended a beautiful daughter-naming service after which close friends "catered" a se'udat in the new parents' home. The parents had no hosting responsibilities. Rather, everyone brought part of the meal, served it, and helped to clean up while the parents contentedly rocked their new daughter in the midst of the celebration in her honor.

Sometimes a daughter-naming celebration is extended outside of the home or synagogue. One morning when Dick was invited to an office in Israel, his meeting was interrupted for a feast much larger than the usual Israeli *aruchat-eser* (10 A.M. meal). Everyone from executives to maintenance personnel enjoyed a splendid array of food and wine in celebration of the birth of the granddaughter of one of the staff.

Brit (Covenant)

Traditionally a baby boy is named during his circumcision ceremony. Although circumcision was widely practiced throughout the ancient world, Jews attached a special holy significance to this act, which the Book of Genesis ascribes to the time of Abraham. In Genesis, Abraham is told that circumcision is the sign of a covenant between God and him, and all of his descendants:

> This is my covenant which you shall keep between me and you and your descendants after you; every male among you shall be circumcised. . . . He that is eight days old among you shall be circumcised in the flesh of your foreskins, and it shall be a sign of the covenant between you and me . . . any uncircumcised male who is not circumcised in the flesh of his foreskin shall be cut off from his people; he has broken my covenant (Gen. 17:10–14).

Abraham, it is said, circumcised himself at age ninety-nine on Tishri 10, Yom Kippur, the holiest day of the year. Thus, rabbinic tradition has allowed that circumcision take place on the eighth day following birth, even though it may fall on Shabbat or on Yom Kippur. There is no real agreement among scholars as to the origin of the circumcision custom. Some think that it was originally a puberty rite, as it was in some ancient societies; others believe it to have been a kind of magic-related firstling sacrifice. The ancients sacrificed the first of the herds and crops to the heavenly powers in hopes of protecting the whole of the cattle or the fruits. This sacrifice of the "first" of the male reproductive organ may have been thought to protect the rest of the organ from damage or disease.[6] One rabbinic interpretation is that the covenant, symbolized through circumcision, uses the penis—organ of regeneration—to signify that the commitment is transmitted from generation to generation.

Because circumcision is now generally thought to be a hygienic practice, most American baby boys are circumcised today. Whether the ancients recognized the hygienic aspects of circumcision is in dispute among general and medical historians. Whatever its origins, however, circumcision has been practiced faithfully through the ages by Jews without regard to their level of observance of other Jewish practices.

In biblical times flint knives were used to circumcise (Exod. 4:25; Jos. 5:2–3). By Roman times, our ancestors had switched to metal knives for the ritual act.[7]

The location in which the circumcision and attendant ceremony take place has come full cycle. During ancient times the ceremony was performed in the home. In the Middle Ages it was moved to the synagogue. In early modern times circumcision took place in the hospital. Nowadays, as women curtail their hospital stays to a few days, once again the brit is most frequently performed at home.

Watchnight

The watchnight, a vigil held over the baby the night before the brit, is an ancient custom rarely practiced today. Folkloric interpretation is that its original purpose was to prevent attacks of evil spirits, particularly those of Lilith, the mythic first wife of Adam, who left him because of his domination. Lilith and her attendant spirits were believed to harm new babies and mothers during and after childbirth. Many candles were lit throughout the house on Watchnight to frighten away the evil spirits, and a feast was prepared to attract positive forces. In later years, the watchnight became more an occasion of joyous anticipation—a kind of pre-brit party—than one of worry and concern.

Ceremony and Celebration

The brit is usually performed in the morning (according to rabbinic tradition this is a mitzvah—divine precept—which we eagerly perform and therefore hurry to do early in the day). The mother bathes her baby. Other women friends and relatives may help. Even the act of putting one cup of warm water on the baby is considered a mitzvah. After dressing him, the mother passes her baby to his godmother (a close relative or friend selected for the honor in advance of the ceremony). The baby's mother is not required to remain in the room during the ceremony and often does not. I can understand why. When I was godmother at my nephew's brit it was my responsibility to pass him to his godfather, who in turn passed him to the mohal (person specially trained to perform the surgery). I was overcome with fear and wanted to run out the door—carrying the baby. For at that moment I instinctively identified with the pagan women of ancient times who had to throw their first-born sons into the fire as a sacrifice to their gods. Once I recognized what had frightened me I relaxed, and since then have appreciated more than ever that child sacrifice was never a Hebrew belief.

In Orthodox Jewish families ten men over age thirteen are required to form the *minyan* (minimum group necessary to say certain prayers) for the service attendant to the ceremony. Among other branches of Jewry, where women are counted in the minyan, ten persons over the age of thirteen are required.

After the baby is passed to the mohal he is placed on a chair called the Chair of Elijah, which has been prepared with pillows. The chair was added to the brit ritual in post-Talmudic times and was already an integral part of the ceremony by the ninth century C.E. Rabbinic reasons for the use of this chair include God's command that Elijah be present at every circumcision ceremony. Folkloric interpretation holds that in ancient times a guardian angel was necessary to ward off evil spirits, potential attackers of the newborn baby; the chair was originally for that guardian angel, and was later through rabbinic reasoning thought to be occupied by Elijah.[8]

The mohal takes the baby from the Chair of Elijah and places him on a pillow on the knees of the *sandek* (assistant to the mohal). When the brit was transferred from the home to the synagogue in the ninth century the sandek—whose name is derived from the Greek word for godfather[9]—was added to the brit ceremony. The sandek holds the baby while the mohal uses the baby's name publicly for the first time, thereby naming him. Following the surgery, the baby is generally given a drop of wine to quiet him and help him fall asleep.

Se'udat Mitzvah

While the cause for the celebration lies in his bassinet, friends and relatives enjoy a feast in his honor. The menu varies from wine, juice, herring, kichel, and sweets to a full-scale brunch. Unless the mother had an amniocentesis, and thus has had several months' notice to fill the freezer, the food is usually brought by relatives and friends, or simply purchased at a bakery or delicatessen.

Herring is traditionally served at a brit, probably because of the association of fish with fertility. I often bring marinated herring, made Grandma Bess's way, to a brit. It's easy to make, can be brought ready to serve, and is wonderful with kichel, crackers, or thick rye bread.

Grandma Bess's Marinated Herring

4 (12-ounce) jars cut-up herring in brine sauce
2 cups sour cream
1 tablespoon vinegar
1 tablespoon sugar
1 orange, sliced thin
1 lemon, sliced thin

Drain the brine from the herring. Place the herring in a bowl. In a separate bowl, mix the sour cream, vinegar, and sugar. Add to the herring and mix well. Add the sliced orange and lemon. Refrigerate 2 days or at least overnight. Serves 24.

Usually, for two practical reasons, the entire brit celebration—ceremony and se'udat mitzvah—does not exceed a couple of hours: a prolonged party could be exhausting for the new mother; also, since the brit is held in the morning, people generally need to get back to their work.

Perhaps the brit celebration is especially meaningful because it takes place under circumstances that are frequently less than ideal—when the new parents are tired and the members of the minyan and other guests have often interrupted busy schedules in order to attend. I remember one brit where the new parents were both students, as were most of their friends. The brit fell on the morning of the father's final Ph.D. oral exam, scheduled months before his son arrived three weeks early. The new father participated in his son's brit, then went immediately from the festivities to his examination. One of the other minyan participants, a childhood friend of the new parents, who was interning at a nearby hospital and had been up all night, arrived—still in his whites—just in time for the ceremony.

Pidyon Ha-ben

Ceremony and Celebration

The ceremony of pidyon ha-ben, redemption of the first-born male, which takes place thirty-one days after birth, shows even more clearly than the brit ritual that our Hebrew ancestors developed a morality different from that of the surrounding cultures.

Whereas in the ancient world the first-born, particularly the first-born son, was sacrificed because he was believed to belong to the deities, the Hebrews reinterpreted both the belief and the practice. The first-born son had a special obligation to the God of Moses and thus "belonged" to the priests to assist them in the sanctuary. The Hebrews developed a means for "buying the child back," whereby the child could retain his obligations yet live with his family. The ceremony ordained in the Book of Numbers is observed on the thirty-first day after the baby's birth.

> The first issue of the womb of every being man or beast, that is offered to the Lord shall be yours [meaning the priests']; but you shall have the first born of man redeemed . . . take as their redemption price from the age of one month up, the money equivalent of five shekels by the sanctuary weight, which is twenty gerahs (Num. 18:15–16).

Although friends and relatives are customarily invited, the only person required for the brief ceremony other than the baby and his parents is a Kohen, who performs the necessary "priestly" functions. (Essentially, all Jews are classified as Israelites. Some Israelites are descended from the tribe of Levi. Some of these descendants are Kohanim and they perform the "priestly" functions. Rabbinic explanation of these divisions is that they were developed to ensure the performance of various functions within the Temple. The responsibilities were passed down from father to son so that continuity would be maintained. There is no pidyon ha-ben for the son of a Kohen or Levi parent.)

During the pidyon ha-ben ceremony a dialogue, developed in the Gaonic period (sixth to eleventh centuries), takes place, in which the Kohen asks the father whether or not he will give up his son for priestly service. The father responds that he prefers to keep him and he pays the Kohen five silver coins.[10] In Talmudic times the priests began returning the money to the father, a custom still followed today. The Kohen recites the appropriate blessings, the wine and challah are blessed, and then friends and relatives who have witnessed the ceremony enjoy a kiddush, or full festive meal.

In recent times some members of Conservative, Reform, or Reconstructionist congregations have argued that central to the pidyon ha-ben is the celebration of the first-time opening of the mother's womb, which is certainly done as effectively by a daughter as by a son. In their essay "The Birth of a Daughter," Myra and Daniel Liefler of Chicago share the pidyon ha-bat ritual that they created for their daughter.[11] It is based on, but not identical to, the pidyon ha-ben. Particularly innovative is their donation to charity of eighteen dollars rather than a five-silver-coin "redemptive price" paid a Kohen (eighteen is Chai—Life—in Hebrew).

Tree-planting

A minor ancient ceremony that applied equally to boys and girls was the custom of planting a tree when a child was born. It has returned in new form since the establishment of the State of Israel. Originally, a cedar was planted for a boy and a pine for a girl. When a couple married, their respective trees were cut down and used in the construction of the *huppah* (bridal canopy under which the bride and groom exchange their vows).

This custom, mentioned in the Talmud, was not specific to the Jews but rather has been practiced in countries throughout the world, including Switzerland, Sweden, and Germany.[12] One idea was apparently that the child should grow from seed to adulthood like a tree, another that the child's and the tree's destinies were somehow bound—that as one grew strong so would the other.

Nowadays, most of us change locations so frequently that if we observed this custom in its ancient form, our yards would be orchards honoring other families' children. However, a modern interpretation of this custom is to plant a tree in Israel (either in person or through the Jewish National Fund) in honor of the birth of a new baby—either one's own or as a new baby gift. We have done this frequently as new babies have been born to friends. And, although I never made it to the synagogue to name our daughters, I had the wonderful experience of going with them, Dick, and my mother to a forest overlooking Jerusalem where we planted a tree each in honor of Miriam, Rachel, and Rebecca.

Death

Death presents theology with its greatest challenge, because its explanations and interpretations affect all of life. For, if we're going to die anyway, why live in a particular way, according to a particular code?

Various religions confront the problem in different ways. Since earliest times Judaism has viewed life from the standpoint of inevitable death, and constructed an ethical way of life in death's face. Whereas others in the ancient world were in constant search of the same immortality as that enjoyed by their gods, the Hebrews accepted their mortality. In the biblical account of Noah's Ark, there is no question of personal immortality, rather the message is that man will die but *mankind* will continue. It is through this philosophy of personal mortality, yet of the eternal continuity of the generations, that Judaism has survived.

Judaism predicates its death rituals upon this philosophy of the continuity of the generations. The deceased is tended to immediately, prepared for burial, buried quickly and simply. Mourning is extended, its various stages enabling the mourner first to believe the death, then to grieve, to be comforted by others who care, and gradually to return to regular matters of daily life. But mourning never completely ceases. The anniversary of the death of a loved one is observed throughout the lifetime of the relatives. In addition, all the departed are remembered collectively at certain festival services throughout the year. In this way we acknowledge our lasting connection to those whose lives have been inseparable parts of our own.

Observances

In the ancient world, and the Hebrews were no exception, a corpse was considered a defilement and therefore buried immediately.[1] Many folklorists connect fears and aversion for the body of the deceased with the ancients' belief that evil spirits immediately inhabited the body of the dead. In Hebrew homes, as in the homes of the surrounding people, certain rituals were performed to rid the house of those spirits as soon as death was evident. The windows of the house were opened, all the standing water in the house was poured out, as was the water in the three houses on either side of the deceased's home. While the ancients may have explained illness and ultimately death as the result of evil spirits (which we now call viruses or bacteria), their methods of attempting to air and clean the house were nonetheless sound.

Today, as in ancient times, traditional Jewish burial takes place as soon as possible. The funeral is generally the day following the death; only very rarely is there a time lapse of over thirty-six hours between death and burial. That usually occurs if Shabbat or a festival intervenes since burial does not take place on those occasions. Traditionally, someone stays with the body from the moment of death until burial.

Funeral Preparations

In biblical times the family prepared and buried its own members in sepulchers without coffins. In Babylonia, where the land did not lend itself to burial of the dead in chambers of cave and mountain, Jews dug graves and buried their dead in cemeteries.[2]

In Palestine during the Roman period, Jewish communities founded burial brotherhoods to announce the death, prepare the body for burial, arrange for pallbearers, and plan the funeral. This was a forerunner of the *chevra kadisha* (sacred society; burial brotherhood), which began in the Middle Ages.

We have come full circle in the modern era. The chevra kadisha, important for centuries throughout Europe, was supplanted in this country by the funeral parlor, complete with funeral director, ornate caskets, and elaborate services. Recently, some congregations throughout the country have formed their own burial societies because of congregants' desires to return to older, more personal forms of caring for the dead. So once again members of the community bathe the body, use simple wooden caskets, and even make burial garments.[3]

Shroud

In biblical times, it was customary to bury the dead in several expensive garments. Religious leaders, such as Rabbi Gamaliel, concerned about the great burden this placed upon the poor, asked that they themselves be buried in simple inexpensive garments. Such requests led to the establishment of the precedent for the inexpensive single burial shroud, which is still used today.[4] (It can be obtained through funeral homes or handmade.) In addition to the shroud it is customary for a man to be buried in his tallit, in which a tear is made to symbolize that it will not be worn again for prayer.

Casket

Traditionally, the body is placed in a simple wooden casket. Often a scholar was buried in a casket made from the table upon which he studied. The principle of burial in plain cloth and in simple wood is that the body should be allowed to decompose as naturally as possible. The return to the dust from which one came is not to be retarded by man-made impediments.

Funeral Service

From Second Temple until modern times the simple funeral service took place either in the home or at the cemetery.[5] Nowadays it usually takes place in a synagogue chapel or sanctuary, or at the cemetery, but almost never at home.

The short service usually consists of psalms, a eulogy, and a memorial prayer. In biblical times the eulogy was given by a close family member. For instance, Abraham is said to have eulogized his wife, Sarah. Only in later times was the honor of giving the eulogy accorded the rabbi. Today, occasionally, family members once again give eulogies themselves. Sometimes the family knows that the deceased would have preferred no eulogy, and simply requests a few minutes of silence instead. Each mourner silently speaks his own eulogy and recalls the departed in his own way.

It is considered an honor to accompany the departed to his grave. If one can attend the funeral service held in the synagogue, but is not able to accompany the procession to the cemetery, one may symbolically do so by following the procession for six or eight feet.

At the cemetery, mourners wait until the casket is lowered into the ground, then place some earth upon the casket before leaving.

Mourning Customs

Rending the Garments

Ancient peoples, the Hebrews included, slashed their own flesh when a loved one died. In all likelihood this was the precursor of the custom of rending one's garments (known as *keriah*), which is still practiced today.[6]

Son, daughter, mother, father, sister, brother, and spouse are considered mourners and in Orthodox Judaism are obligated to tear their garments. The death of a parent is symbolized by tearing the garment across the heart; for all other relatives the tear is on the right side. In Conservative congregations, the mourner rarely tears his clothes. Instead, just prior to the funeral, he is provided with a slashed black ribbon (symbolic of the torn garment) to wear for the duration of the mourning period.

Meal of Mourning

The mourners return from the cemetery accompanied by relatives and close friends. They are met by other friends who prepare a light dairy meal in their own homes and bring it to the home of the mourning. The only constants are bread—the staff of life—and hard-cooked eggs, symbolic of the circle of life since ancient times, and of mourning since the destruction of the Second Temple of Jerusalem. The mourners and those who have come home from the cemetery with them sit and eat. They are served by the friends who brought the meal. A meal of mourning is customary in many societies as a means through which the mourners may begin to reforge a broken chain. The meal serves as a symbol: although a link is missing, the family will continue.

Sitting Shiva

Shiva, seven days of intensive mourning, interrupted only by Shabbat and major festivals, begins immediately upon the mourners' arrival home from the cemetery. Mourners do not work, attend school, or pursue any usual activities during this period. Rather, it is essentially a time of transition between the funeral and the resumption of normal activities during which the mourners stay at home while the outside world comes to them. Friends, relatives, and other concerned members of the community come to the home during this period to pay their respects to the deceased and offer sympathy to the living.

In traditional Judaism when the mourner sits, it is on a stool of lower height than any of the other furniture. According to rabbinic interpretation, the low stool signifies the mourner's desire to be closer to the earth in which his loved one is interred. Folklorists hypothesize that this, along with other mourning customs such as walking barefooted and covering the head, was not originally associated with mourning itself, but rather was connected with survivors' fears of ghosts of the dead. To confuse these ghosts, it behooved the living to disguise themselves and their normal habits until they couldn't be recognized.[7]

On the late afternoon or early evening of the funeral day, the mourners say their first kaddish at home. (Kaddish, originally an Aramaic prose-poem, is a prayer of sanctification of God which is recited by mourners throughout their period of bereavement.) A minyan—quorum of ten—is required, so close friends usually make it a special point to arrive in time for the home service during which the kaddish is recited.

Friends and relatives continue to come to visit the bereaved for the next six days. (Although the traditional period of shiva is one week, nowadays it is frequently shortened to three days due to family preference or extenuating circumstances.) Shiva provides the mourner with the chance to be shown caring by practically everyone he knows, and enables him to return to regular activities knowing that those around him are concerned. By the time shiva is concluded, the mourner has been visited by members of the world outside to the point where he is much more ready to return to interact with them than he was immediately after the funeral.

Throughout the week of shiva friends and relatives bring food to the mourner, who is relieved of the need to think about, or prepare, meals. Those closest to the mourner arrange among themselves to bring and serve dinner on shiva nights.

In addition, other friends often bring food when they come to pay shiva calls. It's amazing what solace a plate of homemade cookies, a cake, or a nut bread can bring. It not only shows caring on the part of the friend who brings it but also symbolizes ongoing life.

Sometimes someone asks, "Should I go to shiva? After all I don't know him that well . . ." It is always appropriate to pay a shiva call. I've heard many mourners remark after a shiva evening—"I'm really so touched that he came . . ." or "I am so surprised and glad she made the effort to come . . ." The total outpouring of caring which "gets one through" the week of shiva helps to ease the transition back into regular activities. The love, care, and concern that are shown during shiva are of immeasurable help in enabling the mourner to begin the long process of emotional reconstruction.

Sheloshim

The thirty days after the funeral of a loved one, designated sheloshim (thirty), are special days of mourning. The first seven days comprise the shiva period, the rest are days during which the mourner attempts to return to normal activities but recognizes that he or she is still deeply grieved. In traditional Judaism, kaddish is said during the regular morning and evening daily services during this thirty-day period.

Year of Mourning

Attendance at daily services to say kaddish is obligatory for all seven categories of mourners during sheloshim, and for those who have lost parents, for eleven months. Even when not obligatory, many mourners choose to say kaddish for the longer period. In secular society psychologists and sociologists recently began forming death support groups for mourners to meet to deal with their losses. Attending daily services to say kaddish has enabled Jews to have the support of such groups since early times.

In the year following my father's death, I found attending daily services gave me a prescribed time for channeling my grief so that it didn't become repressed, and suddenly overwhelming. I met others who were also saying kaddish for a loved one, and thus formed immediate bonds of commonality with them. One young woman and her mother came every evening as I did. When I first saw them I assumed they were saying kaddish for a husband and father, but it turned out that he had died several years previously. This time they were mourning a son and brother. Knowing them helped to prevent me from becoming consumed by self-pity and enabled me to see others who were also grieving, some of whom had been left in circumstances more difficult than mine.

Commemoration

After the year of mourning Judaism provides specific days of commemoration during which we remember our departed loved ones.

One of these occasions is the yahrtzeit, the anniversary of the death, and the other is the yizkor service, which occurs several times during the year.

YAHRTZEIT Ashkenazic Jews call the anniversary of the day of death (as marked on the Jewish calendar) yahrtzeit, while Sephardic Jews call it Annos. On this occasion one lights a lamp or long-burning candle at sundown, and lets it burn until the next sunset. The kaddish is recited during morning and evening services. There is no prescribed family ceremony.

Some families, however, develop their own yahrtzeit ceremonies. When author Bel Kaufman, granddaughter of the late Sholom Aleichem, spoke in Jerusalem in June of 1980, she reminisced with great love about the grandfather she remembered both from personal recollections and from the ceremonies held annually on the anniversary of his death. During his life he stated that he hoped his friends and relatives would gather each year at the anniversary of his death, to reread some of his stories and to laugh. The family has done so.[8]

This seems to me to be a beautiful idea. On the yahrtzeit of a loved one there is both a resurgence of grief and feelings of joy at all the happy memories which come to the surface. So why not share those happy memories with others who loved the person as well, and hear some of their recollections? The first years may be too soon to do this, but later the time may feel right. Then spending an evening with close friends of the loved one to tell and hear happy stories of his life re-told may be uplifting for all.

YIZKOR The yizkor (remember) service, held in the synagogue on Yom Kippur and on the last day of each of the three pilgrimage festivals—Pesach, Shavuot, and Sukkot—gives us a time to remember our departed as a community. Yizkor is appropriate on Yom Kippur, the solemnest day in the Jewish year. It is equally fitting that the prayers are also recited on the final day of each of the pilgrimage festivals—holidays of great joy and festivity—when even in the midst of happy celebration we recall our loved ones.

Bar Mitzvah, Bat Mitzvah

Judaism marks the passage from childhood into the teen years through the Bar Mitzvah and Bat Mitzvah ceremony. According to the Talmud, a boy becomes Bar Mitzvah on the day after his thirteenth birthday, and a girl Bat Mitzvah on the day after her twelfth birthday. The terms "bar" Mitzvah and "bat" Mitzvah literally mean son and daughter of the commandment, and originally referred to the attainment of maturity within the religious community: "He has become Bar Mitzvah" meant "He has come of age." Today, Bar and Bat Mitzvah also refer to the *occasion* on which maturity is reached. "He has celebrated his Bar Mitzvah," means "He has participated in the Torah service."

Origin

Because of the heavy emphasis contemporary Jewry places on the ceremony of Bar Mitzvah and Bat Mitzvah, one might assume this rite of passage to have deep historical roots. The Torah, however, does not mention any puberty rite. In fact, the age of majority is mentioned in the Torah as twenty, for at that age "anyone who is numbered in the census from twenty years old and upward shall give the Lord's offering" (Exod. 30:14), and every male from twenty years and upward was "able to go forth to war" (Num. 1:3).

Historians disagree as to when age thirteen became the age of majority and when the ceremony celebrating attainment of the age of majority came into vogue. Some argue that the rite of circumcision was the ancient Hebrew puberty rite, which in later times was moved back to the age of eight days. Others say that the status of obligation for boys of thirteen was an old norm which later became formalized.

Many scholars argue that there could not have been a ceremony to celebrate the attainment of majority in Talmudic or even early medieval times because in those days a minor was allowed to participate in religious ritual, such as Torah reading, from the time he was able to do so.[1] Since boys received intensive Jewish educations from very early ages, they were capable of participating in most parts of the service from the time they were quite young.

In the mid- or late Middle Ages, when religious rights which had traditionally belonged to the minor were revoked, the age of majority began to take on new importance in Jewish life. A boy could no longer simply read from the Torah as soon as he was able. This act, which had originally been his birthright, became a privilege delayed until he reached age thirteen.

The attainment of Bar Mitzvah meant the coming of age with regard to religious responsibilities, and imposed obligations on a man. From age thirteen on he had to perform religious acts, such as attending daily services, at specific times of day. Coming of age never imposed these kinds of responsibilities on a woman. Because of pregnancies, deliveries, nursing, and all other responsibilities connected with child-bearing, she was exempted from religious mitzvot that had to be performed at particular times of day.

Because her coming of age was not connected with the performance of any religious rites within the synagogue, there seemed no need for a Bat Mitzvah ceremony.

However, in later times, though historians are not sure just when, the custom of the Bat Mitzvah arose in France and Italy, then spread through Europe.[2] The Bat Mitzvah took various forms and sometimes was held at school or in the home rather than in the synagogue. When it was held in the synagogue the girl usually read Haftorah (selections from the prophets) but did not read from the Torah. Such was the case with Judith Kaplan (Eisenstein), the oldest daughter of Mordecai Kaplan, founder of the Reconstructionist Movement, who was the first girl to celebrate a Bat Mitzvah in this country.

Ms. Eisenstein relates that her Bat Mitzvah was "my father's bravery, not mine," and recalls her two grandmothers sitting in rocking chairs the evening before her Bat Mitzvah each telling the other, "Convince your child not to let her do it." But Judith Kaplan did it and was quickly followed by a group of her friends, daughters of members of the Society of the Advancement of Judaism, who celebrated their Bat Mitzvot as she did.[3]

Preparation

Preparing for the Bar Mitzvah or Bat Mitzvah is an excellent way for a young person to begin taking adult responsibilities. Almost every *havurah* (small group of like-minded participants) or congregation, within which the child will celebrate this occasion, is flexible enough for the child to put his or her own imprint on preparations for and celebration of this important day.

Many rabbis believe that a child should be encouraged to participate in as much of the service as possible—through selection of particular readings, original compositions, an original prayer before the ark, translation of his or her Torah and Haftorah reading; as well as by deciding, with parents, whom to select for an aliyah (honor of reciting a blessing over the Torah) during the Torah reading.

Some congregations—particularly havurot, or small Reform or Reconstructionist groups—are extremely flexible in enabling the Bar Mitzvah or Bat Mitzvah to construct his or her own service. For instance, we attended a beautiful Bat Mitzvah service in Chicago where the Bat Mitzvah and her mother, both talented musicians, played guitars and sang original prayers during the service.

Invitations

The Bar and Bat Mitzvah ceremony and festivities are an expression of a family's inner values. Time spent discussing who is to be invited to share in the occasion is time well spent, for the family then decides together to whom it feels closest, and to whom it will extend the honor of sharing the occasion.

In earlier decades in this country parents often used their child's Bar Mitzvah as a time to entertain all their friends, acquaintances, and business associates; but this trend is on the wane. Replacing it is the realization that this is essentially the celebrant's day—that he should be surrounded by loving relatives and friends with whom he has grown up. When the guest list is comprised of those close to the celebrant and his family, the atmosphere is caring and informal, as it should be for welcoming a child into the adult community.

If invitations are oral, the Bar Mitzvah or Bat Mitzvah can do the telephoning. If written, the child has an opportunity to place his or her imprint on the invitation by selecting the wording and making an original design utilizing Hebrew symbols, his or her Hebrew name, a picture or photograph . . . the possibilities are endless, and instant-printing machines make them inexpensive. What's important is that the invitation come from the celebrant as an expression of personal involvement and desire to include the recipient.

We've received some very meaningful invitations over the years, including one where the Bar Mitzvah drew a picture relating to his Torah portion (Moses at Mount Sinai), another where the Bat Mitzvah designed a Torah scroll with her Hebrew name underneath. For her Bat Mitzvah invitation, Rachel used a photograph she took in Jerusalem of the huge menorah outside the Knesset. Underneath she wrote the biblical quotation "and they shall no more be plucked out of the Land which I have given them" (Amos 9:15). Bilingual English-Hebrew invitations are becoming increasingly popular in this country as they already are in Israel.

Ceremony and Celebration

Although a Bar Mitzvah or Bat Mitzvah candidate may participate in services when the Torah is read on Monday or Thursday mornings or on Rosh Hodesh (New Moon), almost every Bar Mitzvah and Bat Mitzvah in this country is held on Shabbat morning. In Conservative and Reform congregations males and females generally participate equally in the service. Thus, the celebrant is called to the Torah to read a part or all of the Torah portion for the Shabbat. In addition, the child may lead the Shacharit service (the morning service that precedes the Torah reading), chant Haftorah, and/or lead the concluding service.

Some congregations have a set amount of service in which the Bar Mitzvah or Bat Mitzvah is allowed to participate; other congregations encourage the boy or girl to do as much as possible. During the Torah reading, in many congregations, members of the celebrating family are called to the Torah for an aliyah, so the ceremony becomes a whole family affair.

Each congregation has its own local customs with regard to particular aspects of the Bar Mitzvah and Bat Mitzvah ceremony. In one congregation, the parents walk to the ark with their son, recite a Shehecheyanu with him, and drape his tallit around his shoulders for the first time; in another congregation the mother gives a short talk and presents a gift of Jewish significance to her daughter; in some congregations at the conclusion of the service, an older sibling congratulates the new Bar Mitzvah or Bat Mitzvah and welcomes him or her into the adult congregation. In other synagogues the congregation sings a congratulatory song to the celebrant at the conclusion of his or her Torah reading.

The Bar Mitzvah or Bat Mitzvah often recites an original prayer before the ark. This derives from an older custom in which, during the Middle Ages, the Bar Mitzvah delivered a *derashah* (Talmudic discourse) at the banquet served in his honor. During the talk he thanked his parents for all they had done for him, and his guests for having joined him for the celebration.

In recent times some people have sought to broaden the concept of Bar and Bat Mitzvah from that of the child's reading from the Torah within the synagogue, which confers membership in the adult Jewish community, to a more general Jewish rite of passage. Some families have their child's Bar Mitzvah or Bat Mitzvah service at home, or use camp or retreat facilities when they are not being used for other purposes. They are then free to invite only those with whom they choose to share the service. (When the Bar Mitzvah or Bat Mitzvah is held within the context of the synagogue the entire congregation or any portion thereof may well be present.) The families are then completely free to write their own service, without being bound by an existing liturgy or framework.[4]

Se'udat Mitzvah

Delicious food served on joyous occasions is synonymous with Judaism. Just as each Shabbat and festival is a time for a special meal so is each simcha—brit, Bar Mitzvah or Bat Mitzvah, and wedding—of the life cycle.

Good food, however, does not necessitate preparation and service by caterers in expensive restaurants and clubs. Just as the family prepares and serves Shabbat and festival meals, it can prepare and serve a meal for a simcha at home or at the synagogue.

At first thought parents of the celebrant often ask, "How can we possibly cook for a hundred people . . . We'll have to hire caterers." Actually, cooking for a hundred is no more difficult than cooking for ten, it's just ten times as much. And, as anyone who has ever cooked in quantity for a simcha knows, it's ten times as much fun because it's so exhilarating. One gets the feeling that one can feed the whole world if necessary—something that many Jewish cooks could probably do.

The se'udat mitzvah can be held either in the synagogue social hall or at home. In some congregations members of synagogue sisterhoods help the celebrating family shop, cook, and serve on a reciprocal basis, so that each member helps with a certain number of celebrations each year. In other synagogues, the family and friends come in and do all the cooking themselves. (Some synagogues employ a person to oversee *kashrut*—kosher food—regulations. That person also often helps the celebrating family bake and cook.)

The major advantages of holding the festivity in the synagogue are that the facilities for food preparation are usually much larger than those in homes, there is generally much more space than at home, and guests are right there so a luncheon can be served immediately after services.

I've helped friends cook for their children's Bar Mitzvah and Bat Mitzvah festivities in their synagogues and it's always a delight. Once eight of us, in less than three hours, made a delicious lunch that included salmon salad, noodle kugel, beautiful fruit and vegetable platters, and cakes and ices.

The advantage of having the festivities at home is that there is nothing comparable to offering hospitality in one's own surroundings. Some families also find preparation there more convenient. When one does have the se'udat mitzvah at home, friends usually volunteer, or are happy to be asked to help. "We'd love to join you . . . what can I bake?" or "We wouldn't miss it for anything . . . when do we cook?" are frequent replies friends give one another when invited to a Bar Mitzvah or Bat Mitzvah.

We attended an evening festivity in honor of the Bat Mitzvah of a close family friend, where almost every one of the guests brought something. The parents had set a large table in the middle of their recreation room on which friends put a splendid array of salads, cheeses, casserole dishes, and baked goods. "I bake or cook for my friends when they have a simcha," the hostess said. "And now they have all done it for me." Their home is not large, and the guests were many, so we all stood, or sat on the floor. Because the atmosphere was so casual and relaxed, and the hosts were having as much fun as their guests, we found the evening much more enjoyable than many a sit-down dinner.

On another occasion we attended a sumptuous se'udat mitzvah in honor of the Bar Mitzvah of the son of Israeli friends, temporarily living in the States. The family and friends cooked and baked for weeks in advance. About eighty guests enjoyed a real feast in the hosts' home, followed by an evening of singing and dancing.

What does one serve when eighty come over for dinner? "Many different things," our hostess laughed. She chose a varied buffet, with such hot dishes as fruited chicken wings and stuffed grape leaves. Accompaniments included rice-mushroom-almond casseroles and a variety of salads. Later in the evening she cleared and reset the buffet table, this time with a huge fresh-fruit centerpiece surrounded by trays of sweets. Among them was this Middle Eastern delicacy:

Almond Pastries

Dough: 2 cups flour
½ cup butter
3 tablespoons water

Filling: ½ pound almonds
½ teaspoon ground cinnamon
¼ cup sugar
Powdered sugar (for rolling pastries)

In a large bowl, blend together the flour, butter, and water until the dough is soft. Roll into 4 or 5 dozen small balls—about the size of a jumbo olive. To make the filling in a blender or food processor, whirl the almonds until fine. Transfer to a bowl and mix the almonds with cinnamon and sugar. Punch each ball to make hollow place; put some filling into it and work dough back around to form ball. Bake the balls in a 350°F. oven for 20 minutes until they are light gold; don't let them turn brown as they will become too hard. Let cool, then roll the balls in powdered sugar. Store for days in a covered container.

When serving a crowd, some hostesses prefer a set menu in which only a few varieties of foods are cooked in quantity. An easy-to-prepare luncheon or dinner menu, which I served for the one hundred friends and relatives who came to our home the evening of Miriam's Bat Mitzvah, consisted of sweet and sour meatballs, pineapple-noodle kugel, fresh vegetable platters, watermelon boats, and sweet trays. I spent a few hours sometime during the month preceding the Bat Mitzvah preparing and freezing the meatballs and kugels, and a couple more hours the day before the festivities preparing the vegetables while a close friend prepared the fresh fruits. The girls and I baked during the preceding months. Friends and relatives baked for us as well.

We used plastic plates and utensils and the entire party was done very easily—with a minimum of set-up. Two friends volunteered to refill platters and clean up, so that we could all be free to greet and mix with our guests.

Sweet and Sour Meatballs for 100

20 pounds ground round steak
6 cups cooked rice
8 eggs
3 onions, chopped
1 tablespoon salt
1 teaspoon pepper
1 teaspoon thyme
10 (28-ounce cans) tomato sauce
4 (8-ounce) jars apricot marmalade

Mix the meat, rice, eggs, onions, and seasonings together in a large roasting pan. Form the meat mixture into small balls. (Have everyone in the family help.) Place in four large (12″ × 12″) disposable aluminum foil pans. Mix the tomato sauce and jam together in the now-empty roasting pan. Then pour pitcherfuls of the mixture over the meatballs. Cover the pans tightly with foil. Bake in a preheated 400°F. oven for 1½ hours. Cool. Freeze.

Festival Kugel for 100

12 (12-ounce) packages wide egg noodles
24 eggs
8 (24-ounce) cans pineapple tidbits in juice
3 cups honey
2 tablespoons ground cinnamon
1 tablespoon nutmeg
4 cups white raisins
24 apples, peeled and chopped

In several big pans, simultaneously or in several batches, boil and drain the noodles according to package directions. Set aside. In a large bowl, beat the eggs. Add the juice from 2 cans pineapple; drain juice from other 6 cans. Add the honey, spices, and raisins and mix. Add the pineapple and chopped apples to the egg-pineapple juice mixture. Blend. Grease six 12″ × 20″ aluminum foil pans. Put 1/6 of the noodles in each, mix well with 1/6 of the liquid mixture. Cover each pan with aluminum foil and bake in a preheated 350°F. oven for 1 hour. Cool and freeze. Each batch will yield about 24 large squares of pudding. Delicious served either piping hot or cold.

One night we attended a Bar Mitzvah se'udah in the Old City of Jerusalem. The Bar Mitzvah, his five brothers, and their parents live in what was originally part of a Crusader compound. Neglected for centuries, it was rebuilt by the Israelis after the 1967 reunification of Jerusalem.

The home is situated at the top of a tiered garden from which one can see the Western Wall of the destroyed Temple, the holiest site in Judaism. As we ate and talked with the hosts and other guests (many of them Orthodox Jews dressed in traditional black long coats and top hats), we felt completely immersed in the timelessness of Jewish history. It was thrilling to see the Bar Mitzvah boy come of age, as have centuries of boys before him, with the tremendous pride of being part of his own land. Although the mother works full time, and the father, like many Israelis, has two jobs, it didn't stop the family from preparing the huge variety of fish, meats, salads, and sweets themselves.

One of the many wonderful treats we enjoyed was a carrot-lemon-raisin salad. This recipe serves twelve and can be multiplied to serve any number of guests.

Jerusalem Salad

6 cups grated carrots
1 cup dark raisins
1 fresh lemon, thinly sliced
1/2 cup sliced pitted green olives
1/4 cup fresh lemon juice
1/8 cup sugar
1 head romaine lettuce, washed and dried

Mix all the ingredients except the romaine in a bowl. Refrigerate overnight. Serve on a bed of fresh romaine leaves.

Gifts. When Miriam became Bat Mitzvah I was very uncomfortable with the feeling that, although we'd limited the guest list to family and close friends, an invitation still seemed equivalent to a request for a gift. However, I've grown to accept the fact that gifts are now an integral part of the tradition and even feel that a Bar Mitzvah or Bat Mitzvah gift can be very positive in both Jewish content and as a reminder of an important and happy event.

Our daughters have given and been given many Jewish books, which will last a lifetime. Many of their friends have received needlepointed kepot with Judaic designs which they love wearing to services. Jewish jewelry, such as the Magen David (Star of David) or Chai (symbol of life) worn on chains around the neck, is a popular Bar or Bat Mitzvah gift. Many boys receive a Kiddush cup as a Bar Mitzvah gift, while girls receive candlesticks.

When a child receives money as a gift, the Bar Mitzvah or Bat Mitzvah is an appropriate occasion for him or her to give a portion of it to charity, since the giving of tzedaka is one of Judaism's highest values.

Weddings

In biblical times a man bought a bride. More specifically, a young man's father bought him a bride through often-complex arrangements with her father. Since the bride and groom would live with his parents after marriage, there would be one more worker in his parents' kitchen and fields, and one less in hers; therefore, monetary compensation seemed necessary.

The families of the bride and groom met to negotiate the *tena'im* (conditions of marriage agreement), which would provide for the financial futures of their children. After the initial purchase, when the groom's family paid a certain *mohar* (price) for her, the bride was betrothed to him. During the betrothal period of not less than one year the bride continued to live in her own home.

The marriage ceremony—since ancient times referred to as the chuppah—took place after the year's betrothal. Amid great rejoicing the bride was led, by friends and members of her family, to the wedding canopy (called the chuppah or tent of the groom), where the bride and groom consummated their marriage relationship.

The wedding and betrothal remained two distinct events from biblical times until the Middle Ages. During the intervening centuries, the bride was not always purchased, however—at least, not quite so obviously. Rather, the mohar paid by the groom's family came to be considered more a gift than a purchase price. In fact, it was a gift that was expected to revert to the bride herself, as part of her dowry. In addition to money, gifts, or property given by the groom's father to her father, and then to her, the bride frequently came to the marriage with her own property as well.

By the twelfth century, beginning in Germany and France, the betrothal and chuppah ceremonies were fused so that a long betrothal period was no longer necessary. Both economic and social reasons are often cited for this. In difficult economic times the merging of these two events saved the expense of two huge feasts, one for the betrothal and another for the actual marriage. Because the futures of the Jews were not secure from year to year, the dissolution of the betrothal period removed the problem of what to do with a betrothed woman whose family (or whose potential partner's family) had to flee the country.[1]

Prior to the merger of the betrothal and marriage ceremonies conditions were always taken very seriously by both the bride's and groom's families, but were conducted orally. After the fusion of the betrothal and the marriage ceremonies, the conditions were put into writing. The Sephardim developed standard forms for this during the eleventh century, and the Ashkenazim did similarly in the twelfth century. A ceremony was developed during which the forms were read and signed. The document was called the *te-nai shidukhin* and was a "condition" for what we would now call engagement. This form was referred to as the "first conditions" while the *ketubah,* the binding marriage contract signed by both bride and groom in the presence of witnesses at the marriage ceremony itself, was known as the "last conditional agreement."[2]

The site of the wedding ceremony has undergone several changes throughout the ages. Scholars believe that during biblical times the ceremony was performed outdoors on the premises of the groom's family. By Talmudic times, marriage was considered a religious as well as a legal institution, and certain blessings required a minyan of ten men in attendance, but it was still a home ceremony. It wasn't until the fifteenth century that the marriage ceremony was transferred to the synagogue to be performed by a rabbi.[3]

By that time the bride was no longer led into the chuppah to remain with the groom. Rather, the bridal canopy (still called the chuppah), under which the bride and groom stand during the marriage ceremony, became the symbolic substitute for the original bridal chamber. The rabbis said the chuppah situated in the synagogue now signified the bride's passage from her father's home to that of the groom's family. This interpretation never really gained popularity because by that time period customs had changed, and the bride and groom generally lived in the home of the bride's family, rather than the groom's.

In the sixteenth century it became customary to hold the wedding ceremony outdoors in the courtyard of the synagogue, under both a chuppah and the stars, where the rabbis said that the bride and groom so married "should multiply like the stars in the heavens." Three hundred years later Reform Jews, finding courtyards too small, brought the wedding ceremony back into the synagogue.

Throughout the ages certain days of the week have been considered best (or less desirable) for the wedding ceremony. Monday was considered an unlucky day for marriages since in the biblical Creation story, God didn't even say once on that day that "it was good." On the third day after creation the Bible relates that God said twice how "good it was." Thus, Tuesday has traditionally been considered a lucky day for Jewish weddings, so much so that in our own times on late Tuesday afternoons in Jerusalem so many brides, grooms, and photographers flock to the Western Wall that one wonders if any single women and men remain in the town. We have twice lived in a Jerusalem apartment above a wedding hall and every Tuesday night we fell asleep to the strains of beautiful music, mixed with much laughter, as celebrants downstairs enjoyed a wedding feast.

Wednesday was often the preferred day for the marriage of virgins, since, if it turned out that the young woman did not show adequate evidence of her maidenhood, the courts met on Thursdays, and the marriage could be annulled. Thursdays were considered appropriate days for a widow to remarry since her husband could devote the next three days to her. Friday was frequently the wedding day because the Shabbat meal could also be the wedding feast. Weddings are not held from sundown Friday through Shabbat, but are permitted after the sun goes down. In earlier times, Sunday was not a customary day for weddings, because no preparation could be made on Shabbat. However, it's become a very popular day for weddings in the Western world.

Until relatively recently parents were responsible for selecting their children's mates. Either the father, or the professional matchmaker—known since the Talmudic period as the shadkhan—arranged the match. Although by shtetl times the matchmaker was often a comic character, such as Yenta in *Fiddler on the Roof,* from the Talmudic period through the Middle Ages matchmaking was a highly respected vocation. In fact, yeshivah teachers and even rabbis were members of the profession. Since the bride's family preferred education over all other qualifications in her mate, a rabbi or yeshivah scholar, who would know the young, marriageable yeshivah students, was a sought-after shadkhan. For his help, the shadkhan generally received a percentage of the dowry, sometimes paid at the time of the betrothal, other times delayed until the chuppah ceremony.

(Interestingly, the matchmaker has reappeared throughout the United States in recent years. In our own community, two women began a Jewish matching service which has met with such success that they receive calls from all over the country—not only from prospective clients but from persons interested in starting dating services in their own cities.)

The Wedding Ceremony

Nowadays in Orthodox and Conservative wedding ceremonies the bridegroom covers his head with a kepah as he would on any other day. From ancient times through the Middle Ages, however, the groom wore a crown of flowers, myrtle, and olive branches, intertwined with brightly colored stones and threads. He was colorfully dressed, or sometimes wore a special white robe. Today the bridegroom wears a suit, or for a very formal wedding, a tuxedo.

Today a bride may choose a long, white dress, traditional symbol of purity. However, she may choose other colors or lengths with ample historical precedent. Through the ages Jews of the East have traditionally worn colorful and sometimes beautifully embroidered bridal costumes of bright reds, purples, and golds.

Today's traditional wedding ceremony is much the same as it was in medieval times after the betrothal and nuptials were fused into one service. The guests assemble in the bride's home, garden, or in the synagogue. The chuppah, four posts secured to the floor, or held by friends of bride and groom, is covered with fabric, perhaps trimmed with flowers, or simply covered with a tallit.

Music, frequently Israeli melodies, which are becoming increasingly popular both for the processional and recessional, is played as the wedding party begins to walk down the aisle. (As we Diaspora Jews become more acquainted with Jewish music, Mendelssohn is used less and less at our weddings.)

The groom is escorted to the chuppah—his symbolic tent—by both of his parents, where he waits for his bride to join him. In the traditional Diaspora wedding ceremony, when the groom arrives under the chuppah he stands facing Israel; in Israel he awaits his bride facing Jerusalem; and in Jerusalem, he waits facing the Temple site.

The bride is escorted by both of her parents, a custom thought to be the last vestige of the ancient procession in which the bride's family led her to the original chuppah—the bridal chamber. In recognition of the role played by both parents in raising their child, Judaism has given both of them the honor of escorting their daughter down the aisle to the chuppah. The bride, groom, rabbi, and two witnesses stand beneath the chuppah.

The ceremony is divided into two parts, the first of which was once the betrothal ceremony, and the second, the actual nuptials. During the first, the bride and groom drink in turn from a cup of wine. The groom then proposes to the bride by reciting the marriage formula, "Behold, thou art betrothed unto me, with this ring, in accordance with the Law of Moses and Israel."

After her reply he places a ring on her finger. (Traditionally the ring goes on the pointer finger of her right hand, presumably to facilitate her showing the witnesses her acceptance of it, and of all that it signifies.)

The ring, thought to have become part of the betrothal ceremony during the seventh or eighth century, is a token substitute for the money once given by the groom to the bride's family. It is made of plain metal, preferably gold, and contains no precious stones (lest the bride presume imitation stones to be precious ones, find out later that she was wrong, and nullify the wedding).

Next the ketubah—the marriage contract written in Aramaic—is read aloud, as a divider between the betrothal and the nuptials. One of the earliest legal documents, the ketubah is thought to date to the period following the Babylonian exile.[4] Many ketubot are exquisitely hand-calligraphed pieces of scribal art decorated with colorful Jewish historical motifs.

The second part of the ceremony is brief. The rabbi recites the seven wedding benedictions *(sheva berakhot)* over a glass of wine. The bride and groom drink from the glass, then the groom smashes it with his foot. A variety of interpretations are given for this ancient custom. Most historians agree that it must have originated with the desire to drive away evil spirits, since smashing various kinds of pottery at or before the wedding was relatively common practice in the ancient world. The rabbinic interpretation is that in the midst of gladness we always recall our sorrows, and that we break the glass to remember the destruction of the Temple. Thus, the Jewish wedding concludes, as it begins, with Jerusalem in mind.

Immediately following the ceremony some couples observe the ancient custom of *yihud* (togetherness), going together into a private room for a few minutes. Whereas this, like the chuppah, is a vestige of the couples' retiring to the bridal chamber, today it is a time for the couple—if they have fasted all day in accordance with traditional rabbinic custom—to break their fast. If they have not fasted, it's a time for a few minutes of privacy before they receive congratulations from friends and relatives.

Celebration

Se'udah

Weddings have always been festive events. In Genesis (29:22) Laban "gathered together all the men of the place, and made a feast" to celebrate his giving Leah to Jacob. The Bible speaks of "completing the week," which commentators interpret to mean the week of celebration which was customary following a wedding in ancient times.

Throughout the Middle Ages and on into nineteenth-century Europe it was usual that the week following the wedding was one in which guests repeatedly feasted, and bride and groom were honorary "king" and "queen."

Sometimes families who could afford to hosted two feasts: one for relatives and friends, and the other for paupers. On the day prior to the wedding, or on the morning thereof, the celebrating family gathered together the town's poor and served them a festive meal. The guests were seated at a table with the bride and groom and were served by the bride's family. Afterward the bride and groom danced with their guests, then distributed coins to them.

In Eastern Europe, the entire community was in a state of hectic preparation for weeks in advance of the wedding. In the United States, during earlier years of this century, the Jewish, like the non-Jewish, wedding was planned largely by the parents and was often an occasion for them to entertain (in addition to family and close friends) acquaintances and business associates while bride and groom looked on. Today, while still a major family event, the wedding essentially belongs to the bride and groom, since couples often marry later and neither may be living at home at the time of the marriage. The extravagant, wedding se'udah with huge numbers of guests, opulent menu, and noisy band is diminishing in popularity. Today's trend is toward smaller, simpler, warmer, and more personal weddings. As both celebrant and a guest, I find that the simpler the wedding se'udah, both in numbers of guests and in menu, the more enjoyable the occasion.

When Dick and I were married in the late 1950s the large catered wedding se'udah was very much in vogue. We picked our wedding date just three weeks before the wedding when Dick received army orders that would otherwise have delayed our marriage by several months. My mother was out of town at the time (Dick's mother had passed away several years before). But, Daddy and Dick's father stopped all else and proceeded, individually and in conference, to make their guest lists. By the time Mother flew home two days later they had compiled over eight hundred names of friends they had to have to the wedding. Since time was short they were prepared to issue telephone invitations (in fact, to this day I suspect they had begun doing so before Mother arrived home).

Daddy and Dick's father immediately greeted my mother with their lists. Then Dick and I gave her ours, on which there were eighteen names. We intended to invite only the immediate family, with ceremony and dinner at home. Mother liked our plan much better, and finally effected a compromise with our fathers. We ended up with fifty people at a synagogue chapel service followed by dinner. It was a warm, lovely occasion and we've always been glad that we kept it small.

We've attended other memorable weddings over the years. Perhaps the loveliest was a wedding held in a synagogue on the shores of Lake Superior late on a summer end-of-Shabbat evening, after three stars were sighted in the sky. The groom's family gave a Shabbat dinner the night before for family, out-of-town guests, and the wedding party. The next day the bride's aunt served Shabbat lunch in her home. The wedding ceremony was held that evening after Havdalah, followed by a festive se'udah. The entire weekend seemed to be what both Shabbat and a wedding should be—time away from ordinary time, time spent within a close intimate community, bride and groom beginning their life together amid those about whom they care the most.

Simplicity of atmosphere and menu is not necessarily synonymous with a small guest list. We attended an informal, yet large wedding in Israel one spring when friends visiting Jerusalem from Tel Aviv stopped in to see us on their way to a kibbutz wedding. "Come on along," they offered. "We can't," we said. "We don't know the bride or groom or either of their families. You can't bring strangers to a wedding."

"That's not so in Israel," our friends laughed. "And especially it's not true on a kibbutz. You come, you won't be sorry. The whole kibbutz will be there." We went and we certainly weren't sorry. The bride's mother greeted us as if we were old friends, as did the bride, groom, and the rest of the family. The ceremony was held outdoors under a cloth chuppah made by kibbutz members; close friends held each of the four poles that supported the cloth. After the ceremony, the colorfully costumed children of the kibbutz performed special dances to joyous music. Everybody enjoyed the picnic supper, danced and talked for the rest of the evening.

A new wedding custom, which originated in the kibbutzim and is gaining popularity throughout Israel and the Diaspora, is that of the showing of "parallel pictures" of the bride and groom during the post-ceremony festivities. A member of the bride's family operates one projector; someone from the groom's family runs another. They show pictures of the bride and groom at similar stages of development from babyhood on through the years.

This custom is rooted in oral tradition. For, in centuries past, the badchan, a musician-entertainer-storyteller-jester, was part of nearly every Eastern European wedding festivity. Among the stories he told were those of the bride and groom as children. First a story about the bride as a baby, then about the groom as a baby; the bride as she grew and played; the groom as he did so. Now that modern technology has made possible the preservation and sharing of the childhood memories of bride and groom through pictures as well as through stories, the custom of showing "parallel pictures" may well become a permanent part of our tradition.

Wedding Gifts

Originally, the bride's parents were responsible for providing a dowry, the goods needed to run a household. The wedding gift developed as a way of friends and relatives helping to "dower" the bride and enable the young couple to form their new home. Many couples greatly appreciate receiving a gift of Jewish significance to help them create a particularly Jewish home.

Shabbat and festivals provide plenty of gift opportunities. We've given such wedding gifts as Shabbat candlesticks, a Kiddush cup with wineglasses, and a brightly colored Israeli-designed challah cover.

Because we've so enjoyed the hanukiyot brought us from Israel by close friends at the time of our wedding, we gave our newly married cousins a modern hanukiyah, which they light on Hanukkah and display all year. There are so many magnificent hanukiyot available that it becomes really difficult to choose. The same is true of Seder plates, which make another wonderful wedding gift.

The wedding itself gives parents or close relatives a chance to present the bride and groom with perhaps the most personal gift of all—a hand-done ketubah. With the revival of interest in all Jewish scribal arts and the ketubah in particular during the past decades, many Jewish artists both in the Diaspora and in Israel now specialize in creating personalized ketubot. Their own ketubah is perhaps the most visually magnificent and meaningful gift a couple will ever receive.

Anniversary Celebrations

Although there is no universal Jewish wedding anniversary custom, in recent years some synagogues have instituted the custom of reading the names of the anniversary couple on the Friday evening or Saturday morning closest to their anniversary on the civil calendar. Then the couple or couples are blessed by the rabbi. At the close of the service, one or more of the couples may sponsor a kiddush for the entire congregation in honor of their anniversary.

Some couples choose their anniversary as an occasion on which to give a special gift to a favorite charity. Tzedakah (charity), always appropriate, is frequently given in honor of a happy event.

Building the Family Bookshelf

Among the many sources researched for this book I discovered some excellent books with which I wish I'd have been familiar years ago, and which are now permanently on our family bookshelf. I recommend these books for the richness which they can add to every Jewish family's knowledge of its heritage.

Included are two of my favorite general sources, which cover Shabbat and all of the ancient festivals; several recommendations for Shabbat, recommendations for each festival and life-cycle celebration, cookbook and music book suggestions, and my favorite guidebooks to Israel.

General Sources

The two books which proved to be of tremendous over-all help to me in understanding the roots of Shabbat and the ancient festivals are *The Jewish Festivals from Their Beginnings to Our Own Day,* by Hayyim Schauss, and *Festivals of the Jewish Year,* by Theodore H. Gaster. Although I used hard-cover library copies for the research, and the footnotes in this book are keyed to them, I found both later in complete paperback editions, which means that for under eight dollars a family can own them both.

Hayyim Schauss's book is the best single source that I have

found on Shabbat and the festivals for two reasons. First, it is written in a scholarly, yet highly readable fashion; the book reads like a novel. Second, it is the only source I found that delineates various phases of the development of each festival into ancient times, Temple period, Eastern Europe (where the author recalls celebrations), and modern times. The book is beautifully researched; the footnotes in themselves are as interesting to read as the text. This is truly a classic.

Festivals of the Jewish Year, by Theodore H. Gaster.

Theodore H. Gaster, a Professor of Comparative Religion at Dropsie College, looks at Jewish customs with an anthropologist-folklorist eye. His work adds a dimension to the study of festival customs that one doesn't find elsewhere for he keeps one constantly aware that festivals didn't originate in a vacuum, but rather were developed by human beings with basic human feelings and concerns.

Sources Particular to Shabbat

The following books are excellent Shabbat guides, references, and all-around reading.

Sabbath: The Day of Delight, by Abraham E. Millgram.

This is probably the best available volume on the Sabbath in terms of the historical research that has gone into its preparation, its clear style, and unbiased approach. It has the scope of an anthology—sections on children's stories and Sabbath poetry written by various authors are included along with a thorough treatment of historical reasons for Shabbat interpretations and customs, Shabbat home ceremonies and music. The section "The Sabbath in History" includes extremely interesting chapters on "The Jewish Sabbath and the Christian Sunday" and "Sabbath Observance in the Far-Flung Jewish Communities." A truly marvelous book for every family member.

The Sabbath: A Guide to Its Understanding and Observance, by Dr. Dayan I. Grunfeld.

In less than ninety pages Grunfeld gives an excellent explanation of the traditional theological interpretations of the Sabbath. In simple language he removes Sabbath restrictions from either a preachy or a practical level and places them in the philosophical context for which he argues they were originally intended. This is an exciting volume that gives Sabbath restrictions many new dimensions.

Life Is with People: The Culture of the Shtetl, by Mark Zborowski and Elizabeth Herzog.

This thoroughly readable, delightfully informative depiction of shtetl life takes us into the villages, homes, and families of Eastern Europe and allows us to experience the lives lead there by many of our ancestors. More than merely reading about a place and a people, one is there with them. The chapter called "Remember the Sabbath" gives a beautiful dimension to the Eastern European Sabbath.

The Shabbat Catalogue, by Ruth Brin.

This useful and instructive book is aimed at families with young children, many of whom are in the process of beginning to formulate Shabbat observances in their homes. It includes Sabbath dialogues in which the whole family can participate, Sabbath songs, recipes, and creative approaches to various aspects of the day. One of its great strengths is its appeal to children who love the many arts and crafts projects and other Sabbath preparation ideas included.

Festival Sources

I have found one, sometimes two or more books that are especially useful for a particular festival, which I highly recommend to other families.

ROSH HASHANAH/YOM KIPPUR *New Year: Its History, Customs and Superstitions,* by Theodore H. Gaster.

As in his *Festivals of the Jewish Year,* Gaster delves where others fear to tread. Here Gaster gives an anthropological folkloric base to festivals of the New Year, placing the Jewish Year into the total context of religious historicity. Gaster presents the best psychological interpretation for the keeping of Yom Kippur that I've read anywhere.

Days of Awe, by S. Y. Agnon.

This book is referred to by many scholars as *must* reading on the subject of Rosh Hashanah, Yom Kippur, and the days in between. At first reading I didn't see what the accolades were about, although I'm a devotee of Agnon's fiction. However, after researching the festivals I reread the book and greatly appreciated many of the vignettes and passages to the point that I would agree it is excellent reading *after* one has some initial background.

Heart of Wisdom, Volumes I and II, by Rabbi Bernard S. Raskas.

Rabbi Raskas begins with Rosh Hashanah and takes the reader from Tishri 1 through each day of the Jewish calendar year with warmth and wit. When the day is a holiday, the author provides a fresh look at an ancient occasion through pertinent insight, historical information, wisdom, and humor.

SUKKOT/SIMCHAT TORAH *Sukkot,* by Hayim Donin. This book is part of the Popular History of Jewish Civilization series. Beautifully illustrated and simply written, it is packed with useful information.

The Sukkot and Simchat Torah Anthology, by Philip Goodman.

This is a good book to have on hand at the time of the festival and from which to read children's stories aloud. The fiction is of variable quality, so it's a good idea for parents to read through the stories first.

There is a great deal of fascinating information in the history sections. I was particularly intrigued by the scholarly disagreements on the use of the etrog, the theories on how this fruit may have come into being, and with a section on a group of American Indians who have long celebrated a festival identical in almost every way to Sukkot.

HANUKKAH *Books of Maccabees I and II:*

I found it most interesting to read both books before reading their various historical interpretations.

The Hanukkah Book, by Mae Rockland.

This is the best over-all Hanukkah book detailing the festival's history and celebrations that I found for the family bookshelf. In addition, Ms. Rockland is an immensely talented artist whose book is a gem for Hanukkah arts and crafts ideas. She gives detailed information on making everything from one's own hanukiyot to Hanukkah wrapping paper.

The Jewish Catalogue, Richard Siegel, et. al.

The volume has a very good section on dreidel-making for anyone interested in making one.

PURIM *The Book of Esther*

This is a delightful rendition of a hope for a time which may someday come, as much as a chronicle of a time which may have been.

Purim or the Feast of Esther: An Historical Study by N. S. Doniach.

Doniach is frequently footnoted by scholars writing about Purim. I can understand why. His is a thoroughly researched resource for anyone interested in an in-depth analysis of various theories on the development of Purim.

The Purim Anthology, by Philip Goodman.

My favorite of all the Goodman anthologies, this is an excellent compilation of everything you would want to know about Purim celebrations the world round, from the earliest festivals to modern times. Included are several sections of Purim literature, short stories, poetry, and plays; excellent music sections giving some Purim music history along with Hebrew, English, and Yiddish songs; and a great deal on the interesting and varied history of the merriest of all the merry Jewish festivals.

PASSOVER *A Feast of History* by Chaim Raphael.

There is probably more literature on Passover than on all the other festivals combined. However, this source is outstanding for its clear, readable explanations of the development of the festival from ancient times to modern days. Because Raphael is particularly interested in the Greco-Roman period, his book adds a whole dimension, rarely found elsewhere, to the development of the Seder. As if all this weren't enough, the book is beautifully presented with excellent colored photographs throughout.

Haggadah Me-ir Ay-nai-yim by Jacob Freedman.

This is a marvelous source book on the development of the haggadah. It is color-coded according to historical periods so that one can see which additions were made to the haggadah during which periods.

Biblical Archaeology, by Ernest G. Wright.

For those who question the historical veracity of such biblical verses as the wonders performed by Moses, or the ten plagues,

Wright, a dean of world archaeologists, discusses archaeological findings which give some scientific explanations of what we might otherwise claim to be in the realm of myth. Wonderful to have on hand for the skeptics at the Seder.

SHAVUOT *The Shavuot Anthology,* by Philip Goodman.

This is undoubtedly the best total family book for Shavuot as it includes stories, poems, songs, plus historical background.

YOM HASHO'AH *The Destruction of the European Jews,* by Raul Hilberg.

This book is considered by many scholars to be *the* major Holocaust history. The book is, in Hilberg's words, "about the perpetrators." It documents, from German records, the plans and actions of the Nazis in their attempt to exterminate the Jewish population. An invaluable resource done with impeccable scholarship.

The War Against the Jews, 1933–1945, by Lucy S. Dawidowicz.

A well-researched documentation of the events of the Holocaust, coupled with the author's attempt to discern what conditions made Europe ripe for Hitler's plan for Jewish annihilation nearly to succeed.

The Final Solution, by Gerald Reitlinger.

A good history in which Reitlinger first gives an overview of how the Final Solution came into being and then a documentation of how each country, as it was overrun by Germany, dealt with its Jews.

So It Was True: The American Protestant Press and the Nazi Persecution of the Jews, by Robert W. Ross.

In this excellent landmark study of Protestant publications during the Holocaust years, Ross details new findings regarding what was known about the Holocaust as it was happening.

YOM HA'ATZMA'UT *My People: The Story of the Jews,* by Abba Eban.

Eban, who had a central political role in Israel's fight for statehood, writes Israel's history with skill and passion. This is an excellent reference for those wanting a basic understanding of Israel.

O Jerusalem! by Larry Collins and Dominique Lapierre.

In a factual drama that reads like a novel, these non-Jewish, non-Arab journalists present an exciting, even-handed picture of the struggle for Jerusalem that culminated in the '67 war. This book is a must for those who wish a perspective on the most exciting, sought-after, spiritual city in world history—Jerusalem!

The Jewish State: An Attempt at a Modern Solution of the Jewish Question, by Theodor Herzl.

This pamphlet, written by Herzl in 1895, is frequently cited by historians in their documentations of the beginnings of the Jewish state. It's most interesting, however, to read in Herzl's own words his analysis and solution to the Jewish question.

Herzl, by Amos Elon. Elon, a leading Israeli journalist, has written a thoroughly intriguing and penetrating biography of modern Israel's founding father. This is an excellent source both for learning more about Herzl and the factors leading up to the establishment of the State of Israel.

Life-cycle Sources

Several general sources were of great help to me in enlarging my understanding of the universality of life-cycle ceremonies, and of expanding my appreciation of the particular touches Judaism has applied to those universals to make them unique.

The Rites of Passage, by Arnold Van Gennep.

Van Gennep is a well-known anthropologist credited with coining the phrase "rites of passage" to denote those ceremonies that various societies use to help their members through what he calls "life crises." This is an excellent reference in which life-cycle ceremonies are placed in conceptual context.

The Lifetime of a Jew Throughout the Ages of Jewish History, by Hayyim Schauss.

As in his *The Jewish Festivals from their Beginnings to Our Own Day,* Schauss distinguishes between anthropological/folkloric and rabbinic reasons for our various customs and ceremonies. In *The Lifetime of a Jew* Schauss takes the reader from cradle to grave in a readable, sensible chronicle of what it was like to enter the world, grow, marry, and die within a Jewish community in biblical, medieval, and Eastern European times.

The Holy and the Profane, by Theodore H. Gaster.

Here Gaster gives the reader a picture of the role played by the ancient superstitions, myths, and beliefs of the surrounding cultures in shaping Jewish life cycle concepts and events.

A Book of Jewish Concepts, by Phillip Birnbaum.

Birnbaum provides readers with expanded definitions on a variety of Jewish subjects, including many customs and ceremonies of the life cycle.

BIRTH, BAR MITZVAH, AND BAT MITZVAH

I found the above books, particularly *The Lifetime of a Jew* by Hayyim Schauss, to be the best sources available on the specific subjects of birth, Bar Mitzvah, and Bat Mitzvah as well as on the general life cycle. In addition, I found a number of other excellent sources on both death and weddings.

DEATH *A Plain Pine Box,* by Rabbi Arnold Goodman.

A clearly written sourcebook that details the way in which members of Rabbi Goodman's congregation, Adath Jeshurun, Minneapolis, Minnesota, formed the Chevra Kevod Hamet to return to Halachic prefuneral, funeral, and burial procedures. Other congregations around the country have already instituted similar groups that predicate their procedures on the Adath Jeshuran model. An excellent resource.

The Jewish Way in Death and Mourning, by Maurice Lamm.

Lamm's now-classic work gives a broad traditional explanation and interpretation of Jewish attitudes toward death. A well-organized resource book as well as one which can be read from cover to cover.

WEDDINGS *The Jewish Marriage Anthology,* by Philip and Hanna Goodman.

An extensive compendium of Jewish marriage customs in various countries of the world throughout the ages.

The Ketuba: Jewish Marriage Contracts Through the Ages, by David Davidovitch.

A beautiful book with explanations and full-color plate illustrations of Jewish marriage contracts from earliest times to today.

A History of Jewish Costume, by Alfred Rubens.

An excellent book of color illustrations of Jewish dress throughout the ages. I particularly enjoyed the Jewish wedding costumes and the explanations in the captions for the pictures.

The Jewish Wedding Book, by Lilly S. Routtenberg and Ruth R. Seldin.

A nonjudgmental modern American Jewish etiquette book.

The Jewish Way in Love and Marriage, by Maurice Lamm.

Lamm explains the traditional marriage customs in a direct, occasionally humorous way. He tackles many modern American male/female mores putting them into traditional Jewish perspectives, often passing judgment on them. An excellent sourcebook whether or not one agrees with all of his views.

Cookbook Sources

Because, along with recipes, I wanted to provide background on where, when, and how the custom of eating a particular food for a certain occasion developed, I read scores of Jewish cookbooks. While most proved to be simply recipe books, I found several excellent sources that would be welcome additions to any family's bookshelf for the history and folklore they offer as well as for the delicious food preparation suggestions.

The Jewish Holiday Kitchen, by Joan Nathan.

This is a thoroughly researched, wonderfully written book for anyone who likes to read about the history of the folklore of food, who is interested in knowing why a certain food is customary on a given occasion, or who likes to cook. There are about 200 recipes in this well-illustrated book; many of them give step-by-step procedures.

The Israeli Cookbook: What's Cooking in Israel's Melting Pot, by Molly Lyons Bar David.

Israeli cooking derives from many lands. This book gives history and lore about the origin of the 700 recipes it contains. Ms. Bar-David researched the book from a variety of sources, including interviews with Israeli immigrants from all over the world.

Jewish Cooking Around the World, by Hannah Goodman.

This book is organized according to various countries in which Jews live or have lived. Recipes from each Jewish community are given along with some interesting sketches of the composition of those communities.

Music Sources

The Board of Jewish Education of Greater New York and Tara Publications under the supervision of Velvel Pasternak have produced an excellent series of Shabbat and festival songbooks.

Since each soft-cover booklet is relatively inexpensive, a family can order enough of them so that—like a haggadah—each person can have a copy when everyone is sitting around the table singing. One can purchase an optional tape to go with each booklet as well; a great learning and sing-a-long device.

Israel in Song, compiled and edited by Velvel Pasternak.

This is a wonderful table, piano, or guitar book for everyone in the family. In addition to some of the familiar favorite tunes are many new ones.

Two songbooks have been a part of our family for so many years that I can't remember being without them. They have come on car trips with us, and through the years have been used at the piano and at the table on Shabbat and festivals. They are:

The Songs We Sing, edited by Harry Coopersmith.

The New Jewish Song Book, edited by Harry Coopersmith.

Guidebooks to Israel

A trio of guidebooks were extremely helpful to us during our first trip to Israel, providing us with all the information we needed for "self-guided" touring throughout the land.

The Guide to Israel, by Zev Vilnay.

This book by Israeli Professor Zev Vilnay is the best available guidebook for the history and geography of the country. Vilnay packs a tremendous amount of information into his compact volume, enabling one to realize that with each step one takes, one travels over thousands of years of history.

The American Traveler's Guide to Israel, by Abby Rand.

This guidebook best captures the spirit of the Israeli people and vividly describes their friendliness and hospitality. Rand's enthusiasm is so contagious that she makes one want to drop everything and take the next plane to Israel. She gives suggestions for allocating priorities and time so that one can see not only the best-known sites, but also some of the less well-known, equally beautiful and interesting places. However, because the book was published a decade ago many of the prices and listings are outdated.

Israel on $20 A Day, by Arthur Frommer.

The latest update on price information, lodging, restaurants, etc., is provided in the Arthur Frommer series. Arnold Sherman and Sylvia Brilliant also provide history and commentary along with their appraisals of the places for food and lodging.

Notes

A Shared Shabbat

1. Abraham E. Millgram, *Sabbath,* pp. 339–41.

2. Hayyim Schauss, *The Jewish Festivals from their Beginnings to Our Own Day,* p. 5.

3. Ibid., p. 6.

4. Ibid., p. 9.

5. Ibid.

6. Theodore H. Gaster, *Festivals of the Jewish Year,* p. 271.

7. Elizabeth Herzog and Mark Zborowski, *Life Is with People,* pp. 38–60.

8. Schauss, *Jewish Festivals,* p. 290, note 25.

9. Millgram, pp. 16–17.

10. Gaster, *Festivals,* p. 274.

11. Schauss, *Jewish Festivals,* p. 33.

12. Ibid., p. 291, note 30.

13. Millgram, p. 16.

14. Ibid., p. 17.

15. Gaster, *Festivals,* p. 284.

16. Joan Nathan, *The Jewish Holiday Kitchen,* p. 45.

17. Millgram, p. 18.

18. Ibid., p. 19.

19. Ibid., p. 21.

The Ancient Fall Festivals

1. Hayyim Schauss, *The Jewish Festivals from their Beginnings to Our Own Day,* p. 121.

Rosh Hashanah

1. Segal, *The Hebrew Passover,* pp. 127–28.

2. Hayyim Schauss, *Jewish Festivals,* pp. 116–17.

3. Ibid., p. 123.

4. Freda Reider, "Kabbalistic Holy Day Breads," pp. 24–25.

5. Theodore Gaster, *The New Year,* p. 81.

6. Ibid., pp. 80–81.

7. S. Y. Agnon, *Days of Awe,* p. 71.

8. *Encyclopedia Judaica,* Vol. 15, p. 830.

9. Schauss, *op. cit.,* p. 162.

Yom Kippur

1. Theodore H. Gaster, *Festivals of the Jewish Year,* p. 138.

2. Hayyim Schauss, *The Jewish Festivals from their Beginnings to Our Own Day.* p. 165.

3. Joan Nathan, *The Jewish Holiday Kitchen,* p. 99.

Sukkot

1. Hayyim Schauss, *The Jewish Festivals from their Beginnings to Our Own Day,* p. 171.

2. Theodore H. Gaster, *Festivals of the Jewish Year,* p. 84.

3. Schauss, *Jewish Festivals,* p. 183.

4. Hayim Halevy Donin, *Sukkot,* p. 44.

5. Richard Siegel, Michael Strassfeld, and Sharon Strassfeld, *The Jewish Catalog,* pp. 129–39.

6. Tapes with companion songbooks may be obtained from Tara Publications, 29 Derby Avenue, Cedarhurst, New York.

7. Lulav and etrog may be obtained from almost any synagogue by ordering several weeks in advance of the festival.

8. Dr. Joseph Hertz, *Daily Prayer Book,* p. 792.

The Ancient Winter Festivals

Hanukkah

1. Hayyim Schauss, *The Jewish Festivals,* p. 223.

2. *Encyclopedia Judaica,* Vol. 7, p. 1,284. "The custom of Simchat Bet Ha Soevah with its kindling of torches and lamps in the courts of the Temple and the city of Jerusalem seems likely to have been transferred as well from Sukkot to Hanukkah."

3. Schauss, *Jewish Festivals,* p. 183.

4. *Encyclopedia Judaica,* Vol. 7, p. 1,283.

5. Ibid., Vol. 11, pp. 909–11.

6. Hayim Halevy Donin, *Sukkot,* p. 29.

Purim

1. Theodore H. Gaster, *Purim and Chanukah in Custom and Tradition,* p. 18.

2. Philip Goodman, *The Purim Anthology,* pp. 35–36.

3. Ibid., p. 286.

4. Hayyim Schauss, *Jewish Festivals from their Beginnings to Our Own Day,* p. 270.

5. N. S. Doniach, *Purim or the Feast of Esther,* p. 103.

6. Ibid., p. 150.

7. Goodman, *Purim Anthology,* p. 211.

The Ancient Spring Festivals

Passover

1. Chaim Raphael, *A Feast of History,* p. 87.

2. Ibid., pp. 67–68.

3. Ibid., pp. 79–80.

4. Ibid., p. 76.

5. Ibid., pp. 95–96.

Shavuot

1. Theodore H. Gaster, *Festivals of the Jewish Year,* p. 77.

The Modern Spring Festivals

Yom Hasho'ah

1. Lucy S. Dawidowicz, *The War Against the Jews,* p. 145.

2. Rabbi Bernard S. Raskas, *Hitler's War Against the Jews,* p. 5.

3. Irving Greenberg and David Roskies (eds.), *A Holocaust Commemoration for Days of Remembrance for Communities, Synagogues, Centers for Home Use.* Committee on Days of Remembrance, 425 13th St., Washington, D.C.

4. "Miracle of Denmark." Copies may be requested through the National Conference of Christians and Jews, 43 West 57th Street, New York, New York 10019.

5. Miriam I. Cardozo, "The Phoenix," p. 2.

Yom Ha'atzma'ut

1. Rabbi Bernard Raskas, *In Their Own Words: A Brief Zionist Primer,* p. 1.

Life-cycle Ceremonies

Birth

1. Theodore H. Gaster, *The Holy and the Profane,* p. 34.

2. Hayyim Schauss, *The Lifetime of a Jew Throughout the Ages of Jewish History,* p. 13.

3. Ibid., p. 44.

4. Ibid., p. 47.

5. *Encyclopedia Judaica,* Vol. 12, p. 811.

6. Gaster, *Holy and the Profane,* p. 47.

7. *Encyclopedia Judaica,* Vol. 5, p. 570.

8. Schauss, pp. 34–35.

9. Ibid., pp. 37–38.

10. Leo Trepp, *The Complete Book of Jewish Observance,* pp. 231–33.

11. Myra Liefler and Daniel Liefler, "The Birth of a Daughter," in *The Jewish Woman,* edited by Elizabeth Koltun, p. 210.

12. Gaster, *Holy and the Profane,* p. 40.

Death

1. Hayyim Schauss, *The Lifetime of a Jew Throughout the Ages of Jewish History,* p. 224.

2. Ibid., p. 248.

3. Arnold Goodman, *A Plain Pine Box.*

4. Schauss, *Lifetime of a Jew,* p. 232.

5. Maurice Lamm, *The Jewish Way in Death and Mourning,* p. 37.

6. Ibid., pp. 38–39.

7. Schauss, *The Lifetime of a Jew Throughout the Ages of Jewish History,* pp. 287–88.

8. Bel Kaufman, lecture at the Center for Conservative Judasim.

Bar Mitzvah, Bat Mitzvah

1. Hayyim Schauss, *The Lifetime of a Jew Throughout the Ages of Jewish History,* p. 114.

2. *Encyclopedia Judaica,* Vol. 4. pp. 243–46.

3. Judith Kaplan Eisenstein, lecture, Temple of Aaron Synagogue, St. Paul, Minnesota.

4. See *The Second Jewish Catalog,* edited by Sharon and Michael Strassfeld, pp. 68–80, for specific alternative Bar and Bat Mitzvah celebrations and names of those persons willing to share information on ceremonies that worked well for them.

Weddings

1. Maurice Lamm, *The Jewish Way in Love and Marriage,* p. 147.
2. Ibid., p. 177.
3. Hayyim Schauss, *The Lifetime of a Jew Throughout the Ages of Jewish History,* p. 161.
4. David Davidovitch, *The Ketuba,* p. 1.

Glossary

aliyah: Literally, to go up. A term applied both to being called to the Torah in the synagogue, and to immigration to Israel.

Ashkenazic: Jews whose ancestors settled in Eastern Europe after the dispersion (Ashkenazim: plural of Ashkenazic).

Babylonian Exile: In 586 B.C.E., Judah was conquered by Babylonia and the population exiled.

badchan:* A jester; particularly at traditional Jewish weddings in Eastern Europe.

Balfour Declaration: A letter sent by the then British Foreign Secretary Arthur Balfour to Lord Rothschild, November 2, 1917, which expresses British sympathy with Zionist goals.

Bar Mitzvah:* The ceremony marking the initiation of a boy at the age of thirteen into the Jewish religious community.

Bat Mitzvah: The ceremony marking the initiation of a girl into the Jewish religious community, which can take place anytime after the age of twelve.

*The definitions of words marked with an asterisk are reprinted from the *Encyclopedia Judaica.*

blintzes: Crepes with cottage cheese filling, which are traditionally served at Shavuot.

brit: A covenant. The word "brit" has become synonymous with circumcision, the act of fulfilling God's covenant.

chag: Holiday.

Chai: Literally, live; Symbol of life.

challah: In biblical Hebrew, a round loaf or cake. Refers to the cake of new dough which the Israelites were required to give as a Temple offering. Colloquially, a white bread, usually for Shabbat and festival meals.

chevra kadisha: A sacred society; burial brotherhood.

cholent: A long-simmering stew, begun before sundown on Friday, which is served hot on Shabbat noon.

chol hamo'ed: The intermediate days of the festivals during which time certain kinds of work are forbidden.

chuppah: The bridal canopy.

Diaspora: Dispersion of the Jewish people from their homeland; also, the places Jews live outside Israel.

eruv: Literally, mixing, blending, or intermingling. A term applied to rabbinic legislation that makes permissible acts that would be otherwise prohibited on Shabbat and festivals.

etrog: A citron; one of the Four Species used on Sukkot together with the lulav, hadas, and aravah.

Feast of the Unleavened Bread: A holiday celebrating the beginning of the barley harvest; a forerunner of Passover.

First Temple: A central building for the worship of God by the Israelites, on Mount Moriah, Jerusalem; 10th to sixth century B.C.E.

Four Species: The lulav (palm branch), etrog (citron), hadas (myrtle), and aravah (willow); symbols used on Sukkot.

gelt: coins given to children on Hanukkah.

groggers: Noisemakers used on Purim.

Haftorah: A selection from the prophets read after the Torah reading each Shabbat, festival, and fast day.

haggadah: Askenazic Jews refer to the book used for the Seder service as the haggadah (the "telling"), while Sephardic Jews call the entire ceremony of the first night of the Pesach celebration the haggadah (haggadot: plural of haggadah).

hakafot: The ceremonial processional circuits made around the synagogue by congregants carrying Torah scrolls on Simchat Torah.

Halachah: The Talmudic code; a generic term for the whole legal system of Judaism encompassing all the laws and observances.

hamantaschen: Literally, "poppy seed pockets"; a fruit- and honey-filled triangular cookie.

Ha-Motzi: The blessing said over the bread.

hanukiyah: A nine-cupped candleholder used on Hanukkah (hanukiyot: plural of hanukiyah).

Hanukkah:* The eight-day celebration commemorating the victory of Judah Maccabee over the Syrian King Antiochus Epiphanes, and the subsequent rededication of the Temple.

haroset: A mixture of fruit, wine, spices, and nuts eaten at the Seder; it symbolizes the mortar and bricks the Israelites made in Egypt.

Havdalah: Literally, "distinction"; the ceremony at the closing of Shabbat and festivals to distinguish the sacred from the everyday.

Hellenism: The cultural tradition of that part of the Roman Empire that spoke Greek; the influence of Greek civilization on other areas, the Hellenistic period between about 300 B.C.E. and about 30 B.C.E.

Holocaust:* The organized mass persecution and annihilation of European Jewry by the Nazis (1933–1945).

Kabbalah: Jewish mysticism.

kapparot: An ancient Yom Kippur custom wherein a person's sins are supposedly transferred to a fowl, usually a chicken.

Karaite:* A member of a Jewish sect originating in the eighth century which rejected rabbinic Judaism and claimed to accept only Scripture as authoritative.

kepah: Skullcap

ketubah: A marriage contract, stipulating a husband's obligations to his wife.

Kiddush: The "sanctification"; the prayer recited over a cup of wine at beginning of Shabbat or a festival.

kitniyot: The collective name for the seven grains from which bread could be made.

Knesset:* The parliament of the State of Israel.

Kohen: A Jew of priestly descent (Kohanim: plural of Kohen).

Kol Nidre: Literally, "All Vows." The "All Vows" prayer, sung at the beginning of the first service on Yom Kippur.

kumsitz: A gathering by an open fire, usually with food and song.

latke: A fried potato pancake.

Levi: One of Jacob's twelve sons; also a tribe; the class of attendants to the priests.

lulav: A palm branch. One of the Four Species used on Sukkot, together with the hadas, aravah, and the etrog. (Colloquially, the term "lulav" applies to the palm branch, hadas, and aravah together.)

Maccabees: The members of Judah's family; also, the Hasmonean (priestly) dynasty as a whole.

Magen David: The six-pointed Star of David.

maggid: The telling of the story of the Exodus in the haggadah.

maror: The bitter herbs used at the Seder.

matzah: Unleavened bread (matzot: plural of matzah).

Megillah: "Scroll"; the Megillah commonly refers to the Scroll of Esther, which is read on Purim.

menorah: Seven-cupped candelabra.

minyan:* A group of ten male adult Jews, the minimum required for communal prayer.

mishlo'ach manot: Sending gifts of food on Purim.

Mishnah: The written collection of Jewish oral laws and ethics compiled in the third century that forms the basis of the Talmud.

mitzvah: Divine precepts; specific commands contained in the Torah. There are a total of 613 (Mitzvot: plural of mitzvah).

mohel: The official who performs the circumcision.

Mourner's Kaddish: A prayer of praise for God recited by the mourners at the conclusion of synagogue services during their period of bereavement after the death of a close relative.

Neilah:* The concluding service on the Day of Atonement.

Omer, Counting of the: The forty-nine days counted from the day on which the omer (first sheaf cut during the barley harvest) was offered in the Temple, from the second day of Pesach until Shavuot; a period of semi-mourning.

Passover: See Pesach.

Pesach: Passover; the eight-day spring festival commemorating the Exodus from Egypt, which begins on Nisan 14.

Pesah meal: A "firstling festival" predating the Hebrews' entrance into Egypt; a forerunner of the Pesach festival.

pidyon ha-ben: The redemption of first-born male at thirty-one days.

Purim:* A festival held on Adar 14 or 15 in commemoration of the delivery of the Jews of Persia in the time of Esther.

Purim Katan: "Little" or minor Purim.

Rosh Hashanah: The Jewish New Year; literally, "head of the year."

sandek: The assistant to the mohal at a circumcision.

Second Temple: A central building for the worship of God by the Israelites; built in 520 B.C.E. after return from Babylonian Exile. Destroyed by Romans in 70 C.E.

Seder: Literally "Order"; Ashkenazic Jews call the special meal and attendant ceremony of the first night of Pesach the "Seder." For Orthodox and Conservative Diaspora Jews, the first two nights are called the Seder (Sedarim: plural of Seder).

Sekhakh: The natural material that is cut to roof the sukkah.

Sephardic: Of or pertaining to the Jews whose ancestors settled in Spain or Portugal after the dispersion (Sephardim: plural of Sephardic).

se'udah sh'lishit: The third Shabbat meal, served late Shabbat afternoon.

se'udat mitzvah: The meal following a prescribed ceremony.

Shabbat: The Sabbath; the day of rest; seventh day of the week. It begins at sundown on Friday, and ends at sundown on Saturday.

shalach mones: Sending gifts of food on Purim (Yiddish). See mishlo'ach manot.

shamash: The "servant" Hanukkah candle, which is used to light the other candles.

Shavuot:* Pentecost; the Festival of Weeks, second of the three annual pilgrim festivals, commemorating the receiving of the Torah at Mount Sinai.

Shehecheyanu: The blessing for having reached a particular festival or other joyous occasion.

sheloshim: The thirty-day period of mourning after the death of a relative.

shiva:* The seven days of mourning following a burial.

shofar:* The horn of the ram (or any other ritually clean animal except the cow), sounded for the memorial blowing on Rosh Hashanah and other occasions.

siddur: The prayer book.

Simchat Bet Hasho'evah: In Temple times, a nightly torch dance ceremony held during Sukkot.

Simchat Torah:* The holiday marking the completion in the synagogue of the annual cycle of reading the Pentateuch; Eretz Israel observes it on Shemini Atzeret (outside Eretz Israel on the following day).

sufganiyot: Israeli Hanukkah food—doughnuts fried in oil.

sukkah:* The booth or tabernacle erected for Sukkot when, for seven days, religious Jews "dwell" or at least eat in the sukkah (Lev. 23:42) (sukkot: plural of sukkah).

Sukkot:* The festival of tabernacles; the last of the three pilgrim festivals, beginning on Tishri 15.

tallit: A four-cornered prayer shawl that has fringes at each corner.

tashlich: A ceremony held near an ocean or stream on the afternoon of the first day of Rosh Hashanah.

tena'im: The conditions of the marriage agreement.

Torah: The Five Books of Moses. Torah is also taken to mean the entire body of Jewish law from the Five Books of Moses through modern Halachah.

tzedakah: Charity.

Warsaw Ghetto Uprising: Most famous act of Jewish resistance during the Holocaust. A revolt against the Nazis by the inhabitants of the ghetto that began on the first day of Passover in 1943.

watchnight: A vigil held over the baby the night before the brit.

Yad Vashem: Israel's official museum for commemorating the Holocaust and Jewish resistance.

yahrzeit: The anniversary of the day of a person's death.

yeshivah:* A Jewish traditional academy devoted primarily to the study of rabbinic literature.

yizkor: From the Hebrew "remember." A prayer in memory of departed relatives that is recited on the last day of Passover and Shavuot, and on Yom Kippur and Shemini Atzeret.

Yom Ha'atzma'ut: Israel Independence Day, celebrated on the fifth of Iyar, commemorating the day Israel became an independent state, May 14, 1948.

Yom Hasho'ah: Holocaust Day of Remembrance, Nisan 27.

Yom Kippur: The Day of Atonement, Tishri 10; generally considered the holiest day of the Jewish calendar.

zemirot: Shabbat table songs that became popular during the sixteenth century.

Zion: A hill and stronghold in Jerusalem; it has become synonymous with Jerusalem.

Bibliography

Agnon, S. Y. *Days of Awe.* New York: Shocken Books, 1948.

Arzt, Max. *Justice and Mercy: Commentary on the Liturgy of the New Year and the Day of Atonement.* New York: Holt, Rinehart and Winston, 1963.

Bar David, Molly Lyons. *The Israeli Cookbook: What's Cooking in Israel's Melting Pot.* New York: Crown Publishers, Inc., 1964.

Becker, Ernest. *The Denial of Death.* New York: Free Press, Macmillan Publishing Co., Inc., 1973.

Birnbaum, Phillip. *A Book of Jewish Concepts.* New York: Hebrew Pub. Co., 1964.

Board of Jewish Education of Greater New York and Tara Publications. *Hanukah Melodies.* Cedarhurst, N.Y.: Tara Publications, 1977.

———. *High Holy Days and Sukkot Melodies.* Cedarhurst, N.Y.: Tara Publications, n.d.

———. *Seder Melodies.* Cedarhurst, N.Y.: Tara Publications, 1977.

———. *Shabbat Melodies.* Cedarhurst, N.Y.: Tara Publications, 1978.

———. *Tu Bi-Shvat Melodies/Purim Melodies.* Cedarhurst, N.Y.: Tara Publications, 1978.

Bright, John. *A History of Israel.* Philadelphia: Westminster Press, 1959.

Brin, Ruth. *The Shabbat Catalogue.* New York: Ktav Publishing House, 1978.

Cardozo, Miriam I. *The Phoenix.* Minneapolis: Holocaust Commemoration Committee, May 1981.

Cargas, Dr. Harry J., ed. *A Holocaust Commemoration For Days of Remembrance.* Washington: United States Memorial Council, 1981.

Charles, R. H., ed. *The Apocrypha and Pseudepigrapha of the Old Testament in English.* Vol. 1. London: Oxford University Press, 1965.

Collins, Larry, and Lapierre, Dominique. *O Jerusalem!* New York: Simon and Schuster, 1972.

Coopersmith, Harry. *The New Jewish Song Book.* New York: Behrman House, Inc. 1965.

Coopersmith, Harry, ed. *The Songs We Sing.* New York: United Synagogue Commission on Jewish Education, 1950.

Davidovitch, David. *The Ketuba: Jewish Marriage Contracts Through the Ages.* Tel Aviv: E. Lewin-Epstein, Ltd., 1968.

Dawidowicz, Lucy S. *The War Against the Jews, 1933–1945.* New York: Holt, Rinehart and Winston, 1975.

Doniach, N. S. *Purim or the Feast of Esther: An Historical Study.* Philadelphia: Jewish Publication Society, 1933.

Donin, Hayim Halevy. *Sukkot.* New York, Paris: Leon Amiel, 1974.

Eban, Abba. *My People: The Story of the Jews.* New York: Behrman House, Inc., and Random House, Inc., 1968.

Edidin, Ben M. *Jewish Customs and Ceremonies.* New York: Hebrew Publishing Company, 1941.

Eisenstein, Judith Kaplan. *Heritage of Music: The Music of the Jewish People.* New York: Union of American Hebrew Congregations, 1972.

———. Lecture. *Temple of Aaron Synagogue.* St. Paul, Minnesota. May 1981.

Elon, Amos. *Herzl.* New York: Holt, Rinehart and Winston, 1975.

Encyclopedia Judaica. Jerusalem. Keter Publishing House Ltd., 1973.

Engle, Fannie, and Blair, Gertrude. *The Jewish Festival Cookbook.* New York: Warner Books, 1954.

Frazer, Sir James George. *The New Golden Bough.* New York: Doubleday & Company, Inc., 1961.

Freedman, Jacob D. *Haggadah Me-ir Ay-nai-yim.* Springfield, Mass: Jacob Freedman Liturgy Research Foundation, 1974.

Frommer, Arthur. *Israel on $20 A Day.* New York: Frommer and Pasmantiar, 1980.

Gaster, Theodore H. *Festivals of the Jewish Year.* New York: William Morrow and Company, Inc., 1953.

———. *The Holy and the Profane; Evolution of Jewish Folkways.* New York: Sloan Associates, 1955.

———. *Myth, Legend and Custom in the Old Testament.* New York: Harper and Row, Publishers, Inc., 1969.

———. *New Year: Its History, Customs and Superstitions.* New York: Abelard-Schuman, 1955.

———. *Purim and Chanukah, in Custom and Tradition.* New York: Henry Schuman, 1950.

Gilbert, Martin. *Exile and Return. The Emergence of Jewish Statehood.* Jerusalem: Steimatzky's Agency, 1978.

Glatzer, Nahma, ed. *The Passover Haggadah.* New York: Schocken Books, 1953. (Rev. ed. 1969).

Goodman, Arnold. *A Plain Pine Box. A Return to Simple Jewish Funerals and Eternal Traditions.* New York: Ktav Publishing House, Inc., 1981.

Goodman, Hanna. *Jewish Cooking Around the World.* Philadelphia: Jewish Publication Society of America, 1976.

Goodman, Philip. *The Passover Anthology.* Philadelphia: Jewish Publication Society of America, 1961.

———. *The Purim Anthology.* Philadelphia: Jewish Publication Society of America, 1949.

———. *The Shavuot Anthology.* Philadelphia: Jewish Publication Society of America, 1975.

———. *The Sukkot and Simchat Torah Anthology.* Philadelphia: Jewish Publication Society of America, 1973.

———, and Goodman, Hanna. *The Jewish Marriage Anthology.* Philadelphia: Jewish Publication Society of America, 1965.

Grayzel, Solomon. *A History of the Jews: From the Babylonian Exile to the Present.* New York: New American Library, 1968.

Greenberg, Irving, and Roskies, David, eds. *A Holocaust Commemoration for Days of Remembrance for Communities, Synagogues, Centers for Home Use.* Washington: Committee on Days of Remembrance, 1980.

Greenstone, Julius H. *Jewish Feasts and Fasts.* New York: Bloch Publishing Co., 1946.

Grunfeld, Dr. Dayan I. *The Sabbath: A Guide to Its Understanding and Observance.* Jerusalem: Feldheim Publishers, 1972.

Hertz, Dr. Joseph H. *Daily Prayer Book.* New York: Bloch Publishing Co., 1957.

Herzl, Theodor. *The Jewish State: An Attempt at a Modern Solution of the Jewish Question.* London: H. Pordes, Fifth Edition, 1967.

Heschel, Abraham Joshua. *The Sabbath: Its Meaning for Modern Man.* New York: Hayer Torchbooks, 1966.

Hilberg, Raul. *The Destruction of the European Jews.* Chicago: Harper and Row Publishers, Inc., Quadrangle Books, Inc., 1961.

Hoenig, S. B. "Circumcision: The Covenant of Abraham." *Jewish Quarterly Review,* Vol. 53, No. 4, 1963, pp. 322–34.

Jones, Tom B. *Ancient Civilization.* Chicago: Rand McNally and Company, 1964.

Kaplan, Mordecai, ed. *The New Haggadah.* New York: Behrman House, 1942.

Kaufman, Bel. Lecture. Center for Conservative Judaism. Jerusalem, Israel. June 1980.

Kitov, Eliyahu. *The Book of our Heritage.* Vol. 1. Jerusalem, New York: Feldheim Publishers, 1978.

Klein, Isaac. *A Guide to Jewish Religious Practice.* New York: Jewish Theological Seminary of America, 1979.

Koltun, Elizabeth, ed. *The Jewish Woman; New Perspectives.* New York: Schocken Books, 1976.

Lamm, Maurice. *The Jewish Way in Death and Mourning.* New York: Jonathan David, 1969.

———. *The Jewish Way in Love and Marriage.* New York: Harper and Row, 1980.

Levin, Nora. *The Holocaust: The Destruction of European Jewry 1933–1945.* New York: T. Y. Crowell Co., 1968.

Mendes, Henry P. *Bar-Mitzvah for Boyhood, Youth, and Manhood.* New York: Bloch Publishing Co., 1956.

Millgram, Abraham E. *Sabbath: The Day of Delight.* Philadelphia: Jewish Publication Society of America, 1944.

Nathan, Joan. *The Jewish Holiday Kitchen.* New York: Schocken Books, 1979.

Pasternak, Velvel, ed. *Israel in Song.* Cedarhurst, N. Y.: Tara Publications.

Potok, Chaim. *Wanderings: Chaim Potok's History of the Jews.* New York: Alfred A. Knopf, Inc., 1978.

Pritchard, James B., ed. *The Ancient Near East.* New Jersey: Princeton University Press, 1958.

Rand, Abby. *The American Traveler's Guide to Israel.* New York: Charles Scribner's Sons, 1972.

Raphael, Chaim. *A Feast of History. Passover Through the Ages as a Key to Jewish Experience.* New York: Simon and Schuster, 1972.

Raskas, Bernard S. *Heart of Wisdom.* New York: The Burning Bush Press, 1962.

———. *Heart of Wisdom,* Vol. II. New York: The Burning Bush Press, 1979.

———. *Hitler's War Against the Jews.* St. Paul, Minnesota: Temple of Aaron, May 1981.

———. *In Their Own Words: A Brief Zionist Primer.* St. Paul, Minnesota: Temple of Aaron, 1978.

Reider, Freda, "Kabbalistic Holy Day Breads," *Hadassah,* October, 1978.

Reitlinger, Gerald. *The Final Solution: The Attempt to Exterminate the Jews of Europe 1939–1945.* South Brunswick, N. J.: T. Yoseloff, 1965.

Riemer, Jack. *Jewish Reflections on Death.* New York: Schocken Books, 1975.

Rockland, Mae. *The Hanukkah Book.* New York: Schocken Books, 1975.

Ross, Robert W. *So It Was True: The American Protestant Press and the Nazi Persecution of the Jews.* Minneapolis: University of Minnesota Press, 1980.

Routtenberg, Lilly S., and Seldin, Ruth R. *The Jewish Wedding Book.* New York: Harper and Row Publishers, Inc. 1967.

Rubens, Alfred. *A History of Jewish Costume.* New York: Crown Publishers, Inc., 1973.

Saadia Ben Joseph, Gaon. *The Book of Doctrines and Beliefs.* Translated by Alexander Altmann. Oxford, U.K.: East and West Library, 1946.

Sachar, Howard M. *A History of Israel, from the Rise of Zionism to Our Time.* New York: Alfred A. Knopf, 1976.

Schauss, Hayyim. *The Jewish Festivals from their Beginnings to Our Own Day.* Cincinnati: Union of American Hebrew Congregations, 1938.

———. *The Lifetime of a Jew Throughout the Ages of Jewish History.* Cincinnati: Union of American Hebrew Congregations, 1950.

Segal, Judah Benzion. *The Hebrew Passover, from the Earliest Times to A.D. 70.* London, New York: Oxford University Press, 1963.

Shirer, William L. *The Rise and Fall of the Third Reich; A History of Nazi Germany.* New York: Simon and Schuster, 1960.

Siegal, Richard; Strassfeld, Michael; and Strassfeld, Sharon. *The Jewish Catalogue.* Philadelphia: The Jewish Publication Society of America, 1973.

Spiro, Jack D. *A Time to Mourn. Judaism and the Psychology of Bereavement.* New York: Block Publishing Co., 1967.

Strassfeld, Sharon, and Strassfeld, Michael. *The Second Jewish Catalog.* Philadelphia: Jewish Publication Society of America, 1976.

Trepp, Leo. *The Complete Book of Jewish Observance.* New York: Behrman House Inc., Summit Books, 1980.

Van Gennep, Arnold. *The Rites of Passage.* Chicago: University of Chicago Press, 1969.

Vilnay, Zev. *The Guide to Israel.* Jerusalem: "Hamakor" Press, 1977.

Wilson, John A. *The Culture of Ancient Egypt.* Chicago: University of Chicago Press, Phoenix Books, 1963.

Wright, Ernest G. *Biblical Archaeology.* Philadelphia: The Westminster Press, and London: Gerald Duckworth and Co., Ltd., 1962 (reprinted 1970).

Zborowski, Mark, and Herzog, Elizabeth. *Life Is with People: The Culture of the Shtetl.* New York: Schocken Books, 1976.

Indexes

Songs

Recipes

Blessings

Subject/Name Index